UNDERSTANDING LEISURE

Second Edition

LES HAYWOOD
FRANK KEW
PETER BRAMHAM
JOHN SPINK
JOHN CAPENERHURST
IAN HENRY

Stanley Thornes (Publishers) Ltd

Originally published in 1989 by Hutchinson Education

Reprinted 1990 by
Stanley Thornes (Publishers) Ltd
Ellenborough House
Wellington Street
CHELTENHAM GL50 1YD

Reprinted 1991
Second edition 1995

British Library Cataloguing in Publication Data
A catalogue record for this book is available from the British Library.

ISBN 0 7487 2059 6

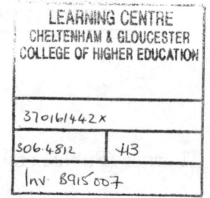
Typeset by GCS, Leighton Buzzard, Bedfordshire
Printed and bound in Great Britain

CONTENTS

PREFACE TO SECOND EDITION

During the seven years since the first edition of this book was in preparation there have been significant developments in both leisure *per se* and in leisure studies. For example, market-driven policies have made further inroads into public sector provision, while the introduction of British National Lottery has not simply re-written the rule book on State involvement in gambling, but has caused a major re-think on the public financing of sport, the arts and national heritage.

Meanwhile, there have been concomitant developments and debates within leisure studies on how social/leisure theory can best explain these institutional changes and take account of the increasingly pluralistic and individualistic consumer and leisure lifestyles of the late twentieth century.

The first edition of *Understanding Leisure* was designed as a conceptual framework through which substantive aspects of leisure could be studied. The second edition maintains this approach, but takes on board the ways in which leisure practice – provision and policies – and leisure theory – ideas and explanations – have developed since 1989.

Les Haywood
Frank Kew
Peter Bramham
John Spink
Ian Henry
John Capenerhurst

February 1995

PREFACE TO FIRST EDITION

Two decades ago few books had been written on the topic of 'leisure'. There were then no academic or professional courses on leisure, and few Leisure Departments in local government. There were no workers who called themselves leisure professionals, and national bodies, such as the Institute of Leisure and Amenity Management and the Leisure Studies Association, were not formed until the 1970s.

These developments are one indication of significant social and economic changes. Some argue that these changes are so radical that a new 'society of leisure' is evolving. Others indicate that basic problems of economic growth, of the environmental impact of industry, of material and social inequalities have not changed, and that issues about leisure are of secondary importance.

Nevertheless there is substantial evidence to suggest that, for many people, time for leisure is increasing, as is participation in leisure activities. Many people have shorter working weeks, longer holidays, and longer periods of retirement. For others, the demands of work are increasing and some people choose more work, such as overtime and second jobs, not more leisure. Whatever choice individuals make about their working lives, opportunities for leisure have increased significantly in post-war Britain.

The aim of any enquiry into social life is to enrich personal knowledge and provide perspectives which extend understanding and, in some cases, undermine previously held assumptions. This text is no exception. The aim is to introduce the reader to a range of perspectives upon leisure, and to provide a clear framework within which key issues can be addressed. To achieve this aim, material is introduced in an accessible jargon-free way based upon an assumption that readers will not have an extensive acquaintance with academic studies of leisure. Exercises and discussion topics listed at the end of each chapter invite the reader to relate the general issues discussed in the text to substantive instances of leisure activity, and to consider data which might either confirm or indeed undermine some of the analyses offered in the text.

This text is divided into seven chapters. Chapter 1 outlines and assesses the utility of different *conceptions and dimensions* of leisure through which the relationships of leisure to play and to work are examined.

Chapter 2 focuses upon the differences between *activities* conventionally labelled as leisure and presents a typology to distinguish between those which demand a more active involvement in the production of leisure experience and those which are characterised by a more passive reception or consumption of activities produced by others.

Chapter 3 provides a framework to explore the range of opportunities available to *participants* in leisure activity. The argument offered is that each individual's leisure lifestyle is the outcome of his or her own choice together with the constraints which circumscribe that choice.

Chapter 4 is devoted to an analysis of the *spatial* dimension of leisure. Relative land values have a crucial effect upon the location of leisure facilities and the types of activity provided.

Chapter 5 examines the complex and changing relationship between the commercial, voluntary, and public sector of leisure *provision*.

Chapter 6 considers the ways in which contemporary social and economic change might have an impact upon leisure. Just as the present is the culmination of the past, so the *future* will be the outcome of the present. How can we analyse the present in order either to predict or forecast the future?

Finally, Chapter 7 invites the reader to assess the utility of broad strands of *contemporary social theory* for understanding leisure. Each of these (figurational sociology, cultural studies, feminist studies and postmodernism) provides insights into leisure which have yet to be fully explored within leisure studies. The perspectives provide an analysis of experiences and meanings within particular leisure activities yet acknowledge the impact of social contexts.

This problem is central to much of the text. To understand leisure requires an acknowledgement of the distinctiveness of this aspect of social life. Without being able to distinguish 'leisure' from non-leisure there would be no subject-matter and the term would have no meaning, nor could one say anything specific about leisure forms, leisure experiences, leisure provision, etc. But, to understand leisure also requires an acknowledgement that leisure is *not* a separate, self-contained sphere of life. It can only be fully understood with reference to the social and cultural life of which leisure is but one element.

The text is the outcome of the collective work of six people. This collaborative exercise, involving a sharing of ideas and knowledge, has been a valuable learning process, enriching our own understanding of leisure, and informing our own teaching and research.

Les Haywood
Frank Kew
Pete Bramham
John Spink
Ian Henry
John Capenerhurst

Ilkley 1988

DIMENSIONS OF LEISURE

Introduction

A random sample of people, asked what they understand by leisure, would produce a number of different replies. Some might think that leisure is time left over after work and/or other duties and obligations. Others might talk about particular activities such as watching television, taking part in sports, going out for a meal, gardening or any other of the myriad activities which people find interesting.

Still others might indicate a particular quality of experience; that leisure provides the main opportunity in their lives to 'do their own thing', to have fun, to exercise free choice, to develop their own interests, to have experiences which are not available in the rest of their lives. Related to this, some people might regard leisure as rest and recuperation from work, and as an antidote to the stresses and strains of modern life.

The variety of these answers illustrates that leisure has different meanings for different people, and that this aspect of human experience is very complex. In order to unravel these complexities, this introductory chapter is organised around three major issues. These are:

1 Conceptions of leisure
2 The relationship between leisure and play
3 The relationship between leisure and work

Leisure is viewed in different ways, each of which emphasises particular characteristics to the neglect of others. The utility and the limitations of each of these conceptions is assessed later. In Section 2, we acknowledge that one aspect of the meaning of leisure is intimately connected with the characteristics, experience and purposes of play. In Section 3, however, the nature and meaning of leisure in contemporary society is also inter-related with work.

Underpinning each of these approaches is a recognition that leisure, leisure activities and leisure experiences cannot be fully understood as a self-contained sphere of life separate from the societal conditions within which leisure is experienced and structured.

1 Conceptions of leisure

Leisure as residual time

Here, leisure is viewed as unobligated time, as discretionary time to use in relatively freely chosen ways, when the obligations of work and subsistence have been met. This conception of leisure is typically to be found in industrialised societies where work has become the dominant factor of daily life and the clock rules our lives. It is relatively easy to determine and calculate hours of paid work during a day, or week, numbers of weeks worked during the year, lengths of paid holidays and so on. Since the middle of the nineteenth century social scientists have charted factors such as reduction in hours worked and growth in statutory paid holidays as evidence of the growth of time available for leisure, and even as a herald of the coming society of leisure. There is, for example, a long tradition of time–budget research which seeks to identify the ways in which people structure their days around such dimensions as domestic duties, subsistence, sleep, employment and leisure.

A major criticism levelled at this type of research, and at the 'residual time' conception of leisure in general, is that it reflects a 'man made' view of the world, and that consequently women's experience of leisure is at best undervalued and at worst ignored. This critique revolves around the centrality of men's work historically inherent in the residual time concept; the failure to take account of private domestic labour as a legitimate form of work; and the different meanings of 'discretionary or unobligated time' experienced by women and by men. These issues are discussed again later in this chapter, in the context of work-leisure relationships, and in Chapter 3.

What are the strengths and weaknesses of the 'residual time' concept, and how is it used? Table 1.1 (p. 3) summarises these issues.

Leisure as activities

This conceptual model is clearly related to the first definition since leisure is seen as a range of *activities* in which people *choose* to participate during their free *time*. The emphasis shifts, however, from the person, to the nature of the activities undertaken, e.g. sports, television, arts, dancing,

Table 1.1   Leisure as residual time

Dimension	Strengths	Weaknesses
Identifying time free from work as leisure.	Easy to calculate for *paid* employees. Data available on long term basis. Comparisons possible across time, occupations, countries, etc.	Difficult or impossible to calculate for unpaid work, e.g. unemployed people, housewives. Major segments of the population are thus ignored/invisible.
	Diaries of 'duties and obligations' such as eating, family concerns etc. can be constructed in order to identify 'free time' left over.	Difficulties in defining 'obligations and duties' (e.g. when does eating become more than a subsistence activity? Is playing with the children a duty or freely chosen?).
Understanding the nature of modern leisure.	Identifies in broad terms the *quantity* of time available for leisure for selected groups in society, and how this time is *distributed*.	Tells us nothing about the *content and quality* of leisure experienced. Marginalises certain groups not in paid employment.

Uses
Planners and policy makers in identifying long term trends in the availability of leisure time (e.g. Sports Council; local authorities) in order to allocate resources.

Managers of leisure facilities in organising and structuring their programmes for different groups (e.g. sports halls, theatres, museums, etc.).

The tourist industry in determining holiday, hotel, and travel schedules, etc.

Commercial providers in identifying groups with large quantities of free time and disposable income (e.g. youth markets).

hobbies, holidays, gambling, drinking. Frequently these activities are characterised as playful and pleasurable, and are often referred to as recreations. (In this book, however, the term 'recreation' is reserved only for certain categories within the broad field of leisure activities – a point discussed more fully in Chapter 2.)

A further important feature of this concept of leisure is its relationship to work. A central element in describing an activity as leisure lies in its apparent opposition to work; as freely chosen instead of obligatory and done for its own sake instead of for instrumental reasons. Ironically this apparent opposition to work betrays the dominance of employment, creating these activities in the forms in which we know them today. The activities, as much as the conception of leisure as residual time, are products of an industrial society, and are shaped in the image of such societies. This had led some critics to regard the conception of leisure as 'activities' as a contradiction in terms – a negation of leisure – an issue to which we shall return in due course. However, at this point let us examine in Table 1.2 the uses of the activities conception of leisure, and its strengths and inadequacies.

Leisure as functional

Closely allied to the model of leisure as a range of activities, is the conception of leisure in functional terms. This views leisure activities as performing useful functions for individuals, and more particularly, for society. Leisure is thus conceived as a *means* to achieving socially desired and approved ends, and is consequently frequently described in such positive terms as 'therapeutic', 'remedial' or 'training', or more negatively, as 'compensatory', 'sublimatory', or 'social control'.

This sort of evaluative view of leisure differs in character from conceptions of leisure in 'time' and 'activity' terms, because it is less concerned with defining how leisure is best identified and measured, than with how leisure is *used*. Defining leisure is thus not regarded as particularly problematic, but people's leisure lifestyles are. Again we find strong echoes of the role of leisure as a servant of work – as the dependent variable in a work-centred world. A clear example is the derivation of the word 'recreation', which in its original form implied 're-creation' of a readiness to return to work. Equally, the idea of leisure as compensatory or as a safety valve (a frequent justification for sports), is at root a commentary on the centrality of work in general, and in particular on the inadequacies of industrially dominated working-life as a fulfilment of human potential. However, work centrality is not the only issue here, for positive views of leisure in functional terms are often associated with, for example, health and fitness for its own sake; with self-fulfilment through the mastery of skills and knowledge; with social cohesion through the sharing of common interests; and with community development through collective action and sociability.

In summary the functional view of leisure may be seen in Table 1.3.

Leisure as freedom

Conceptions of leisure as an end in itself requiring no instrumental jus-

Table 1.2 Leisure as activities

Dimension	Strengths	Weaknesses
Identifying leisure as relatively freely chosen activities.	Easy to understand common sense way of thinking of leisure.	Ignores *passive* leisure. Uncertain status of activities such as religion, DIY, charity work. Difficult to calculate for certain groups, e.g. professional artists, sports personnel.
Understanding the nature of modern leisure.	What people do in their free time; focuses attention on the content of activities and thereforefore on their potential quality as individual/social experiences; highlights the importance of play.	Over-emphasises the importance of institutionalised leisure forms such as sports and the arts; excludes informal, unorganised leisure forms. Tends to be rooted in the past. Difficulty coping with change.

Uses
Planners and policy makers analyse trends in leisure in terms of patterns of participation in selected *activities* by social categories (e.g. gender, age, socio-economic group). The General Household Survey is a prime example of such data.

Facilities are constructed to accommodate popular activities and managed or programmed to provide for the groups most likely to participate. Problems arise when new activities emerge which are of uncertain durability (e.g. skateboarding); or when activities are identified with certain groups to the exclusion of others (e.g. many sports are male dominated); when activities become ossified and administrators are oblivious to changes in lifestyles of their clients/participants (e.g. football and cinema).

---

tification, contrast sharply with the idea of leisure expressed in functional terms. One is at leisure when one is free from the trammels which circumscribe other spheres of life and, therefore, leisure is concerned with autonomy, with the capacity to be and develop oneself. Historically this conception of leisure has been associated with elites, who have had the time and economic independence to allow them to develop leisured lifestyles under ideal circumstances.

Table 1.3   Leisure as functional

Dimension	Strengths	Weaknesses
Identifying leisure by its functions.	Focuses on the content and social consequences of leisure.	Does not necessarily discriminate between leisure and other activities, except by implication.
Understanding the nature of leisure.	Attempts to explain the functions of leisure for participants and for society. Focuses on the importance of policies for leisure and the rationales of leisure providers.	Sees leisure in utilitarian, instrumental terms. Tends to ignore, or under-rate intrinsically motivated leisure done for its own sake – for unjustified fun.
	Highlights changes in the use and abuse of leisure over time (e.g. leisure as social control or social service).	Overemphasises the societal dimension at the expense of the the individual (see Chapter 7).

Uses
By policy makers and planners (politicians, managers, etc.), especially in the public sector, to justify their decisions about what is good for their constituents (claims that leisure provision promotes social control, and reduces vandalism and discontent, have proved a powerful lever in prising funds from central and local government since at least the 1930s).

Conversely, by academics and theoreticians in analysing and criticising the decisions of leisure policy-makers and practitioners, and more positively, in studying motivation for the adoption of leisure life-styles.

Public bodies such as the Sports Council and Health Education Council in promoting and marketing their activities (e.g. sport for health).

The Latin word *licere*, from which 'leisure' is in part derived, implies both choice (licence to do something) and constraint (licensed in the sense of regulated).

An implicit distinction has often been made between societies where this freedom has been used positively or negatively. The Ancient Greeks, for example, are frequently praised for the model of leisure they evolved as 'free men', which stressed such qualities as harmony, excellence in mind and body (the cultivation of music and gymnastics), contemplation, and public service. In medieval times the 'Age of Chivalry' saw the

development of similar traits as indicative of the 'gentleman' and provided a model for conduct which still has links (even if somewhat strained)
in the 1990s, with the concept of the 'right use' of leisure, embodied in
notions of fair play and gentlemanly conduct in sports; an important
quality in activities done for their own sake – for intrinsic rewards.

These conceptions of leisure behaviour are strongly gender-biased, reflecting the power of male elite-groups to define the parameters of leisure
in different historical settings. Negative examples often refer to leisure in
the later stages of the Roman Empire, where excessive free time and
wealth was linked to exploitative leisure pursuits typified by games and
circuses, in which bloodshed and degradation developed as a grisly form
of public entertainment. A more recent example, less extreme in nature
but no less critical, is to be found in the writings of T. Veblen (1899) who
scathingly condemns the leisure practices of the new 'leisure class' in the
late nineteenth century USA as 'conspicuous consumption' – the wasteful
worship of style and opulence by the nouveau-riche American elite, in a
public display of their freedom from necessity.

Fears that attainment of free time may lead to debased and mindless
forms of pleasure rather than to creative leisure (to consumption and not
concerts; Gladiators not Glyndbourne) are also to be found in critical
writing from such diverse sources as T. S. Eliot (in defence of elitism in
the arts) and H. Marcuse who bewails the public's seemingly
unquenchable pursuit of 'false needs'.

Negative views of the conception of leisure as freedom – as *not* providing opportunities for the fulfilment of human capacities for skill, for
expression, for contemplation, *but* twisted into degenerate forms are,
however, relatively few. More common is the view that leisure is an
ideal, has humanistic qualities, and that freed from the constraints of
work and necessity some human beings may attain a higher state.

This almost mystical view of leisure was particularly strong in America
in the 1950s and 1960s, and is typified by such statements as:

Anybody can have free time. Free time is a realizable idea of democracy. Leisure
is not fully realizable and hence an ideal not alone an idea. Free time refers to
a special way of calculating a special kind of time. Leisure refers to a state of
being, a condition of man which few desire and fewer achieve.

(De Grazia, 1962)

Such views found sympathy among some cultures seeking alternative
lifestyles in the so-called permissive 1960s, and in some parts of the USA
and Western Europe, the phenomenon of the 'drop out' seeking a con-
templative existence in an idealised leisured world became almost commonplace. More conventionally, an emphasis on the quality of
leisure – on the cultivation in leisure of higher human values, as demon-

strated in the fine arts and literature, for example, has been a continuing indicator of an ideal leisure lifestyle. Clearly such a view reflects an elitist conception of leisure, as there is little room here for mere sports and pastimes, let alone gaming and gambling.

It is paradoxical that a conception of leisure based on a form of freedom to pursue interests and activities for intrinsic rewards (for their own sake), should be subverted for purposes of defining what is desirable and good, as against what is vulgar and bad in leisure. What this highlights of course, is that the 'qualitative' conception of leisure is anything but neutral; it reflects a value judgement, based in the main, on the world view of successive cultural elites of what leisure *ought* to be, rather than what it is. Despite this obvious flaw (in the eyes of the egalitarian cynic of the late twentieth century at least) the conception of leisure as offering freedom and autonomy for intrinsically directed self-development remains an important one for many leisure theorists, because it points to the opportunity which leisure gives for the expression and nurturing of higher human values. Table 1.4 summarises the validity and uses of the conception of leisure as freedom.

Summary

We have overviewed four consistently recurring themes in the conceptualisation of leisure:
- leisure as residual time;
- leisure as activities;
- leisure as functional;
- leisure as freedom.

Some writers have attempted to combine these into a compound definition, so that leisure is seen as a construct embodying a number of characteristics. For example, Max Kaplan (1975) states:

Leisure consists of relatively self-determined activity/experience that falls into one's free-time roles, that is seen as leisure by participants, that is psychologically pleasant in anticipation and recollection, that potentially covers the whole range of commitment and intensity, that contains characteristic norms and constraints and that provides opportunities for recreation, personal growth and service to others.

The problem with such a definition, as Kaplan himself recognises, quite apart from its unwieldiness, is that these characteristics may also be present in many other activities/experiences, and therefore it provides no real basis for distinguishing leisure from non-leisure. A more useful approach is to recognise that:
(a) there are a number of different ways of conceptualising leisure, of

Table 1.4 Leisure as freedom

Dimension	Strengths	Weaknesses
Identifying leisure as 'freedom' as 'qualitative'; as 'intrinsically rewarding'.	Focuses on the subjective dimension of leisure; on the quality of leisure experience. Identifies activities which have historically been valued highly as leisure.	Difficult to quantify. Many activities have multiple motivations. Does not *necessarily* distinguish leisure from work and obligations (e.g. religion meets the necessary criteria for leisure, but it may not be perceived as such by participants).
Understanding the nature of leisure.	Forces attention on the intrinsic nature of leisure; on its potential for enhancing the quality of of life. Includes apparently passive forms of leisure. Provides exemplars of leisure forms which are seen as human qualities (e.g. fine arts).	Drawn largely from the study of the leisure pursuits of elites. Highly value-laden view of what is 'worthwhile', 'fulfilling', 'meaningful'; historically and culturally specific (e.g. Ancient Greek lifestyles of no current relevance).

Uses
Lobbyists for the traditional high arts – e.g. theatre, opera, ballet, classical music, stress the importance of the maintenance and development of these leisure forms in their contribution to the quality of cultural life.

Educators (and some politicians and futurologists) stress the role of leisure in realising human potentialities, in a future where work is not central in people's lives, and in which guidelines for the 'proper' use of leisure will be required. Frequently 'proper' use is identified with higher rather than popular culture.

Managers and short term policy makers have had little truck with the qualitative dimensions of leisure in the recent past; their concern has been more with maximising participation, which implies a populist approach. It is possible that the emerging community approach being adopted by some local authorities in the 1990s may require a more serious consideration of the qualitative nature of leisure provision.

Critics of mass culture and of the materialism of consumer societies implicitly adopt this view of leisure.

which the most common revolve around the dimensions of *work and time; activity; function;* and *freedom;*

(b) none of these explanations gives a complete definition of leisure, but each tells us something important about the nature of leisure:

(c) most importantly, they focus attention on the *social origins* of each conceptualisation; on the *values* implicit in defining leisure in a particular way; and on the *current ways* in which leisure is viewed by such decision-makers as politicians, leisure providers and recreation managers.

From the foregoing discussion of differing conceptions and definitions of leisure, two major dimensions may be extracted which merit further consideration. These are:

(a) Relationships between leisure and play focusing primarily on the *intrinsic* qualities of leisure activity and experience (drawing from concepts of leisure as activities and as freedom).

(b) Relationships between leisure, work and unemployment, where the *extrinsic* contextual elements predominate (drawing from concepts of leisure as residual time and as functional).

2 Leisure and play

'Play' is an important characteristic in many aspects of leisure practice. Its use in the language constantly betrays its centrality: we *play* cards, *play* a sport, go to a *play*. Johan Huizinga, perhaps the foremost play theorist, goes as far as identifying play as basic to culture and the development of civilisation. Despite its apparent importance to leisure, 'play' appears bedevilled by confusions about its very nature, due to contradictions between fact and ideal, and between play's qualities and the functions often ascribed to it. It is not uncommon to find alternative explanations of play jostling with each other in the same text, but with few signposts pointing out their significance, differences or relationship. In order to avoid similar pitfalls, we shall initially separate those theories which treat play as a *quality* (as being *intrinsically motivated,* for *fun*), from those which seek the key to understanding play in its *outcomes* (as being *extrinsically motivated,* as *functional*).

Qualities of play

There is broad consensus among these play theories that the primary characteristic which distinguishes play from other areas of social life is its *non-serious* nature. The rest of life is made up with *serious* duties and obligations (work, maintenance of a desired standard of living, etc.).

Members of any given society are socialised into recognition of what is and what is not serious – so that gradually the young child comes to recognise when an activity is, or is not, work, necessity or obligation, and when it is play or non-play. From this primary quality of non-seriousness, or separateness, as Huizinga calls it, other qualities flow:

(a) play is free – it is not an obligation, and therefore if we are compelled to play, it is at best a pale shadow, a simulation of play. In this sense school games would certainly not be seen as play unless they are so enjoyable that the sense of compulsion is lost. (Would it were so!)

(b) play is self-contained – and an end in itself. Because it is non-serious it is not a means to an end; we do it for its intrinsic rewards. The process of playing is what matters, not the end product – in fact in play the means of playing and the outcome of play are inseparable. In this sense play has been described as 'an occasion of pure waste' because its consequences are not carried beyond its immediate confines. The French sociologist Caillois (1961) has further elaborated this characteristic in order to accommodate gambling games within the sphere of play. Aware that gambling may, if one is lucky, have consequences beyond play (we are in the era of the one million pounds pools winner after all), he has suggested that the term *unproductive* be used as an alternative to 'self-contained'. Thus gambling (as any other form of play), is merely an exchange between players – no money is created, it is simply redistributed;

(c) play is regulated or rule-governed – a further characteristic which emphasises its separateness from other aspects of life, is the tendency for play to take on and elaborate its own special rules. These may, in sports, be highly formalised and enforced even more rigorously than the laws of the land. Amateur players are frequently banned from playing for lengthy periods with no appeal to bodies such as industrial tribunals which regulate dismissals in the serious world of work! In actuality, the law of the land can of course override the rules of play, as recent legal cases demonstrate. However, the relative infrequency of legal intervention in play, and the consequent media furore when it occurs (e.g. in 1987 Glasgow Rangers' players were indicted for fighting on the pitch) only serves to highlight the perceived power of the rules of play. Even in very informal play – such as children's games – the sanctity of the rules is paramount. The cheat who deliberately breaks the rules is reluctantly tolerated, but the spoilsport who refuses to recognise the rules at all is 'beyond the pale'! Huizinga believed that the voluntary acceptance of the framework of rules in play gave it an ethical dimension;

(d) play is limited in space and time – the rules of play take on spatial and temporal elements in order to demarcate them more fully. Games typically have boundaries; areas on which play proceeds, and beyond which other rules apply. Evidence from the ways in which these boundaries are treated helps us to gauge the extent to which an activity remains truly playful, or becomes more serious. For example, in the 1980s and 1990s, as some sport participants have become more concerned with winning, and as the laws on the pitch have offered players insufficient protection from physical violence, so the playing area has been seen as less 'sacred' and police have gone on to the pitch to restore order between players. Such actions were virtually unheard of (and unthinkable) in earlier, less utilitarian times. In children's play the spatial element, though less formal than the lines on the pitch, is no less important. Young children know, for example, which space is part of their game, even if their parents are unaware of the fact that the chair they just sat on is, in fact, a railway engine.

The time boundaries of play are also usually marked, so that the players know when play begins and ends. Again, games and sports provide the most clearly structured examples of time specification in play. But in all forms of play there are implicit temporal limitations. When the theatre curtain falls, for example, we return from another psychological time/world, to our own.

A further characteristic of the time element in play concerns *repetition*. In most serious duties and obligations we do not repeat actions merely for the pleasure of repetition – there are other instrumental motives. In play, on the other hand, the same experience or activity is repeated again and again for its own sake. Application of the 'test of repetition' to certain activities which take place in non-work time, and which are frequently termed leisure activities, helps us further to unravel the nature of play, and its relationship to leisure. Take the case of DIY – a major feature of non-work roles in the late twentieth century. Is this play? Wallpapering a room involves some aesthetic judgements, but thereafter it becomes a utilitarian act and it is not repeated immediately for fun. When paper is torn off, it is for serious reasons (of taste and discrimination) not for the opportunity it affords for repeating the act of wallpapering. DIY may not always be entirely economically motivated and it usually takes place in residual time, but by this token, it is not playful. Religion is a more difficult case. Certainly, religious rituals are repeated in the same form with great regularity, and it fits many of the other criteria of play. However, true believers in a faith see its implication extending far beyond its immediate temporal boundaries (maybe even as far as the next world) and in this sense it is certainly not self-contained.

(e) Other characteristics of play – additional dimensions to play have been identified by some writers. Huizinga considers that the 'make-believe' and 'secretive' nature of play is important. In play, people enter voluntarily into a sort of fantasy world with its own special lore and language which further cuts it off from non-play and makes it secret. Caillois thinks that the make-believe element is an alternative to regulations in play. The play-world is circumscribed and demarcated, either by rules (as in sports) or by make-believe (as in drama), but not by both.

A further quality of play regarded as important by Caillois, is its *uncertainty* and the pleasurable *tension* which accrues from its unpredictability of outcome. If the outcome of play is known in advance, players are only going through the motions and their interest quickly dies. Consider, for example, a one-sided game in which the dominant team 'plays with' their opponents rather than 'playing against them'. Equally, in make-believe play, such as drama, the actors and the audience suspend their knowledge of the ending of a familiar play, in order to enjoy the working of the plot. It is a measure of the quality of a classical story (film or play), that it stands repetition even though the outcome is familiar. Tension is still present in the playing out of events and relationships, while external realities of time and space are held in abeyance.

To summarise then, the major qualities of play are: non-seriousness; freedom; self-containment; regulation and/or make-believe; limitation in time or space; and uncertainty of outcome. Two major criticisms have been made of this approach. The first revolves around issues of definition. In the following chapter, problems of defining particular leisure forms are highlighted. Arts and sports can be both forms of work and of leisure. How, for example, can we distinguish between an amateur and a professional sport, when the form of the activity (e.g. golf) is indistinguishable, yet in one case the players are working for a living, while in the other their involvement is for pleasure only? A more fundamental issue concerns the assumption that humans enter another world, a different reality, when they are at play. Critics claim that it is fallacious to conceive of human life as segmented in this way. Life is lived as a whole and we never suspend part of our own person. In a sense, these two broad critiques are linked, as they both concern the complex issue of human motivation and perception, and insist that we look beyond the structure of play to the meanings which individual players invest in their play activity.

This issue is taken up in greater depth in the ensuing chapter's consideration of specific leisure forms, and in the final chapter.

The outcomes of play

Many theories have been advanced claiming to explain play in terms of its function, i.e. what it does for individuals and/or society beyond the immediate experience of playing. Play is analysed in terms of its *outcomes* – its long term *goals* and consequences. These explanations are of three main types: biological; psychological; and sociological. Biological and psychological approaches have tended to emphasise the effects on the individual of play experience, and frequently concentrate on children's play, while sociological approaches have examined the role of play in contributing to culture and social order. In this section some of these major 'functional' explanations are briefly summarised, and finally an attempt is made to examine the relationships between the 'qualitative' and 'functional' accounts of play, and their relevance in understanding leisure.

Play as developmental and educational
Early hypotheses saw play as natural; as an instinct in children which, if given scope for expression, would lead to the development of skills and learning. Similarities were noted between the play of animals and of children; the concept of the *kinder-garten* (child-garden) in which children would develop naturalistically, if left to play, was an inevitable consequence. In more recent times the 'playway' to learning has been the subject of educational debate and criticism – proponents arguing for the benefits in spontaneity, creativity and motivation which would accrue if children were allowed to adopt an exploratory, problem-solving approach to learning. In a different vein, but still focusing on children, the Swiss psychologist Piaget studied the role of play (and especially games with rules), in forming moral judgements and standards. Clearly a developmental function for play is implied here as children learn to accept a need for rules in a game such as marbles (the now-dated subject of his study), to elaborate them and to generalise concepts to other situations.

Play as stimulus-seeking behaviour
Closely linked to educational justifications for play, is the view developed principally by Ellis, that play represents a human need for stimulation. This notion suggests that psychological well-being is dependent on humans being able to experience periodically heightened levels of arousal, and that this stimulus-seeking behaviour occurs largely in the sphere of play. The concept of the level of 'optimum-arousal' is important because fulfilment depends on finding a level somewhere between boredom and over-stimulation. This approach has much in common with the ideas expressed by Csikzentmihalyi and by Elias and Dunning, who similarly ascribe to play the power of providing psychological satisfaction, lying between the *boredom* of under-stimulation and the *anxiety* created by

over-challenging 'demands', or the chaos and hysteria of excessive excitement (the latter well-known to pop concert organisers; the former to England soccer supporters!). This approach embraces adult play as well as that of children and it clearly has some links with the idea of play as self-motivated. However, there remains a strong sense, in the texts quoted, that such play is not merely self-contained but has important utilitarian meanings extending into social life beyond the play experience itself.

Play as socialisation

Many sociologists and anthropologists identify parallels between types of play behaviour found typically in a given society, and the dominant values of the culture of that society. 'Play behaviour' is usually interpreted in practice as the most prevalent forms of games encountered. The structures and practices of these games are then studied for evidence to support the notion that they help to socialise children into the values, roles, practices, beliefs and conventions of society. The mechanisms operating within this process are many and complex, involving relationships between children and parents, child-rearing practices, structures of games, and attitudes towards authority.

G. H. Mead, for example, has identified an important place for play and games in helping children develop a conception of the 'generalised other'. This refers to the ability to move from a very individualistic view of oneself and others (typical of children), towards a capacity to generalise about the roles that people play in society, without necessarily identifying them with specific persons. The notion of a game or society having a set of abstract roles which can be filled by anyone who knows how to play is a difficult concept, rendered accessible through practice.

Roberts and Sutton-Smith (1962) argue that games have the dual function of:

- defusing the conflict that inevitably arises between children and their parents as they are disciplined to conform gradually to the adult world;
- enculturation, as the games themselves are played, since they contain acceptance of rule-governed behaviour, and exemplify values that society holds to be important.

Thus, for example, games of physical skill (which require active physical involvement in competing with others), help children to reduce the anxiety they experience in a training situation where democracy and reasonableness overlay parent power. At the same time, these games, with qualities like equality, fair play, skill and achievement, help to socialise children into desirable qualities.

Games of chance (e.g. bingo requiring a passive acceptance of fate and luck) relate to authoritarian parental control with much emphasis on children taking responsibility very early in life. Here, games provide a means of release from responsibility, and at the same time reinforce belief that control over one's life lies in the hands of fate or the 'gods'. Closely related hypotheses developed by Zurcher and Meadow (1971) shift the scale *wider* still. They suggest that the 'national sport' of the country gives important clues to the central value system of that society. Hence bullfighting, the Mexican national sport, is linked to authoritarian, patriarchal relationships in the Mexican family, and to acceptance of an authoritarian state. The nature and structure of the sport provides a means of sublimating the tension in the family, while at the same time confirming a belief in a rigidly hierarchical society. This explanation attaches highly symbolic meanings to the bullfight and its players – bull, matadors, picadors, president of the corrida and the audience. In a similar manner, in the USA, baseball represents the values of the modal Anglo–American family and reinforces belief in a rule-governed, democratic, egalitarian society. Again the baseball park and its participants are interpreted in a heavily symbolic manner.

These sociologically orientated explanations of play have been criticised for their determinism. Individuals appear to have little choice about their play; they are directed into it by psychological and social forces which imply a degree of stereotyping and generalisation. Nonetheless, they are examples of a strong tradition which seeks to account for the phenomenon of play in socially functional terms.

Play as compensatory and sublimatory
The work of Caillois has been mentioned earlier in relation to the qualities of play, and he certainly interprets these formal characteristics as central to the understanding of play. However, he extends his analysis to explore the psycho-social functions of playing, and in so doing leans strongly towards the view that game-play has an important functional role in providing a means of compensation or sublimation for attitudes and activities which cannot find expression elsewhere in social life: they are interpreted as a channel, a release, as cathartic. In order to explore this more fully Caillois made the following assumptions (*see also* Figure 1.1):

- *all play* manifests itself in the form of games. Games are *four major types* which he calls competitions (agon); chance (alea); make-believe (mimicry); disequilibrium (vertigo);
- the ways of playing games may be located on a continuum from simple to complex which he calls childlike (*paidia*) to structured (*ludus*);
- in games, players *express themselves* in ways which are not readily available to them in other aspects of life;

	Agon (competition)	Alea (chance)	Mimicry (simulation)	Ilinx (vertigo)
Paidia (tumult agitation)	e.g. unregulated contests, athletics, wrestling	e.g. counting-out rhymes, heads or tails	e.g. games of illusion fancy dress, masks, disguises, charades	e.g. roller coasters, dancing (some forms), water flumes
Ludus (control, skill)	e.g. football, hockey, fencing, chess snooker	e.g. bingo, football pools, roulette, lotteries	e.g. theatre, opera, drama, spectacles in general	e.g. skiing, sky-diving, mountain climbing, canoeing, wind-surfing

Figure 1.1 Caillois' classification of games (adapted)

- games may be *corrupted* if the qualities they require are taken to excess;
- the nature of games prevalent in a society, or its subcultures, is a powerful indicator of dominant *values* in society.

The close identification of play with 'games' emphasises the essentially social nature of this interpretation. The classification of games into the four major types is intimately bound up with the players' reasons for playing (the psycho-social rationale). Thus *agon* games are those in which competition with opponents is central, and the outcome is determined through the exercise of skill, judgement, endurance, and intelligence. The players are actively in control in a situation of equality not necessarily available elsewhere. Major examples are sports, and board games such as chess.

Games determined by *chance* (alea) differ greatly from *competition* (agon) since players are passive, have no control over the outcome once play is under way, and abandon themselves to the action of others, or to luck. Major examples are gambling games such as bingo, horse racing, and football pools. Here players again find an equality unavailable elsewhere in that the odds of success exactly match the degree of risk or loss, and fair play operates under ideal circumstances.

Games characterised by *make-believe* (mimicry), allow the adoption of a different personality. An alternative world is simulated, for the pleasure of being another and as an escape from reality. Examples may be found in a simple form such as fancy-dress, or in more complex drama and theatre. Players are not attempting to deceive others or themselves since the adoption of another self is conscious and temporary.

If an alternative reality is not sought via regulated competition, chance, or make believe, we can always abandon ourselves to the novel world of physically induced games of *vertigo* (ilinx), or imbalance. Here, reality is literally turned on its head through the exploitation of gravity and friction. The fairground is the most obvious example where complex gravity-defeating mechanical rides induce dizziness and sickness, or reduced friction allows the illusion of freefall. Current leisure provided in theme parks and swimming pools attempts to produce ever more spectacular loop-the-loops and water flumes.

Implicit in Caillois' model is the belief that play, through its manifestation in games, has important social functions to perform, and that without the availability of play, as a means of compensation or sublimation for potentially destructive forces, social order will be jeopardised. Furthermore, games themselves may be corrupted if the motivation which drives them is carried to excess, or is short circuited in pursuit of instant pleasure, like the quick fix.

Thus competition is corrupt when the desire to win becomes obsessive and rules are flouted. Chance becomes corrupt when fatalism takes control, e.g. absolute belief in astrology. Mimicry becomes corrupt when people believe in their alter-ego, living two or more personalities (in chronic form schizophrenia). Vertigo becomes corrupt when the alternative psycho-physical world is sought through internal chemical change – as in drug taking – rather than through external changes in the physical environment.

Caillois' analysis and classification is important not simply because of its contribution to the study of the effects and functions of play, but also because it provides an important model for the classification of forms of play which are recognisable as major forms of leisure (*see* Chapter 2). Furthermore, because it is concerned with both the qualities of play and with its purposes, it leads us towards a resolution of the apparently conflicting distinctions which we noted early in this section, between theories of play emphasising its intrinsic non-utilitarian nature and those favouring extrinsic, utilitarian explanations. In so doing it helps to clarify the relationship of play to leisure, and it provokes a number of questions about the role of play in contributing to the quality of leisure experiences. We therefore conclude this section with consideration of a model for the synthesis of play theories.

The duality of play: intrinsic and extrinsic dimensions

One of the primary qualities of the experience of play is that it is 'disinterested'; it is activity for its own sake, for no ulterior interest. Children play for no other reason than to play. On the other hand, play is often valued precisely because of the purposes it might fulfil, purposes which have little to do with the playing itself. This duality of play – the interlinked intrinsic and extrinsic dimensions – has important implications for leisure which are outlined in Figure 1.2

This model enables us to examine the ways in which the functional or purposeful meanings and goals ascribed to play are intimately related to, and dependent upon, play's intrinsic qualities. This relationship can be identified on four levels.

Level 1   This suggests that the initial motivation for play is a basic human attribute (instinct). Humans have a capacity for stimulus-seeking which manifests itself in problem-solving, skill-learning behaviour. In very young children this capacity is not chosen, it occurs naturally and in that sense is obligatory, and it is directed towards mastery of the environment by learning.

At this stage play is conceptually not differentiated from other activities. It is stimulus-seeking activity which to the infant is neither play nor non-play. Gradually children are socialised into learning what adult so-

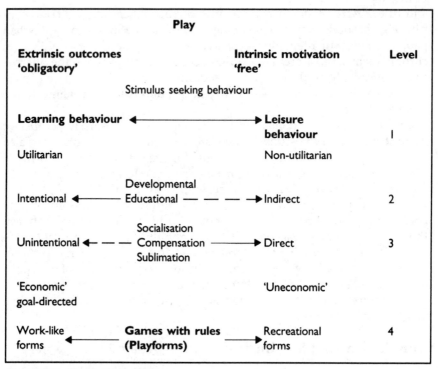

Figure 1.2 The duality of play

ciety regards as play, and what is not play. Activities may still be relatively undifferentiated, but some become associated with obligation and useful learning, others with freedom and fun. Despite the fact that infant school work may be primarily based on a play-like problem-solving approach, it is readily distinguished by children from 'Play-time' which is unobligated. Meanings of activities change according to their context. Thus play in this context moves from level 1 on the model to level 2.

Level 2 Developmental and educational theories of play have emphasised the learning which accrues from early stimulus-seeking activity. They also recognise the usefulness of activities which children begin to regard as freely chosen (as prototypical forms of leisure), as vehicles for learning. Thus games and game-like approaches become part of the formal system of education. At this stage, however, the learning objectives of the activity take precedence over the leisure objectives, and the consequent loss of freedom may extinguish any sense of playfulness. These theories are therefore located on the extrinsic side of the play continuum, but note that it *is* a continuum since they implicitly recognise the importance of playful qualities in meeting learning objectives.

Level 3 Socialisation and compensatory/sublimatory theories are also located on a continuum, but this time biased towards the intrinsic side of the model. These theories recognise the importance of the apparently freely chosen nature of playful activities, as far as the participants are concerned, which are also performing significant social functions. Furthermore, (and paradoxically), according to Caillois, the better the fit of particular activities with the intrinsic qualities of play, the greater their potential as agents of socialisation, and the better their effectiveness in channelling human energies into constructive forms.

Finally, at *level 4* of the vertical axis (the structured end of the play-games continuum) we locate 'games with rules'. This allows us to examine a major set of leisure forms which clearly carry many of the qualities of play, within the extrinsic-intrinsic; obligatory-free framework. Sports, for example, may be played for non-utilitarian, 'uneconomic' reasons, for fun or as recreations, or they may be played seriously in work-like forms in an 'economic', goal-directed way. (Certainly for professionals their play becomes work-like, even though it remains illusory to spectators.) Thus, using this model, we are able to make sense of, and reconcile, the apparent paradox of an activity which has a single form (e.g. football) but different meanings for players, motivated for different reasons.

This model, therefore, provides a way of examining the complex inter-relationships between the intrinsic and extrinsic dimensions of play. Moreover, the relationship of play to leisure can be examined through consideration of the following formulations:

- the greater the freedom allowed to players to choose an activity, the greater its potential as leisure
- the more extrinsically orientated an activity becomes, the lower its leisure potential
- the better the fit with the qualities of play, the greater its functional significance
- the greater the emphasis on play as a vehicle for intentional learning, the lower its leisure potential
- the more structured a play form becomes, the less its leisure potential. This suggests that the greater the degree of organisation in, for example, a game, the lower the degree of freedom/choice available to players.

It is instructive to examine these hypotheses and relate them to experiences of such activities as school sports. Were they ever leisurelike? Equally, the drive to manage and organise ever more complex forms of competition, even in such individually orientated sports as skateboarding, may be harmful to the nature of the activity. How strong is this trend in your local sports centre?

Does the growing commercialisation of televised sports, and their ever increasing emphasis on the needs of spectators, diminish their recreational potential for players?

3 Leisure and work

In the last section we took a play centred view of leisure, arguing that the quality of many leisure activities and experiences is dependent on the purity of the play element in their makeup. In the final section of this introductory chapter, we shall examine some aspects of 'the work-centred' view of leisure, which in many ways has dominated debate on the significance of leisure since the advent of industrial society. As we noted earlier, this view of leisure is strongly related to the 'residual time' and 'functional' conceptions of leisure.

Leisure as a product of industrial labour

In some senses it is accurate to describe our modern conception of leisure as *industrial* – that is to say, the way in which we associate leisure with blocks of free-time and with certain sorts of worthwhile activities, relates essentially to changes which occurred in the combined processes of industrialisation and urbanisation in Britain between 1750 and 1900. This is not to suggest that leisure did not exist before that period, for it most certainly did. There is considerable documentary evidence of pleasure, pastimes, fairs, wakes, feasts, holy-days, markets and recreations in pre-industrial Britain. It *is* to suggest, however, that leisure came to be conceived in a new way during the industrial period, and the most telling characteristic of this new conception is that of work *centrality*.

Work came to dominate people's lives during this time, not simply in the sheer amount of time demanded by the new processes and practices of industrial labour, but much more powerfully, because of changes in the nature of work. This demanded a new way of seeing the world – a new psychological stance – which came to be characterised as the 'work ethic'. Pleasure came a poor second in this scenario, and the modern view of leisure emerging against this background reflects this conception: leisure is dependent on work for its time and its justification. Leisure, though 'separate', paradoxically comes in many ways to resemble work, such is the predominance of the work-centred view of the world. An analysis of the ways in which certain leisure activities changed in form during the major period of industrial growth can provide us with powerful clues to the new concept of work-based leisure (leisure in the image of work). Football is a well documentated example, and we can readily trace the gradual shift from the riotous and unruly street games of the 1820s to the largely rational and regulated forms of the 1870s. The dimensions of this change are important because they illustrate the transformation not simply of leisure forms, but of ways of experiencing the world:

Time

The idea of time changed from cyclical to linear. Clock-time, related to the demands of shift work, replaced the sense of time dictated by the seasons and day and night. Time was organised into blocks of useful work to ensure continuous operation of capital intensive machinery, rather than being flexible to meet the demands of a particular task, such as haymaking or harvesting. Time in this new sense became a commodity – to be 'spent', 'wasted', or 'killed'. Time for leisure, and time in leisure, was equally compressed and packaged. When Saturday afternoons from 2 p.m. were eventually won from work as 'free-time', their use for the newly curtailed winter game of football, lasting until dark, seemed almost natural. The step to formalising it to 90 minutes, neatly divided into halves, was a short one.

Space

Conceptions of space also changed, and in much the same way as time, became compressed and packaged. Space for purposes of popular leisure had been under attack for some time prior to the major phase of industrialisation, as a result of the agricultural revolution which preceded it. The enclosures of common land around the turn of the eighteenth century had already reduced horizons. With urbanisation, the rapid growth of industrial terraced housing crowding around the mill, mine and factory, the process was given a decisive twist. Mental maps became further confined and concomitant forms of recreational activity fitted this reduction in scale. Football became an urban-scale game, contained by boundaries. Gradually these were incorporated into the structure of the game itself, and a sharp demarcation was established between the playing space and the world outside. Spaces for leisure also became incorporated into the commercial sphere, hence street football moved to the football ground and street markets to the market hall.

Discipline

A major requirement of the new industrial work-processes came to be termed 'labour discipline'. Workers had to be coerced and persuaded to adopt a new lifestyle of a more orderly nature. They had to become more like the machinery they were to serve, in order to meet the demands of industrial production. The establishment of police forces and factory discipline helped this process in an overt way, but covert forces were of equal or greater importance. 'Civilisation' and 'respectability' became important watchwords as religious and reformist groups sought to establish the new morality and incorporate it into the industrial world. Leisure activities were especially susceptible to scrutiny, as many of the traditional forms ran counter to this crusade. Violent forms such as animal baiting were banned; other forms, such as football, were regulated. In order to play, it became necessary to conform to the rules, and to a degree this required the exercise of self-control. Ultimately, games like football, in their civilised guise, became suitable for purposes of social and religious education. Thus by the last quarter of the nineteenth century they were sufficiently orderly to be seen as a model form of physical recreation and were incorporated to some degree into the embryonic state education system, and into church youth work as so-called 'muscular Christianity'.

Division of labour
Central to the nature of new forms of industrial work was the division of labour. Industrial tasks were broken down into manageable elements, each of which could be accomplished by individual workers in stark contrast to pre-industrial practices where tasks were normally conceived of in a more holistic form. With the division of labour came specialisation, as particular roles, requiring particular skills became the industrial norm. These changes were echoed in leisure. Football, for example, developed from a formless scrimmage for the ball in which all players pursued undifferentiated roles, into a formalised attack and defence. Play was thus divided; formations developed; and efficiency in the achievement of goals became of heightened importance. Other leisure forms exhibited similar tendencies; for example the old multi-purpose fairs which combined commerce and entertainment gradually gave way to specialisation as commerce was separated into more specific occupations, and the funfair (exploiting the new mechanical wonders) became an entity in its own right.

Leisure and work in nineteenth century industrial society became ultimately related in two major ways. First, leisure-time came to be seen as sharply divided from work-time and subservient to it. Second, many leisure activities took on the qualities which characterised industrial work, and were thus seen as serving the needs of production and psychologically bolstering the work ethic. Writers such as Cunningham and Bailey have questioned the extent to which this process was all-encompassing, and have pointed to resistance to the domination and acceptance of work-centrality. It is impossible, however, to ignore completely the accumulated evidence about major changes which did occur in leisure forms under the impact of industrialisation, and indeed the concept of work-defined leisure lingers into the late twentieth century.

Changing work–leisure relationships

A number of leisure theorists, struck in part by the dependence of leisure on work in early industrial societies, have sought to establish theoretical frameworks for the exploration of work–leisure relationships. These frameworks are of two main types:

(a) those which examine work and leisure in their wider societal context;
(b) those which focus on individuals and their choice of leisure and work lifestyles.

Here we shall examine these frameworks separately for purposes of analysis, but individual lifestyles and wider structural frameworks are related – an issue which is addressed more fully in Chapter 7.

Work and leisure – fusion or polarity
Writers concerned with broad structural processes of change have debated the extent to which work and leisure are like each other (fusion), or are dissimilar (polarity), the terms having been coined originally by Riesman and Blomberg (1957). In primitive societies, it is frequently argued, work and leisure are not distinguishable. South Sea islanders for example fuse together work and play with religion and ritual, and have no compartmentalised idea of leisure. Idealised versions of rural life in pre-industrial Britain also lean towards this view. The opposite standpoint, that leisure bears no resemblance to work, finding its meaning elsewhere, is attributed historically to the Ancient Greeks of the classical period. Indeed the Greek word for work means non-leisure. Only free men were capable of attaining leisure, because leisure was freedom from the necessity to work which was in itself a mark of citizenship. An obvious corollary was that ideal forms of Greek leisure sought to display their independence of work; hence for example, musing and contemplation as 'worthy' leisure. The Greek case, however, is rare, since it was after all based on a massive slave economy, and a small citizen elite. Even wives and daughters of free-born Greeks were not eligible for citizenship. In industrial societies it is difficult to find examples of such polarity, for as we have argued above, work so dominates that leisure forms themselves become involved with its spirit and take on a work-like nature. Even when activities appear to contrast vividly with work (as for example drinking and gambling) it has been argued that they are still work-determined, because they are seen as a deliberate attempt to escape it, or to reverse its values. This view of course relates to Caillois' discussion of the compensatory/sublimatory functions of play discussed earlier.

As the end of the twentieth century approaches, it is difficult to discern movement towards a polarity of work and leisure but many remark on shifts in the strength and direction of the work-leisure relationship. Some writers depict the 1990s as a stage of advanced industrialism or 'post-industrialism' and suggest that it is now more appropriate to think of a leisure–work fusion. They argue that for a majority of the UK population leisure has superseded work as a central life-interest and that the shaping of work and work time to fit leisure needs (rather than vice versa) is now a significant issue. Work is also much more varied than in the early stages of industrial society and there is a shift towards a 'service' economy. Only a minority (fewer than 20%) are employed in manufacturing industry of the traditional type, so that no dominant mode exists to compare with the former overbearing presence of 'mechanical-labour'. With computerisation and automation, most present-day jobs make fewer demands on time, energy and discipline and are seen mainly as a means to a wage packet by many workers, while the power of the work ethic is much reduced.

There are critics of this view of work in advanced industrialism who argue that the organisation of work has resulted in 'deskilling', intensified labour productivity, and new patterns of employment for all workers, particularly the disadvantaged, such as racial minorities, women and the unskilled. Such critics see the 1990s as a period of 'late capitalism' rather than 'advanced industrialism' or 'post-industrialism'. The different terms reflect different views on recent changes in work–leisure relationships. In reply to such doubts about changing work patterns, and in support of the fusion of leisure–work it is stressed that leisure choices have expanded to match newly freed time and energy resources. A new leisure-ethic means that the relative affluence experienced by the majority of the UK workforce since the late 1950s may be spent in a new guilt-free way. Analysis of the growth in paid holidays during this period, the rise of foreign package holidays, and more importantly the adoption of markedly hedonistic holiday styles by the previously 'silent majority', are strongly indicative of this trend. Concurrently with this change, there is evidence of a decline in the older work-based forms of leisure. The decline in football spectatorship as the working man's leisure is perhaps the most stark; average gates having decreased by 75% in the period from 1950–85.

Other regimented leisure forms have also virtually disappeared as popular activities, and have become the province of (often elderly) minorities. Consider, for example, the case of ballroom dancing and the old Butlin's style holiday camps. Of course it would be wrong to attribute all changes in post-World War II leisure behaviour to the demise of work-centrality. The rise of television and other home-based electronic entertainment and the corresponding fall in cinema viewing would appear to be a technologically driven transformation. Equally the power of radio and television to reduce the scale of leisure to the home, and to destroy its communal nature, while at the same time creating a mass culture of its own, is probably not directly related to the nature of work. It has, however, been instrumental in promoting a leisure ethic. This issue is discussed more fully in Chapters 6 and 7.

Some argue then that the fusion of leisure and work has weakened as the centrality of a particular kind of industrial work has declined, and lifestyles have become much less uniform. Leisure has not become independent of work, but the direction of the relationship is changing so that work may now be conceived as the servant of leisure, and that a 'leisure-ethic' is abroad in the world. Economic reasons for working are as important as ever and to that extent work remains central in people's lives. As a moral force, however, work it is argued is in decline, since its status for the majority of people is seen in instrumental terms as paid employment or sold time.

In conclusion it is worth noting that Parker (1983) has questioned the completeness of the division between 'fusion-polarity' and has suggested that a threefold classification may be more appropriate. This would categorise work and leisure thus:

● work and leisure are related and similar in form (identity);
● work and leisure are related but dissimilar in form (opposite);
● work and leisure are unrelated (separateness).

Individual work–leisure relationships

The foregoing discussion has examined broad societal trends in the relationships between work and leisure, but said little about individual human beings and the extent to which they fit these patterns, or deny them. Do people in their everyday lives choose leisure forms with total freedom from the influence of their work? Or does their work shape the nature of their leisure, and if so to what extent? This issue is often referred to as the 'segmentalism-holism' debate. *Segmentalists* conceive lives as a series of elements (home, work, family, leisure) which are essentially separate from each other, while *holists* make no such divisions, but see all aspects of their lives as mutually informing and interconnected. In this sense individuals are capable of choosing how they wish to experience leisure irrespective of broader issues of 'fusion-polarity' work–leisure relationships. This, however, makes life purely a matter for personal philosophy and most social theorists would argue that individual agents are never completely free from structural constraints. It is revealing, therefore, to examine the degree to which work *structures* leisure in different occupations, in its time and energy requirements, and the extent to which members of the same occupation groups conform to any particular pattern.

Early research of this type examined the ways in which work values may *spill over* into leisure, or the capacity of leisure to *compensate* for the shortcomings of work. In either case, leisure was seen as subordinate to work, and reflected a concern with the quality of work rather than of leisure. A more recent and more leisure-orientated set of hypotheses has been progressively developed by Parker (1971; 1983). Drawing from research findings on the work and leisure lifestyles of various occupational groups, he identifies three broad work–leisure relationships:

(a) *extension*: similarity between at least some work and leisure activities and a lack of demarcation between work and leisure, e.g. social workers, successful business people, doctors and teachers;
(b) *opposition*: intentional dissimilarity of work and leisure and a strong demarcation between the two spheres, e.g. miners, oil-rig workers;
(c) *neutrality*: 'usually different' content of work and leisure, and an 'average' demarcation between the two, e.g. routine manual and clerical workers.

Extension and opposition patterns both exhibit an attachment to work – positive and negative respectively – and are associated with work as a central life interest. Neutrality is markedly different because work is viewed in a detached way, and leisure may well be of central concern.

Parker's threefold classification is extended to examine a number of variables within work (e.g. degree of autonomy, social groupings) and outside work (e.g. level of education) and is reproduced in Table 1.5. Some of the studies of the occupational groups on which the typology is based are listed at the end of this chapter for further reading.

A number of criticisms of Parker's hypotheses have been made, which may be grouped as follows:

(a) the analysis *overstates the importance of work* in contemporary leisure behaviour. Work is, for example, much less important than one's gender, stage in the family and life-cycle, except perhaps in the few remaining traditional industries where 'occupational communities' still exist.
(b) the analysis largely *ignores women* in its basic assumptions because it equates work with paid employment and draws its empirical evidence from men's employment. The concept of domestic labour and its influence on women's leisure choices is not addressed.
(c) The analysis *simply classifies activities* in work and leisure, and ignores the difference between their form and meaning. For example, the same activity may carry different meanings for different people. One might play golf to test one's skills competitively; or play for fresh air and exercise and the result is unimportant. We should not therefore expect to find any particular leisure activity populated solely by 'extentionalists', 'oppositionists' or 'neutralists'.

Table 1.5 Types of work–leisure relationship and associated variables (individual level)

(Source: Parker, 1983)

Work–leisure relationship variables	Extension	Opposition	Neutrality
Content of work and leisure	Similar	Deliberately different	Usually different
Demarcation of spheres	Weak	Strong	Average
Central Life Interest	Work	–	Non-work
Imprint left by work on leisure	Marked	Marked	Not marked
Work variables			
Autonomy in work situation	High	–	Low
Use of abilities (how far extended)	Fully (stretched)	Unevenly (damaged)	Not (bored)
Involvement	Moral	Alienative	Calculative
Work colleagues	Include some close friends	–	Include no close friends
Work encroachment on leisure	High	Low	Low
Typical occupations	Social workers (especially residential)	'Extreme' (mining fishing)	Routine clerical and manual
Non-work variables			
Educational level	High	Low	Medium
Duration of leisure	Short	Irregular	Long
Main function of leisure	Continuation	Recuperation	Entertainment

It could also be argued that the weakening of the links between work and leisure in society discussed earlier, together with a growing leisure-ethic, will make such relationships on the individual plane less likely. In a way 'we are all neutralists now' in an era of mass culture and mass consumption. This equates to some extent with the ideas of Daniel Bell on 'post-industrial society', to the effect that in industrial society work, morals, religion and leisure were all of a piece with the work ethic; however, in post-industrial society people are allowed to compartmentalise their lives and not perceive any contradiction or necessary connection between the 'cultural realm' (fun, pleasure, play, consumption) and the 'techno-economic' realm (of employment).

Despite these criticisms, which Parker recognises, his typology remains a valuable device which provides a tool for the analysis of particular work or leisure relationships. It is not intended as a deterministic or causal theory and should not be conceived as such. Used as a template however, against which to evaluate empirical reality, it may extend our understanding of the changing relationships between leisure and work.

Leisure, work and unemployment
Unemployment in Britain rose from under 500 000 people in the 1960s to 3 million by the mid 1980s, and has since fluctuated between 2–3 million. In 1993 about 10% of the potential workforce was unemployed (average for the European Community, excluding Spain at 16–20%). Unemployment in Europe bears heavily on the young and on ethnic minorities. In Britain, for example, in 1993 one in five males and one in seven females under 19 were unemployed. Among black, Pakistani and Bangladeshi populations the rate is 20–25% of the potential labour force. Because unemployment is a 'flow' rather than static, it is possible that 6 million individuals have experienced unemployment at some time during the 1980s and early 1990s.

IS UNEMPLOYMENT LEISURE?
For the majority of people, unemployment is not seen as leisure. Leisure is conventionally still associated with time free from work – with the 'industrial' conceptions which we discussed earlier. This renders unemployment 'non-leisure' on a number of grounds:
- spare time is not conceptually the same as free time from work; it has not been 'earned';
- many leisure activities are complementary to work and not to unemployment;
- most leisure activities are concerned with consumption paid for by work.

Studies of the unemployed have shown that availability of extensive spare time does not, for most people, lead to an increase in their range of leisure activities, but to a decrease both in number and enjoyment. In spite of free recreation and library facilities, time is more likely to be spent in bed or watching TV. A few people, usually the better educated, have chosen unemployment deliberately for the freedom it offers to develop an alternative lifestyle, despite low income. The State, however, does not adopt the view that unemployment may be regarded as leisure, and actively discourages those who attempt to construct an alternative to the work ethic. A recent example is current legislation requiring school leavers not entering employment to take up a Youth Training Scheme place or to forfeit unemployment benefit. Ironically for the unemployed the work-ethic may well be stronger than for those in employment, both symbolically and in actuality.

Paul Willis (1985) has researched into unemployment in Wolverhampton. He argues that the young unemployed are in a state of suspended animation, 'frozen' in a broken transition between leaving school and starting work. The failure to find work and an adequate wage closes the door to adulthood and particularly the consumption of leisure. Black youths experience unemployment more frequently and for longer periods while young women are driven further into domestic and family responsibilities because of inadequate material resources within the family. There are differences in how youth responds to unemployment, state training and work. Roberts' study of Liverpool/London differs substantially from Willis' Wolverhampton study. Roberts suggests that young people are developing new patterns of work and leisure in response to changed circumstances and opportunities. Ken Pryce's study of Afro-Caribbeans in Bristol (1979) provides a vivid account of how black youth copes with being working class and black in the local labour market which offers mainly 'shit-work'. Pryce traces distinct responses, many illegal, to coping with institutionalised racism in local labour markets. He also provides important insights into how Afro-Caribbean social networks are built up around leisure lifestyles which strengthen their own cultural identity – whether leisure is gospel choirs, parties and smoking dope, prostitution or black music (*see* Figure 1.3).

CAN LEISURE REPLACE WORK?

Work, in the form of paid employment, provides tangible benefits of pay and associated conditions for which leisure is clearly no substitute. It also provides other intangible, but psychologically important benefits:

- it helps to define self identity and often confers status;
- it imposes a time structure on the day, week, year;
- it usually provides social contacts, interdependence and group experience outside the immediate family community;
- it links a person to the outside community via an occupational role;
- it requires activity;
- it is regarded as serious, obligated activity by the majority.

Leisure, conceived in its familiar forms of activity, may be able to meet some of these psychological demands which the absence of work will have left unfilled. For example, recreations and crafts can provide social contacts, demand activity, and help create an acceptable self-identity. They may partially help to structure the day. However, except in the few cases where unemployed people are able to re-orientate their values completely, they are no substitutes for work because they still retain their non-serious unobligated meanings (playfulness), with which the (em-

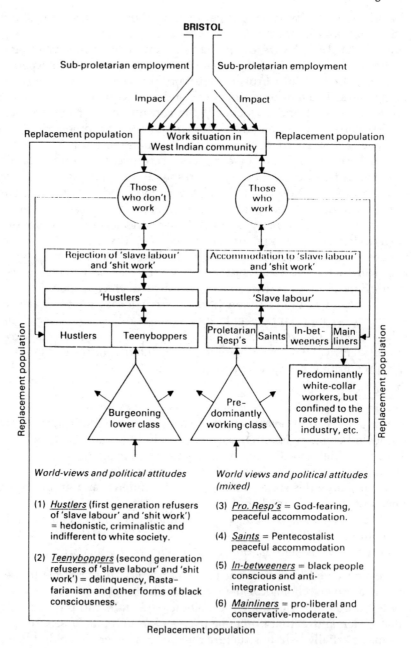

BRISTOL

Sub-proletarian employment | Sub-proletarian employment

Impact | Impact

Replacement population

Work situation in West Indian community

Replacement population

Those who don't work

Those who work

Rejection of 'slave labour' and 'shit work'

Accommodation to 'slave labour' and 'shit work'

'Hustlers'

'Slave labour'

| Hustlers | Teenyboppers | | Proletarian Resp's | Saints | In-bet-weeners | Main liners |

Burgeoning lower class

Pre-dominantly working class

Predominantly white-collar workers, but confined to the race relations industry, etc.

Replacement population

Replacement population

World-views and political attitudes

(1) *Hustlers* (first generation refusers of 'slave labour' and 'shit work') = hedonistic, criminalistic and indifferent to white society.

(2) *Teenyboppers* (second generation refusers of 'slave labour' and 'shit work') = delinquency, Rasta-farianism and other forms of black consciousness.

World views and political attitudes (mixed)

(3) *Pro. Resp's* = God-fearing, peaceful accommodation.

(4) *Saints* = Pentecostalist peaceful accommodation

(5) *In-betweeners* = black people conscious and anti-integrationist.

(6) *Mainliners* = pro-liberal and conservative-moderate.

Replacement population

Figure 1.3 Work–leisure lifestyles: lifestyle map showing the impact of 'slave labour' and 'shit-work' on the lifestyles of West Indians in Bristol

ployed) majority still identifies them. Playing, however seriously, is not a proper job, except in a few cases of professional sports and arts. /

The circle is thus complete, for the very qualities which distinguish leisure from work, and which give leisure its potential to provide human fulfilment, are the same qualities which prevent leisure from replacing work for those who cannot obtain it. Values, however, are not static, and the recognition that full employment in its traditional sense is structurally unlikely to return, may foreshadow a re-definition of the concepts of both work and leisure.

QUESTIONS AND EXERCISES ————————————

1 What conceptions of leisure are implicit or explicit in policy documents produced by:
 (a) The Sports Council ¬
 (b) The Arts Council ¬
 (c) your Local Authority Leisure Services Department? ¬

2 It was suggested earlier that work in industrialised societies has been transformed in time, space, discipline, and division of labour. Further, contemporary leisure activity was constructed in the image of work. How work-like are contemporary leisure activities?

3 Why has Parker's analysis of work–leisure relationships been criticised for being 'gender-blind'?

4 How useful are the characteristics of play (outlined in Section 2) for describing your own leisure activity?

5 Does Parker's typology of extension/opposition/neutrality make sense of:
 (a) your own work–leisure pattern?
 (b) those of your work colleagues?
 (c) those of your friends/acquaintances/neighbours?

6 How does a commercial provider's view of 'leisure' differ from that of a public sector provider?

7 Write down your own working definition of leisure. Can you refine it to exclude non-leisure? How close is your original definition to that of Kaplan?

8 How do 'children's games' inform your understanding of 'play'? Why are particular games 'traditional' and are to be found in different regions of Britain and in different countries?

9 Salaman, G. (1974) *Occupation and Community*, argues that both architects and railway workers are 'occupational communities', and have extension

patterns of work–leisure relationships. Can you think of other 'occupational communities' which have similar work–leisure relationships?

10 How do TV game shows like 'Gladiators' differ from sports such as football on television in presentation and commentary?

Further reading

Most leisure texts contain a section on various ways in which leisure has been defined and conceptualised. Helpful summaries and discussions may be found in the opening chapters of:

M. Kaplan (1975) *Leisure: Theory and Policy*, John Wiley and Sons, Inc.; S. Parker (1976) *The Sociology of Leisure*, George Allen and Unwin; S. Parker (1983) *Leisure and Work*, George Allen and Unwin; K. Roberts (1981) *Contemporary Society and the Growth of Leisure*, Longman; J. Stockdale (1985) *What is leisure? An empirical analysis of the concept of leisure and the role of leisure in people's lives*, Sports Council/ESRC contains a section analysing people's 'common sense' understandings of leisure. G. Torkildsen (1983) *Leisure and Recreation*, E. and F. N. Spon, examines the related concepts of play, recreation and leisure in three separate chapters. A corrective to the predominantly male definitions of leisure may be found in R. Deem (1986) *All Work and No Play: The Sociology of Women and Leisure*, Open University Press, and in E. Green, S. Hebron and D. Woodward (1990) *Women's Leisure: What Leisure?*, Macmillan.

One of the strengths of 'community studies' undertaken in the 1950s and 1960s was to understand people's leisure within the wider contexts of class and community. N. Dennis *et al.* (1968) *Coal is our Life*, Tavistock, and J. Tunstall (1963) *The Fishermen*, George Allen and Unwin, provide clear examples of oppositional work–leisure relationships, whereas Goldthorpe *et al.*'s study (1969), *The Affluent Car Worker*, Cambridge University Press, suggests a more 'neutrality' work–leisure relationship amongst the 'new' working class. Such studies ignored the position of women, see R. Frankenberg (1976), 'In the production of their lives, Men (?) . . .' in *Sexual Divisions and Society: Process and Change*, Tavistock.

LEISURE ACTIVITIES

Introduction

One of the principal concerns of Chapter 1 was to indicate that the word 'leisure' has a number of different meanings. It follows from this observation that an identification of 'activities' which might be described as 'leisure' is fraught with problems, since any activity may have different meanings for participants. Moreover, leisure activities are bewilderingly numerous and diverse, ranging from aerobics and arts, through to yachting and yoga.

One approach to better understand this range and diversity, is to construct a typology by which similarities, differences and relationships between 'types' of leisure activity can be identified. This approach can be adopted and applied to a range of subject-matter. A library, for example, usually classifies books according to their content and author. Librarians could sort the books according to other criteria such as their weight, colour, number of pages, age, or cost. The reason they do not is because such classifications are generally unhelpful for the patrons of the library.

Similarly, leisure activities may be classified according to a range of criteria, each emphasising particular features or aspects of leisure activity, and different relationships between them. Just as the librarian provides information which will route patrons through the library, a typology is presented here which characterises the major dimensions of participation in, and provision for, the myriads of leisure activities. The typology identifies six major types of leisure activity. These are:

1 Recreations (including sports, arts, and countryside recreation);
2 Hobbies, crafts, and education;
3 Tourism and holidays;
4 Entertainments;
5 Commodities and shopping;
6 Gambling and gaming. (*See* Table 2.1.)

The aim of this typology is to provide an understanding of the nature of participation in leisure, the ways in which activities are structured and provided, and the response of governments towards their practice.

To construct this typology and to provide a route through the field, two key dimensions of leisure activities are identified. Every leisure activity has a *formal* dimension and a *contextual* dimension which are interrelated and can only be separated for purposes of comparative analysis. It is important to emphasise that participants' experience of leisure forms is holistic, and is shaped by the interaction of form and context. This will become apparent in the detailed consideration of particular leisure activities later in this chapter.

Formal dimension

This indicates the process which characterises participation in a leisure activity. Each and every leisure activity has particular characteristics which give it 'form', identify it as that activity, and distinguish it from other leisure activities in particular, and other activities in general. In some cases, this process is *active*, as participants are involved in the actual *production* of experience, of skills, of artefacts, or objects, of performance. For example, members of a local operatic society, football club, rambling association, or pottery class are individually and collectively involved in producing a performance, a game, a country walk, an object of utility and an art form.

In other activities the process of participation is more *passive* in the sense that participants are involved in the *consumption* of experiences, knowledge, artefacts, performances, and goods produced by others. This characterisation of the leisure experience applies to the audience of an opera society, the spectators at a football match, or the patrons of a gallery at which the pottery club's works are displayed. Hence the nature of the process of participation might be initially characterised as follows:

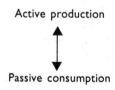

Active production

Passive consumption

Figure 2.1   Participation in leisure

Table 2.1 A typology of leisure activities

Leisure activity	Formal dimension		Contextual dimension				Examples
	Process	Location	Provision/ Management	Provider	State Control		
Recreations (Arts, sports, countryside)	Active production of experience; control over outcome	Outside home	Self-programmed or external provision	Mainly public or voluntary	Encouraged		Sports, drama, outdoor activities
Hobbies/ crafts/ education	Active production of skills or knowledge or objects	Home or outside	Self-programmed or external	Mainly public or voluntary	Encouraged		Gardening, collecting, pottery, reading
Tourism/ holidays	Consumption of experiences (some active production/	Outside home	Mainly external	Commercial	Neutral		Day trips, tourism, packaged holidays
Consuming: entertainments	Active production and consumption of experiences	Home or outside	Mainly external	Public or commercial	Encouraged but licensed/ censored		Dancing, spectating, TV, cinema, theatre
Consuming: commodities and shopping	Consumption of goods	Home or outside	Self-provided or external	Commercial	Licensed		Drinking, eating out, shopping
Gambling and gaming	'Passive production'; no control over outcome	Home or outside home	Mainly external	Commercial	Licensed		Pools, horseracing, bingo, roulette

However, this stark twofold characterisation of leisure activity needs considerable qualification, since production and consumption aspects of experiences are closely inter-related. 'Actively producing' a game of football, for example, also necessarily involves consumption of time, of spaces, of equipment. Similarly, the 'passive consumer' or spectator does not merely absorb the spectacle. He or she is actively involved in interpreting what is happening, reacting with expressions of delight, disappointment or disgust, and might actively attempt to influence the outcome through expressions of encouragement (or in some cases invasion of the playing space). Therefore, while the participant is consuming in order to produce, the spectator is producing in order to consume.

Another related aspect to this formal dimension is the degree of *control* the participant has over the outcome of the activity. In gambling on the football pools, playing bingo or fruit machines, the participant is essentially a passive recipient with little or no control over the outcome. There may be an illusion of control such as studying the 'form' of football teams, or manipulating the 'hold' and 'climb' buttons on the fruit machine, but once the 'bet' is made, the actor surrenders to fate, as a powerless, passive observer. Not all 'gambling' is as 'fateful'. In card games, such as poker, there are skills, tactics and knowledge of other players which might enable the participants to exert some control over the outcome, but not to the same extent as the rambler, in the earlier example, who can control the time, space, and equipment elements of the leisure activity, and hence much of the outcome.

Experiences of leisure activity are, therefore, characterised by differing processes of production and consumption, relative activity and passivity of the participants, together with varying amounts of control exercised by the participant over the process and outcome of the activity.

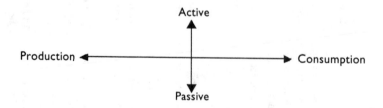

Figure 2.2 Participation in leisure 2

Contextual dimension

This indicates the activity's physical location, how it is provided and managed, and the type and degree of control exerted by government. Building upon the above characterisation of active production and passive consumption, the following major dimensions emerge:

1 The more an activity is characterised by 'active' production rather than 'passive' consumption, and the greater the degree of control by participants over its process and outcome, the more an activity is likely to be provided or managed by the public (or at least the voluntary) sector, and the more the attitude of the government (local and national) will be one of encouragement and financial subsidy.
2 Conversely, the more consumption-orientated the activity and the less the participant is in control, over process and outcome, the more the activity is likely to be provided by the private commercial sector, and the government to intervene to license and circumscribe it. 'Leisure', in these cases takes on the meaning of *licere* as discussed in Chapter 1.

Hence, for example, active production of artistic or sporting participation is subsidised by the Arts Council, the Sports Council, by Local Authorities, by Local Education Authorities, and by a range of other voluntary and public bodies. Conversely, activities developed by commerce for profit such as pop concerts, drinking alcohol, and gambling are circumscribed by licence and subject to taxation by government.

One finds intermediate cases such as tourism where local public and commercial sectors coincide in their interest. The national state, motivated by economic factors at the expense of moral considerations, legislates to subsidise consumption. Investments in tourism, whether 'active and wholesome' or 'passive and decadent' are clear examples of ambivalence on the part of governments. Study of the state's varying interventions in the field of leisure consuming in general, also reveals a degree of equivocation when economics and morality confront each other. Recent parliamentary debates (1986) on Pub Licensing Hours and Sunday Trading provide a fruitful source of information.

Drawing these two dimensions of 'form' and of 'context' together, leisure activities might be characterised thus:

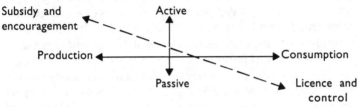

Figure 2.3 Leisure subsidy and licence

The above analysis of formal and contextual dimensions provides a framework within which leisure activity can be viewed holistically rather than as a series of varied and isolated experiences and activities. This typology suggests that there are underlying regularities inherent in the processes of production and consumption of leisure activities which are central to questions of public/commercial provision, state encouragement/licence, and individual freedom/constraint. These issues are considered in greater detail in the remainder of this chapter which is devoted to an analysis of recreations; hobbies; crafts and education; tourism; entertainments; consuming and gambling. In each case, attention is paid to the diversity and range of leisure activities conventionally labelled as sports, arts, tourism, etc., and the problems of definition which are consequent upon this range and diversity. Key issues are identified around the problems of meanings, and around the dimensions of provision and control.

QUESTIONS AND EXERCISES _____

1 Make a list of your own leisure activities. How are these actively produced and passively consumed? Where do they take place? How are they provided? How are they controlled?

2 Do the answers to these questions provide insight into the appeal of these activities for you?

3 Why do you think governments encourage 'active production' and license 'passive consumption'? What would happen if the state did not intervene at all in people's leisure activity?

_____

Sports

In the typology of leisure activities (Table 2.1) sports were identified as 'recreation', which involves the active production of a leisure experience with participants having some control over the process. This applies to participation in sports by a player or performer. However, as leisure activity, sports extend beyond this active involvement of 'producers' to include consumption by non-participants. Hence sports might accurately be described as forms of entertainment, for the spectator at sports events or for the television viewer. Sports are also the object of an extensive gambling industry through football pools and betting on horses or greyhounds. Sports are also an integral part of tourism exemplified in ski package tours and adventure holidays, while many localities or regions market themselves as tourist attractions through the sporting opportunities provided. More broadly, sports are just one of the leisure activities which involve the consumption of goods, services, or products provided commercially. Additionally, sports are an element of education, and some sports can be considered art forms (e.g. ice-dance) or as countryside recreations (e.g. outdoor pursuits). One may conclude that sports are a characteristic feature of most elements of the typology of leisure activities presented earlier.

Sports cannot, therefore, be fully understood solely on the basis of active production since they are characteristic of much leisure consumption. Nevertheless, the primary focus here is upon active involvement and the consequent appeal to participants of particular sports. Through this, providers of sporting experience in any of the sectors of leisure provision, either as coaches or as administrative personnel, may be better placed to meet the needs of their clients.

The Recreational Management Yearbook lists over 120 National Sports Associations in Britain. These associations represent sports of extreme diversity from aerobics and archery through frisbee throwing and fencing, gliding and Gaelic football, to yoga and yachting. Given the variety of forms, it is a difficult task to generalise about the nature or characteristics of sports which are appropriate for every 'sports' practice. However, a useful approach is to ask two deceptively simple questions:

1 What is common to all sports?
2 What are the differences between sports?

The first question invites us to identify those particular characteristics which distinguish an activity as a 'sport', and therefore distance it from other leisure activities. Are there a set of criteria which must be met for an activity to be properly called a sport rather than, for example, a pastime, a game, a ritual, an art form, or an entertainment?

The second question addresses the diversity of sports and invites us to construct a classification of sports. Through this procedure, sports are placed into specific categories according to particular criteria. In the introduction to this chapter, an illustration was given of the different ways books might be categorised by a library. Similarly, sports might be 'sorted' in various ways. For example, individual sports can be distinguished from team sports, expensive from cheap sports, indoor from outdoor sports. Other differences include the characteristics of typical participants according to age, sex, social class, or race. These ways of distinguishing between sports have their uses. However, in this section a typology is presented which seeks to describe the specific demands and challenges inherent in particular forms of sport for the participant. Taken together these analyses of commonality and difference provide insights into the appeal of particular sports and into the nature and extent of sports provision.

The nature of sport

Defining sport
Many writers have attempted to define sport by identifying the range of characteristics which collectively establish an activity as a bona-fide 'sport'. Each of these writers, in their different ways, identify the following as being necessary or essential features of sport:

- they must involve a symbolic test of physical or psycho-motor skills;
- there must be a competitive framework; which requires:
- specific, codified rules which constitute the activity;
- there must be continuity over time – a tradition of past practices.

In combination, these necessary characteristics are sufficient for an activity to be called a sport. They are inclusive in that they identify all those activities which can be called sports, and are exclusive in that they exclude those forms which cannot properly be called 'sports'.

The utility of this approach is that it allows for a distinction to be made between sport proper, and related areas of activity like games, pastimes, recreations, and other play forms. All that is necessary is to apply the 'necessary and sufficient characteristics' of sport to diverse leisure activities and note the match or mis-match.

Applying this procedure it is clear that some of the more common sports such as rugby, netball, athletics, and gymnastics fit the characteristics very well. But there are many others which are marginal sports in that they exhibit some but not all of the criteria. Consider for example, skateboarding, jogging, fox-hunting, darts, fishing, rock-climbing, hang-gliding. Allowing for a more extended and liberal meaning of 'sport', consider alligator-wrestling, body-building, tractor-pulling, poaching and motor-cycle stunts. Each of these has, in various contexts, been described as a 'sport', but they do not meet all of the four conditions outlined above.

Because of the difficulties in defining sport satisfactorily, many conclude that the attempt to do so is misconceived. Sports are so diverse and are perceived and interpreted so differently that any definitional attempt is doomed to failure. Even Peter Lawson, the Secretary-General of the Central Council of Physical Recreation has argued that sports are in the eye of the beholder and best left at that simplistic interpretation.

To terminate enquiry at this juncture, however, tells us little about the nature of sports, or about the range of experiences which they offer through their particular structures. In the introduction to this chapter, it was emphasised that an understanding of any leisure activity must be based upon two interlinked dimensions: the *form* of the activity, and the social *contexts* in which they are practised.

Formal and contextual dimensions

FORM

One of the most popular sporting activities in this country is swimming. Most of it is pursued in informal, often family settings with participants having fun, playing in the water. This activity is not competitive, nor, therefore, does it require codified rules, nor does it involve a symbolic test of psycho-motor skills. Therefore, according to the argument earlier, it is not a sport. In some contexts however, swimming is a highly competitive test of abilities in pre-determined events controlled by a national governing body. Within this context, the activity becomes a sport. Similarly, running can be engaged in as a sport within athletics competitions or as a physical recreation such as jogging. Jogging has no competitive framework, participants set their own aspirations and determine what counts as success or failure.

CONTEXT

According to this account, the same activity *form* can be a sport or a mere physical recreation depending upon the *context* of its practice. This contextual consideration indicates that an activity might be played or pursued in informal settings with a relative lack of organisation, and primarily for fun or relaxation. Conversely, the same activity can be highly regularised, rigidly formalised, and played primarily to achieve an end result such as to win, to better one's previous best performance, or break a record. Many writers have indicated that when this latter, more 'serious' competitive approach occurs, then engagement in the activity rapidly displays characteristics normally associated with work and few which are associated with the qualities of play (e.g. voluntary, self-determined). The activity becomes 'rationalised', meaning that the process is scrutinised and developed in the interests of efficiency and maximising performance outcomes. All professional sports provide examples of this work-like approach, as do many highly competitive amateur sports.

The context of sporting activity is therefore identified by its degree of organisation and by participants' motives and objectives. These dimensions are inter-linked since participants' objectives are deemed to be appropriate or inappropriate according to the relative formality of the organisation of the sport. To play a formally organised competitive sport in a flippant and careless way is as inappropriate as being too concerned

with winning in an informal recreational setting. In short the characteristics of 'sports' in contrast to mere physical recreation *demand* that participants are motivated to achieve particular goals or objectives – and
these can only be met if the activity is formally organised.

To summarise, sport *forms*, like all other leisure forms, are manifested
or realised only through participation. This takes place in differing *contexts*, by different people, and for different reasons. Therefore, an understanding of the nature of sport must hold two dimensions in focus:

Dimension A *Form*
the nature of sports and their particular structural characteristics
Dimension B *Context*
the organisation of the activity
participants' motives/objectives

With respect to dimension A, it has been indicated that sports take many
forms. It is now possible to answer the second question about sports;
what are the differences between their forms?

The diversity of sports forms

Skateboarding, hang-gliding, choukball and American football are relatively recent additions to the list of sporting associations in this country.
What have these sports in common, for example, with ten-pin bowling,
orienteering, judo and netball, except that they are all conventionally
labelled 'sports'? Some sports are provided only by the voluntary sector,
others enjoy funding through bodies such as the Sports Council, others
are developed through the commercial sector. The complexity of public,
voluntary and commercial provision for sport is, in part, an indication of
the disparate demands and requirements of diverse sports. Torkildsen
(1984) argues that sensitivity to the particular demands and requirements
of different sports is critical for mounting effective provision. He states:

The more the manager can learn about the nature of the activities, the more
understanding of the requirements, problems and solutions will be gained.

Torkildsen goes on to consider the differences between sports forms
which are important for leisure providers. These differences which, with
respect to the conventional wisdom of leisure professionals, are considered to be important, include the following:

- those sports played indoors, those outdoors;
- those requiring large spaces, those requiring small spaces;
- those played by young people, those attracting participants from different age groups;

- those attractive to girls, women, boys, men, or relatively neutral in this respect;
- those which have high skill thresholds, those which do not;
- those which require supra-individual organisations, those which do not;
- those which are income-producing, those which are not.

These ways of distinguishing between sports are useful, for sensitising providers to the differential appeal of particular sports amongst identifiable groups of potential participants, and addressing problems and issues relating to their provision. This list is not exhaustive. Similar questions can be asked about providing for different ethnic groups, for participants with a range of disabilities or handicaps, and for participants from different occupational groups. Also the equipment requirements of particular sports pose specific organisational problems. Moreover, the various sectors of provision confront different issues in working effectively. For example, commercial providers will be interested in each of the above ways of classifying sports, but only insofar as they enhance the last item listed above, i.e. producing an adequate return on investment. Clearly the relative import of these ways of mapping-out sports participation will depend upon the objectives of providers.

All the issues listed above focus upon either the organisation and management of sports forms or the differential appeal of sports amongst the population. However, the *form* of sports remains unexamined and taken-for-granted. In the introduction to this section on leisure forms, a distinction was made between the 'formal' and 'contextual' dimensions of participation. To understand the contextual dimension (the nature of the participation) account must be taken of the structural properties of sports forms.

The structural properties of sports

All sports are in varying degrees, deliberately contrived structures. These artificial contrivances differ considerably from one to another in the way they are structured. Moreover, they differ in their historical origins. Some have evolved from pre-industrial folk-games, others have evolved from skills formerly associated with types of work. Other sports have simply been invented, and in some of these cases technological advance has been influential (e.g. hang-gliding). Some sports have been imported from different cultures (e.g. lacrosse, or martial arts).

In all cases, groups of individuals have, at some time in the past, decided upon the form that the sport should take and hence established the rules which, taken together, constitute the sport. Part of the remit of all governing bodies of sports is to preside over the 'form' of the activity. Hence rule committees clarify, modify, or change the rules in order to preserve the contrived challenge that is provided. The challenge can take many forms; some are primarily tests of strength, others tests of skill, or stamina or a combination of all these. Some challenges are between individuals, others between teams. Some take place on land, others in different media such as water or air. Some challenges are posed within direct interpersonal competitive frameworks, in others, the interaction between participants is indirect.

Clearly not all the challenges offered by different sports are equally attractive to everyone, therefore not everyone takes up the challenge. Part of the explanation of the differential take-up of particular sporting challenges is to be found by understanding the range of personal, social and environmental factors which 'filter' people in and out of sports (*see* Chapters 3 and 4). Another part of the explanation is to be found in the nature and extent of provision for sport and people's differential access to such provision (*see* Chapter 5). Yet another explanatory factor, however, is to acknowledge that different sporting challenges offer particular sets of experiences and action opportunities for participants. For example, the experiential possibilities and opportunities for action and interaction within gymnastics contrasts with that offered by the challenge of football. Gymnastics is about individual, non-interactive performance of a range of motor skills in response to the challenge posed by sets of apparatus. Football is about co-operating with team mates in order to compete against opponents for a ball in order to score goals. Both gymnastics and football are cases of sports, but there are considerable differences in terms of what might be variously labelled as their formal characteristics, structural properties or inherent challenges. Consequently, analysis of these diverse structural properties is an essential requisite for understanding the nature of sporting processes and their appeal for different participants. With this consideration in mind, the reader is directed to several classifications which highlight particular properties of sports and games. Roberts and Sutton-Smith (1970) have developed a classification from extensive cross-cultural analysis of 'game forms'. Their concept of 'game' is very wide and includes sports practised in this and other countries. The authors classify 'games' on the basis of the 'outcome attributes' or 'determinants of achievement'. Hence they distinguish between games where the outcome is determined by physical skill, those which are determined by strategy, and those determined by chance. Physical skill, or more broadly psycho-motor skill, is a key characteristic of all sports, although in many cases the outcome is determined by such skills employed within particular strategies, and there are always elements of chance.

Much of Roberts and Sutton-Smith's analysis informs the introductory discussion of leisure forms where distinctions were made with respect to the degrees of individual control over the outcome of activities. Moreover, Caillois' (1961) four-fold classification of the 'essential and irreducible impulse of games' which was introduced in Chapter 1, also provides useful insights into the disparate challenges and properties of particular sports. Caillois and Roberts and Sutton-Smith make us keenly aware that understanding of games and sports is relative to individual cultural experience. This is a key factor for a multi-ethnic society such as Britain where many leisure professionals are charged with providing for groups from diverse cultural backgrounds.

The more general classifications are complemented by Mauldon and Redfern (1969) who provide a culturally specific analysis of sporting games (games where psycho-motor skills are a central feature). Their classification, therefore, is limited to games as a particular species of sports forms, but since such games comprise a major element of sports provision in Britain, their analysis is of particular interest. Mauldon and Redfern state that all sports games involve, either singly or in combination, three elements:

- gaining possession of a ball (catching or collecting);
- travelling with the ball (carrying or propelling); and
- sending a ball away (striking or throwing).

These motor elements are deployed over a terrain or playing space which is either divided or shared between the contestants.

There are considerable differences in the action opportunities and interaction processes between, for example, badminton and rugby. Badminton has divided territory and is principally about striking an object. Rugby has shared territory and has more complex interaction patterns, where everyone can carry, propel, strike, throw, catch, and collect the ball subject to the constraints of the rules. There are far fewer limitations on action and a much higher degree of complexity of interaction which, together, make the activity much more difficult to control. So, different games are subject to varying amounts of constraint and hence allow relative degrees of freedom of action by their form or structure.

Mauldon and Redfern's analysis illustrates the diversity of forms which games take. Yet games only comprise part of sport. Other non-game sports provide different challenges, and other psycho-motor skills are deployed in order to meet these challenges. Haywood and Kew's (1984) characterisation of the structural properties of sports includes games, outdoor pursuits, and other non-game sports (e.g. gymnastics,

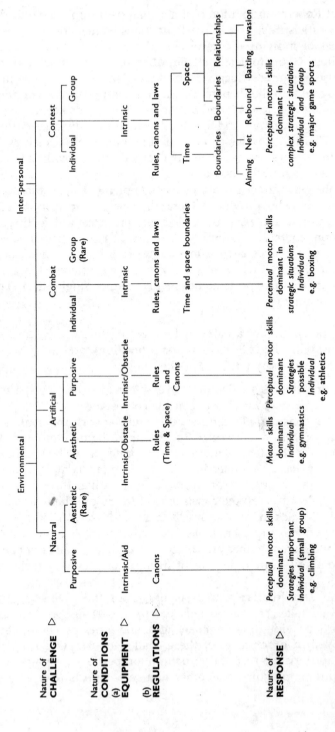

Figure 2.4 Structural properties of sport forms

boxing, judo, swimming). The authors argue that the variety of sport *forms* can be unpacked by posing the following questions:

1 What is the nature of the *challenge*, the problem to be solved?
2 What *conditions* are imposed upon that challenge?
3 What type of *response* is made to this conditioned challenge?

These three inter-related elements; the challenge, the conditions, and the response, can be examined separately, and are summarised in Figure 2.4.

1 *The challenge*

The challenge takes one of two fundamental forms: it is either *environmental* or *inter-personal*. *Environmental challenges* (usually to do with gravity or friction) may be subdivided into those posed by *natural* phenomena (e.g. ice, rock, water) and those which are essentially *artificial* (e.g. trampoline, hurdle). Both natural and artificial challenges may be further categorised, in Best's (1978) terms, as *purposive* or *aesthetic*. This is a specific use of Best's distinction, which in its original form is applied more generally. This distinguishes some sports activities (e.g. canoeing), where the outcome is central, from others (e.g. gymnastics) where the style or manner of performance is crucial. While recognising that 'outcome' and 'style' are linked to varying degrees in different activities, this is a useful distinction. *Inter-personal challenges* may also be subdivided (after McIntosh 1964) into two basic forms, dependent on the exact relationships existing between opponents. In *combat* sports, striking an opponent's body or immobilising it in some way is the objective, and only varying amounts of equipment and simple rules lift these sports above a crude fight. Typically, combat sports are for individuals, team fights being relegated these days to entertainment (e.g. tag-wrestling). *Contest* sports on the other hand, may be individual or group activities and in many ways are much more contrived than combats, since they are characterised by a whole variety of targets; spatial circumstances differ greatly; and crucially, the inter-personal struggle is mediated by some object (e.g. ball, shuttle) interposed between the opponents. What is common to both combat and contest sports is that the outcome is the focus of all action.

2 *Imposing conditions on the challenge*

Conditions imposed upon particular challenges identify or define particular sporting forms within the general categories of environmental and inter-personal sports. Such conditions have two dimensions: (a) equipment and (b) regulations. Equipment may be intrinsic to an activity (like hockey); introduced to create a sphere of gratuitous difficulty; or it may be an aid (as in climbing), either to reduce the scale of the problem or to open up new challenges. The second (regulations) deserves much greater attention.

Different primary challenges characteristically invoke differing forms and amounts of regulation. Again, the nature and extent of such regulations, in part, explains the appeal of different sporting forms for different people. In short, all sports are not subject to the same types or amount of regulation. Inherent in particular forms are differing degrees of choice, differing rewards and sanctions, differing experiences of relative freedom and constraint. Some sports require, by the nature of their conditions, a high degree of conformity to expected norms of behaviour. How, then, are sports regulated? To answer this it is useful to consider two examples – an outdoor pursuit like climbing, and a game like soccer. Climbing has no rule-book. There are no rules laid down by a governing body, which 'consecrate' and legitimate a particular form of activity. Rather the activity of climbing is regulated (often with more success than other sports and physical recreations) by *canons* of acceptable behaviour or action. Such canons are generally held as sacrosanct amongst climbers and their peer group.

In contrast, other sports can be seen as constituted by *rules* which describe necessary behaviour or action. Without such behaviour or action, the sport ceases to exist as that particular sport (e.g. backward rather than forward passing in rugby football). Such sports (and all games come into this category) have legislators who make rules, and referees who police the activity. Therefore the rules lay down the limits to one's action within the context of the particular sport.

A further elaboration of the *rules* of inter-personal sports, but not usually of the environmental ones, is the detailed specification of *time* and *space*. Time constitutes a boundary around the activity, cutting it off temporarily from other social behaviour, while spatial considerations define both the playing area, and in the case of contests, the playing relationships between opponents. For example, contestants may share territory, use it alternately, or attack it. The use of space leads us into Mauldon and Redfern's (1969) classification of 'game-sports'. There are five major types, all of which exhibit major differences in form and content, even though they belong in the same overall contest category; aiming games (e.g. golf); net games (e.g. volleyball); rebound games (e.g. squash); batting games (e.g. cricket); running or invasion games (e.g. football).

3 *The response to the challenge*
This refers to the particular mix of individual and group skills, tactics, and strategies, which are employed in response to the basic challenge of a sport as it is conditioned by particular regulations. Such skills, tactics, and strategies, are the concrete manifestations of sports as experienced by participants. These differ markedly from sport to sport. The skills might be 'fine' or 'gross', they also might be about co-operation or deception, they might be 'open' (i.e. contingent upon environmental circumstances)

or 'closed' (i.e. principally concerned with bodily movement). This suggests that experiences of skilled action differ considerably from sport to sport; differences which again are significant in understanding the appeal of particular sport forms. Figure 2.4 presents a more extended analysis of the structural properties of sports.

Provision for sports

The appeal of sports
Differences in challenge, regulation and response are, in part, explanatory of the particular *appeal* of sport forms because individual structures provide the opportunity for particular experiences in sports. Experiences are related to the unique challenges, conditions and responses of a sport. For example, a game such as netball has an inter-personal challenge, is constrained by rules which limit action in particular ways, allows for precise interaction between players, and provides the opportunity to develop skills and strategies in order to meet the contrived or conditioned challenge of putting a ball into a net. Contrast this with an 'environmental' sport such as gymnastics, or a combat activity like judo.

The experiential dimensions of those three sports (and many others might be contrasted in this way) are crucially different from one another. This provides at least a partial explanation of the enduring motivation to participate in the activity. What might providers for sports therefore gain from an acknowledgement of differences in the forms and hence the appeal of sports?

Providing for diverse sports
In education, in the youth service and in local authority leisure services, there is considerable debate about the nature and place of sports as an element of provision. Sports are no longer unproblematically assumed to be an intrinsic 'good', providing wholesome and beneficial experiences for clients. Much of the debate, publicised (and often misrepresented) in the media, centres around a concern that 'traditional' competitive team sports are inappropriate vehicles to realise social objectives. In schools, for example, the 1980s witnessed a partial retreat from team games towards individual sports such as trampolining, outdoor pursuits, swimming, and games such as volleyball and badminton. Many acres of open space in urban areas (which command enormous real estate values) allocated to educational use for team games are under-utilised as a consequence. National governing bodies such as the FA and RFU are concerned that the schools, so long a nursery for developing talent, are no longer providing that service. Consequently, they are developing initiatives to encourage voluntary associations and clubs to assume the role previously assumed to be fulfilled by schools. The problem is seen to be so acute that private

members' bills have been produced in Parliament by Conservative MPs in an attempt to make team games compulsory in schools! The argument is that such sports provide experience which (a) cannot be had elsewhere and (b) are essential for the well-being of society.

Similarly the youth service has debated the role of sports as an element in boys' clubs, youth clubs and other voluntary associations. The impetus for this debate is the ambivalent attitudes about sport partly stemming from youth workers' experience of sport in their own schooling, and partly from the image of sports portrayed through the media. Modern sports are becoming big business, highly professional, commercialised, and over-serious. The disquiet is that the values they encapsulate are antithetical to those which are deemed to be appropriate for the youth service. Can sports contribute to personal and social development within a social climate which portrays their personnel as only interested in winning, in ruthless pursuit of success, where wholesale violence, cheating and drug-taking seem to be rife? Sports are becoming 'dehumanised'; sportsmen and women valued only insofar as they function successfully as a cog in a machine which is geared solely towards winning by any means. Traditional virtues encapsulated by the terms 'fair-play' and 'sportsmanship' hold no value in the cut-throat, dog-eat-dog business of modern sports. Of course, these professional, deadly-serious attitudes towards sports affect the lower levels of sports practice. Children, in this highly competitive environment, rapidly find out what counts as success and failure, and its intimate connection with winning or losing. Because most sports are organised locally, regionally and nationally on a competitive basis, increasing numbers are effectively debarred from participating.

In both education and the youth service the issue resolves into a simple question: what is the point of encouraging participation in activities which (a) inculcate ruthless attitudes and (b) through the competitive framework are designed to label people as failures either sooner or later? Conversely: how might sports be re-visioned to provide more wholesome experiences?

Within local authority provision for sport, the issues are different, since the primary concern is to encourage participation, maximise use of facilities and thereby provide a successful service to the locality. User surveys of sports facilities undertaken in the 1970s concluded that various socio-economic groups were markedly under-represented. Hence, non-participants were targeted and various strategies devised to encourage sports participation and thereby improve the quality of people's leisure experience. Many of these initiatives have been labelled as 'community' oriented.

In line with other services such as Community Arts, Community Policing, Community Education, Community Health, the rationale behind 'community' sports initiatives is to provide a service which is meaningful to clients and meets their needs, however these might be formulated. Many local authorities such as Sheffield, Leicester, Bradford and Middlesbrough formulated 'community recreation' programmes, the CCPR started a community sports leaders' award scheme and the Sports Council provided funding for 'Action Sport' initiatives. In each case, the key idea is about communication with potential client groups: Out-reach workers are designated to make contact with clients, with voluntary clubs and associations and through consultation, identify their needs and hence encourage participation in sport. Some of these initiatives have succeeded in increasing participation, others have failed. But whether successful or not, each of these initiatives is characterised by attempts to contact client groups and react to their perceived needs.

The concerns of education, the youth service and public leisure provision are different. What is common to these cases, outlined above, is the vehicle with which they strive to realise their separate objectives, namely sports. Sports, as indicated earlier, are crucially different from one another, having diverse structural properties and consequently affording diverse individual and group experiences. An understanding of this diversity can inform provision for sport and encourage professional and voluntary workers to be proactive in providing a range of sporting experiences to appeal to people with different interests and abilities. Effective provision for sport depends not only on empathising with clients, but also on an acute understanding of the nature of sport and the diversity of forms it takes.

QUESTIONS AND EXERCISES _____

1 If you participate in a sport, use the model in Figure 2.4 to identify its structural properties. Does this explain the appeal of that sport for you? Does this explain why others might not be interested in that sport? What explanations of participation are not covered by this model?

2 Participation in many 'environmental' sports is increasing. How might this, in part, be explained in terms of the particular challenges which these activities offer?

3 Using Figure 2.4, identify those types of sporting challenges which:
   (a) were offered to you at school
   (b) are offered at your local sports centre
   (c) are offered at your local youth club.
   How extensive is that provision?

4 A distinction has been made between formally organised competitive sports and informal physical recreations. How useful is this distinction for:

(a) determining coaching strategies?
(b) understanding the appeal of sports?

5 One cannot 'win' in outdoor pursuits in the same way as one can 'win' in inter-personal sports. What does this tell you about the appeal of these different sporting challenges?

Further reading

The typology of sports (Figure 2.4) has been informed by classifications of sports forms presented by the following:

E. Mauldon and E. Redfern (1969) *Games Teaching: a new approach for the Primary School*, MacDonald and Evans.

D. Best (1980) *Philosophy and Human Movement*, George Allen and Unwin.

P. McIntosh (1963) *Sport and Society*, Macmillan.

R. Caillois (1961) *Man, Play and Games*, Free Press, Glencoe.

J. Roberts and B. Sutton-Smith (1971) 'Child Training and Game Involvement' in J. Loy and G. S. Kenyon (eds) *Sport, Culture and Society*, Macmillan.

G. Torkildsen's (1986) discussion of the differences between forms of physical recreation is to be found in *Leisure and Recreation Management*, E. and F. N. Spon; pp. 390–3.

Two further examples of how the typology of sports (Table 2.1) might inform leisure policy are:

F. Kew (1987) 'Sporting Challenge' in *Youth and Society*, May, pp. 16, 18.

L. Haywood and F. Kew (1989), 'Community Recreation: New Wine in Old Bottles' in P. Bramham, I. Henry, H. Mommaas, and H. Van Der Poel (eds) *Leisure and the Urban Processes*, Routledge.

This section has focused primarily upon the nature and diversity of sports forms. Critical perspectives upon sports as leisure forms in contemporary society include:

R. Gruneau (1983) *Class, Sports, and Social Development*, Amherst University Press.

G. Whannel (1983) *Blowing the Whistle: the politics of sport*, Pluto Press.

J.-M. Brohm (1978) *Sport: a prison of measured time*, Ink Links.

J. Hargreaves (ed.) (1982) *Sport, Culture and Ideology*, Routledge, Kegan and Paul.

W. Morgan (1983), 'Towards a critical theory of sport' in *J. Sport and Social Issues*, No. 7, pp. 24–34.

The arts

What is art?

In April 1987 one of Van Gogh's *Sunflowers* paintings sold for £24 million. Why do particular works of art fetch such high prices when auctioned at Christies or Sothebys? Who buys them and why? Are such masterpieces the same as antique furniture or collections of jewellery? Are they differ-ent from priceless collectors' items which range from original manu-scripts, pieces of china and silverware to stamps and motorcars? Why should the National Gallery struggle to raise £3 million to keep an orig-inal Turner painting in the British Isles? Who actually visits art galleries, museums and theatres and what price should they pay on entry? Does it really matter if some works of art were destroyed by fire at Hampton Court?

Such questions raise even more questions about the precise nature of art and art forms and their relationship to other areas of creative practice such as photography, cinema, design, architecture and craft. For example, when and how does a film or a photograph become a work of art? Is a Stradivarius violin the epitome of a particular musical craft or is it a work of art? What happens when a research scientist uses computer technology to reproduce the exact varnish that Stradivarius used to give instruments their tone? Why are some forms of dance but not others regarded as 'artistic'? Why does the Arts Council fund particular art forms, primarily the 'fine arts' and pay little attention to others? What is even more bewildering to some is when art 'experts', working under the aegis of the Arts Council, fund artists, exhibitions or events which appear to some as valueless. Many examples spring to mind – piles of building bricks exhib-ited at the Tate, rubber tyres sculptured into a submarine (later to be incinerated by an 'art lover'), or two individuals, wearing bowler hats, walking around East Anglia balancing a plank on their heads. The fear is not so much the waste of public funds on the arts but that experts seem to value something that lacks artistic skill or technique.

As with other leisure forms, it is no easy task to define the nature of 'Art' or 'the Arts'. To proceed uncritically towards a definition leaves any analysis open to the charge from philosophers of 'the fallacy of essential-ism'. This means that it is impossible to define 'art' in such a way as to exclude all 'non-art'. Academics cannot define arts so precisely that the boundaries of the definition include all art forms and exclude everything else in the wilderness of non-art. It is therefore misguided to think of arts as if it could be distilled into a pure essence. Although both academics and artists may argue over the nature of art, most people have some understanding of what forms can legitimately be included in the umbrella term 'the arts', and what makes those forms artistic. People's understanding of art is partly influenced by the art education they received at school and by the work of the Arts Council which consecrates particular art forms by its funding. As is clear from Chapter 5, the Arts Council historically focused on the 'fine' arts, including opera and ballet, and ignored the artistic work of many other groups; most glaringly absent were racial minorities, working class writers and women. However, recently some local authorities have developed cultural policies or 'cultural politics' which broaden the definition of the arts to include more popular cultural forms, particularly those forms which express the values and interests of working class culture, the women's movement and racial minorities.

Major policy debates within the arts revolve around two policy options which are best described as 'the democratisation of culture' as against 'cultural democracy'. The demand for the 'democratisation of culture' argues that there exists a national cultural heritage in the arts, particularly in the fine arts, which must be shared amongst the whole population. Groups in society are not involved in the arts because of lack of opportunity, education or income. In contrast, the demand for 'cultural democracy' in arts policy argues that there are a variety of art forms in any society and previous policies have valued art forms such as opera, ballet and theatre which have been favoured by a cultural elite. Other artistic forms have been ignored and arts policy should encourage the variety of 'taste publics' in society, as exemplified by the community arts movement which encourages the participation of ordinary people in diverse artistic forms. A good example of this approach is Herbert Gans' depiction of different types of popular culture, none of which are inherently superior to others. Many critics of the Arts Council argue that its funding has overemphasised professional performances in a narrow range of 'fine' arts and has turned its back on a wealth of artistic creativity within hobbies, crafts and popular entertainment.

Those involved with the arts debate their exact nature and function in society. Traditionally the focus has been on the art form itself. In sharp contrast with debates about sport which have paid scant attention to the nature and the diversity of sport, arts commentaries have been preoccupied with the variety of artistic forms. This focus on 'the aesthetic dimension' of human culture seeks to clarify the intrinsic criteria for understanding and judging art. Art is treated as an end in itself which must be valued by internal codes. These codes examine the style, texture, expertise, etc., which often develop into schools of art. Over the centuries there have emerged works of art which have cross-cultural significance because they are exceptional examples of a particular art form. Such worth can be translated into a price such as £24 million paid for Van Gogh's *Sunflowers* oil painting. This celebration of artistic form by traditional aesthetics has been challenged by critics for ignoring the wider context of artistic production and consumption. Such critics demand that art must also exhibit some 'extrinsic' value in that works of art must provide a criticism of society; a truth, or a real understanding of human experience, politics, life or religion. The greatest artist is capable of communicating depths of experience, feeling and understanding which others can share but not necessarily express. The nature of art, the diversity of art forms, artists and artistic activity, as well as their place in the structures of society are crucial issues surrounding funding and provision of the arts. Table 2.2 introduces the arts and relates them to some of the dimensions outlined in the typology used in this chapter. The aim of the table is to encourage the reader to explore the complexity of art in modern society and to think about the diversity of artistic forms which are the product of many cultures spread over centuries of history. All forms of art, dance, drama, literature and music have classical and popular forms and the boundaries between the two are often blurred, contested and changed over time. All forms have both an experiential and a contextual dimension to them. Some forms, such as music or drama, may require a collective context to make artistic forms, such as plays or orchestral symphonies possible.

Certain key points must be borne in mind when using the table:

1 The major areas of artistic practice overlap and are inter-related (e.g. dance would be inconceivable without musical accompaniment of some sort for dancers and audiences to interpret). Innovation in art forms depends upon capturing the fusion of dance/music/drama and re-working art forms to explore creative tensions that exist. For example, the popularity of English National Opera is founded on attracting new audiences which expect to see a more even balance between the opera score and its dramatic interpretation.

2 In understanding leisure forms, it is important to distinguish between the production and consumption of artistic practices. These categories are useful ways of understanding people's involvement in and governmental responses to the diversity of leisure forms. In the arts, there is clearly a difference between attending a live concert, listening to the recording of that 'live' concert later on the radio and hearing a recording of a musical performance for the first time. Conversely, rehearsing a piece of music is clearly different from performing before an audience

Table 2.2 A typology of artistic activities

	Arts	Dance	Drama	Literature	Music
Medium	Visual	Human movement	Human movement/voice	Writing	Voice/instrument
Artistic output/ outcomes	Canvasses, 3D, design, photography	Live performances, notations	Live performances	Texts, manuscripts	Live performances, scores
Reproduction	Prints, lithography, cinema	Memory/tradition, recordings, video, TV, cinema	Memory/tradition, radio, cinema, TV, video, records	Memory/oral culture, publication	Records, tapes, CDs
Location	Art galleries, museums, schools	Theatre, ballrooms, discos/dancehalls	Street theatre, community events, theatre	Home/households, libraries, bookshops	Households, schools, concert halls
Examples of forms	Printing, design, sculpture, photography	Ballet, folk, ballroom, old time, disco, break	Plays, mime, puppetry	Poetry, novels, plays, science fiction, short stories	Opera, choral, song, orchestral, sonatas, symphonies

as a soloist or part of an orchestra. The context or framing of musical performances is crucial; whether practising in the privacy of one's own home, performing before a music teacher, taking a graded examination or competing in a music festival.

3 Wolff (1981) argues that consumption is the completion of artistic production. Drama, dance, music and literature are only realised when consumed by audiences. Yet there is no easy distinction to be found by describing the performance as active and the audience, consuming the artistic practice, as passive. Some writers (e.g. Pick 1981) argue that there is much more of reciprocal exchange, an aesthetic dimension, which is absent in commercial or commodity exchanges. Indeed, much is expected of the audience and there are fierce policy debates about how best to educate the audience to appreciate artistic performance. Nevertheless, to appreciate a performance the audience must *be* there and this involves a substantial amount of human choice as well as portraying the holistic nature of leisure. Consider the example of a night out at the theatre. The individual chooses which play to watch, which night to go, who to go with and how to travel there; anticipates the performance, has a meal and/or drink beforehand, watches the play and discusses the performance afterwards.

4 In any historical period, art can be described as classical or traditional and contrasted with contemporary fads and fashions which may draw their inspiration from popular culture. New art forms in music/drama/theatre challenge traditional styles and conventions of artistic production and reproduction. Martin (1981) describes this process as a 'liminality' – exploring and testing the boundaries of conventional rules, codes and styles. Her analysis examines the expressive cultural revolution of the 1960s – in art, fashion, pop music and design, which questioned conventional ideas about sexuality, work and politics. At that time many feared the collapse of the 'heritage arts' (i.e. drama, opera, ballet) under the new wave of the likes of Warhol, Leary and Lennon. From the perspective of the late 1980s such fears were misplaced yet there has always been a creative tension between traditional art forms and those more deeply embedded in the mass media and popular culture. It is precisely this tension that generates the fiercest policy debates.

The structures of art

It is crucial to examine the context within which practices take place; which frames the performance and possible reproduction and consumption of an artistic performance. People can draw on different authoritative rules and resources depending upon the context of the artistic activity. It is difficult to answer the question 'how good is art?' without referring to the people and institutions that mediate and evaluate its production and consumption. Artists draw on a wide variety of ideas, rules and resources in the production of works of art, art administrators and critics are important channels who organise and evaluate art, while finally audiences are clearly consumers of artistic performances. Some of the audience may even belong to art or music appreciation classes so they may gain a deeper understanding of a particular historical period of art or of a particular composer.

Production	*Reproduction*	*Consumption*
amateur/	critics, arts	audience
professional	administrators	

It is the critic who is crucially important in evaluating artistic performances. Critics represent particular traditions/practices themselves and are located in arts organisations with power. Artistic judgements involve more than witnessing a skilful technical performance or product. Skill and human creativity abound in hobbies, crafts and education classes. Human movement in games or sport forms, such as gymnastics, ice skating and ice dance, may be judged aesthetically. The appeal of an activity is its aesthetic dimension. Nevertheless, art critics remain important gatekeepers as to what counts as 'art' and artistic performance.

Each area of aesthetic practice has developed its own historical traditions, codes of practices which are debated by artists themselves and by critics (of art, music, dance, drama). Although the artist is constrained by artistic codes and traditions, such codes paradoxically permit or enable the artist to innovate. Some writers, notably in Marxist aesthetics, feel that radical potential is only possible if the artist innovates and challenges conventional forms. For example, Brecht's 'radical theatre' broke with tradition in the 1930s by engaging the audience, encouraging them to participate and reminding them that they were after all an audience watching a play.

Tensions between classical and popular art are reflected in sponsorship by both the state and the commercial sector. Certain artefacts and events are accepted as high quality and worth funding, whereas community arts, political theatre and artistic experiments are regarded with suspicion and scepticism. Since 1974, community art has been funded by the Arts Council but only a small proportion of its budget is allocated there, compared to the massive funding of the four major national companies. Since 1979, the commercial sector has been encouraged and is prepared to sponsor prestigious orchestras, like the London Symphony Orchestra, yet pressure may be exerted to perform well-known classical pieces from their repertoires rather than experiment with little known composers.

The primary function of art is to communicate; in a cultural aesthetic exchange between the artist, as producer, and the audience, as consumer. The artist is often presented as an isolated misunderstood genius, an albatross on land, and critics are keen to intervene to interpret such art and educate audiences to appreciate and understand it. Art administrators may be committed to break down the barriers to understanding which can operate within wider society and to counteract structural inequalities of class, gender and race which find their different expressions in localities. What is of concern here is that the function of art is one of signification, i.e. art signifies or stands for something and this representation is communicated by the artist to the audience. The immense diversity of art and artistic practices raises important policy questions about what art forms and artists to support, and how to fund them, and what forms and artists should be ignored and discouraged.

QUESTIONS AND EXERCISES ———————————————————

1 Should local authorities be 'patrons of the arts' as recommended in the Redcliffe Maud report 1976?

2 What policies lie behind the following Arts Council slogans 'The Glory of the Garden', 'The Best For Most', 'Few But Roses'?

3 Why should artists fear Clause 28 of the Local Government Act 1987 and organise against it?

4 How do you explain the apparent neglect of Arts Council funding in the following areas or towards the following groups:
photography; women, cinema; black groups; literature; community groups?

5 Does the fact that publishing companies, TV companies and newspaper groups are each dominated by multinationals, carry any threat to artistic freedom, and censorship?

6 What amateur arts groups exist in your locality? Find out about their history, membership, calendars and events.

7 Imagine yourself to be the manager of a sports and arts centre complex in the inner city. What sort of policies and programmes would you develop and why? Timetable an ordinary working week and justify it to a mixed audience of local politicians, rate payers and community representatives.

8 Why should 'community artists' emphasise the process of artistic production rather than the artistic product?

9 What are the hidden benefits of public subsidy for the Arts? Do the same arguments hold for community arts?

Further reading

R. Hutchison (1982) *The Politics of the Arts Council*, Sinclair, Browne, provides an interesting account of the 'selective tradition' of Arts Council history and pleads for a more open democratic arts policy. Harold Baldry (1981) less critically makes *The Case for the Arts*, Secker and Warburg, as does Owen Kelly (1984) in *Community, Art and the State*, Comedia (1984). Geoff Mulgan and Ken Worpole (1986) offer a defence for a socialist arts policy in *Saturday Night or Sunday Morning?*, Comedia.

J. Wolff (1981) *The Social Production of Art*, Macmillan, provides a so-phisticated theoretical analysis of art and its production. She explores the myth of the artist as a unique creative individual and locates art within wider political, social and historical processes. Raymond Williams (1981) sets himself a similar but broader task in *Culture*, Fontana; whereas Bernice Martin's *A Sociology of Contemporary Cultural Change*, Basil Blackwell (1981) traces the impact of art on popular and youth culture in the 1960s and 1970s.

Countryside recreation

To those who are exhausted by the journey through the complexities of leisure forms of sports and arts, this section on countryside recreation offers no rural retreat. There are a variety of disparate activities encom-passed by the form 'countryside recreation' and, of course, a similar variety of groups to whom the different activities appeal. But the coun-tryside is not exclusively a leisure resource. Many sports and most artis-tic activity are usually practised in spaces primarily designed for that purpose. Leisure activity in the countryside, however, is but one interest in a precious and finite resource. Others include agricultural, industrial and conservation interests. Moreover, most of this resource is in private ownership so that any public use (including leisure) must be negotiated. Many of the problems of countryside leisure stem from this intensive multiple use of a fragile resource. Indeed, there are even conflicts of interest *between* leisure activities. Consider for example, the use of a stretch of river by canoeists and fishermen; or the use of a fell by ram-blers and motor-cycle scramblers.

An understanding of leisure in the countryside must therefore ac-knowledge the following:

1 Different people, in different social and spatial circumstances, have different interests in the countryside. This gives rise to different value-positions or conceptions, ranging from purely aesthetic to purely func-tional interests.

2 The term 'countryside recreation' embraces a variety of leisure activities which attract different people seeking particular leisure experiences. These activities have a differential impact upon the countryside.
3 Different conceptions of the countryside, different interests, and different activities are represented in the leisure field by a range of public, voluntary and commercial bodies. Each of these has to compete with the multiplicity of other interests in the countryside.

These three inter-related dimensions provide a way of understanding key issues about countryside leisure activities.

Conceptions of countryside

Perceptions and definitions of 'the countryside' and 'the rural' are related to whether people are residents, visitors or landowners. For the agricultural labourer, the countryside is a site for work; for the town-dweller a site for leisure and recreation; for the landowner a source of livelihood. Debate about the meanings of 'countryside' is not, therefore, simply an academic exercise. Different perceptions and definitions can have practical consequences in the way land is used. 'Countryside' perceived as a recreational resource will highlight issues quite different from 'countryside' perceived as private property and a means of livelihood. Those who see the countryside as a site for varied flora and fauna will demand policies for land use quite different from those who seek freedom to roam and who regard the countryside as a recreational resource.

'Countryside' is not all the same. Lowland and upland areas differ in appearance, determined in part by physical features and also by land use. Attitudes towards nature change over time. Thus for instance, in the early eighteenth century mountains and upland areas were regarded with horror since they represented the wildness and disorder of nature. Mountainous areas were 'natural' and did not conform to the then canons of 'good taste' which demanded 'planned prospects'. The eighteenth century witnessed wholesale alteration of the English landscape in the deliberate separation of land used for business (i.e. for farming) from land used for pleasure (i.e. for the pleasing prospect of lawns, water, clumps of trees). 'Countryside' was not then a product of farming but a construct of landscape architects who planted thousands of trees in belts and clumps, re-formed the land into knolls, hills and grassy slopes, created artificial lakes and removed villages and their inhabitants from the view of the country home. 'Countryside' in the eighteenth century was not defined by functions, but by aesthetics.

This aesthetic definition tends to dominate perceptions of the countryside held by many town-dwellers. It is a conception which often clashes with the functional approach of many farmers, farm workers and landowners. This is not to suggest that farmers are insensitive to aesthetic considerations, or that all town dwellers share the same vision of rural paradise. Nevertheless, the lowland farmer, however conscious of the aesthetics of landscape, is in competition with those who see farming as 'agribusiness', and will seek efficiency in a functional landscape – in the prairie-like field devoid of useless hedgerows, trees and weeds. In the uplands, as farms amalgamate, dry-stone walls become redundant and are allowed to fall, to be replaced where necessary by the more easily maintained post and wire fence.

Many town-dwellers see these changes as a threat to the 'traditional' English landscape, best illustrated by the increasingly fossilised land-scapes in National Parks like the Lake District and Yorkshire Dales. The image is one of quaint, picturesque countryside with small rural settle-ments served by shaded lanes, set in a mosaic of fields bounded by hedgerows or dry-stone walls. This image is strengthened by the move-ment of many middle-class professionals out of towns into small rural settlements. For these groups, the vision of a rural way of life embodies notions of not only 'traditional' landscapes but traditional crafts and skills, underpinned by ways of life and values which are slow to change, creating thereby a sense of solidity and permanence in contrast to the artificiality, impermanence and volatility of city life. However inaccurate, the vision of rural paradise remains powerful and influential, and lies at the heart of many of the conflicts over countryside recreation.

Conflicts arise between recreational users of the countryside who have differing perceptions of the resource and make different demands upon it. To some the countryside is important for its open spaces, fresh air, sweeping views, sense of tranquillity, peace and solitude. To others, the main attractions are the villages, rivers view-points with summer crowds and visitor services. Others see the countryside as a location for an after-noon's drive; others as the base for some specialised form of recreation. All these groups may find themselves at odds with conservationists who wish to protect flora and fauna from the impacts of visitors, or with ex-town dwellers turned rural residents who may wish to discourage others from visiting a particular location in order to preserve it.

Countryside recreation is then largely an urban-dweller's construct. It can encompass a wide variety of activities pursued in countryside sur-roundings. Figure 2.5 and Table 2.3 from the National Countryside Rec-reation Surveys in 1977 and 1984 give some indication of the range of activities which fall within the term and indicate the continued domi-nance of drives, outings and picnics as major countryside recreations. These activities are more widespread than walking, fishing, organised and informal sports. The range of recreations gives some clue to the complexities of provision required and the conflicts generated both

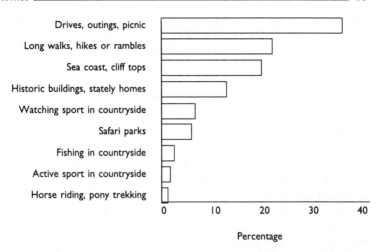

Percentage

Figure 2.5 Proportion of visitors participating in different recreational activities in the countryside

(Source: Patmore, 1983)

amongst recreational users and between recreational and other users of a scarce resource.

Resource and demand-based recreations

Inevitably with such a variety of activities, there are a number of ways of analysing 'countryside recreation'. One method analyses activities in terms of those which are resource-based and those which are demand-based (Clawson and Knetsch, 1966). Resource-based activities are dependent on the nature of physical resources used. Typical activities might be land-based pursuits such as climbing, caving, camping, caravanning, hiking, or water-based activities such as sailing, pleasure-boating, and wind surfing. Demand-based activities are user oriented and emphasise the location of activities and the relationship between location and demand from urban centres.

Concern with the resource directs attention to its quality and the character of its setting. Where other land uses such as mining, forestry, and farming affect the resource and/or its setting, then there is a possibility of conflict. Recent developments in agriculture and husbandry have led to widespread destruction of hedgerows, woods, copses in lowland areas; to the ploughing up of moorland, dereliction of walls and farms in upland areas. Public concern with the countryside as a recreational resource has increased since that resource is the context for a wide range of recreational experiences.

Table 2.3 Activities undertaken by recreational groups in the countryside (percentage of respondents undertaking each activity)

(Source: National Countryside Recreation Survey, 1984; Countryside Commission, 1985)

Activity	Frequency of use of the countryside			
	Frequent	Occasional	Non-user	All respondents
Visit a seaside resort	80	75	30	69
Visit a park or other urban space	76	69	35	66
Visit the sea coast	57	47	12	45
Visit historic buildings	60	47	9	45
Visit country parks	45	33	7	32
Visit zoos/safari parks	29	26	7	24
Visit nature reserves	27	16	3	17
Go on drives/outings	83	71	17	66
Go on long walks	59	41	10	41
Go fishing	10	7	2	7
Go riding	6	3	1	4
Take part in organised sport	27	17	4	17
Take part in informal sport	45	34	8	33
Watch sport	37	24	6	24
Conservation work	5	3	1	3
Pick your own	45	32	8	32
Visit friends/relatives in the countryside	67	50	12	48
Proportion in sample	24	61	15	100

n = 6203

The distinction between resource-based and demand-based activities is not easy to maintain. One difficulty in maintaining boundaries is that demand in this context usually refers to expressed rather than latent demand. Greater publicity of a resource, and increased accessibility, increases the expressed demand. Resources can be purposely developed to encourage demand. The Woburn Abbey Game Park and the Lions of Longleat are examples of attractions created to increase demand. Similarly, while country parks grew out of the increased expressed demand in the 1960s for countryside recreation, many of these parks have now added attractions to encourage a further increase in visitors. The different emphases of a resource-based approach from a demand-based approach is evident in these examples. While the former is concerned with enjoyment of the countryside, the latter is increasingly concerned with providing entertainment in the countryside.

Active and passive recreations

Other attempts to categorise the variety of activities covered by the term 'countryside recreations' have distinguished between active and passive recreation. Passive recreation refers to activities in which experience of the rural setting is of primary consideration and essential for the performance of other activities. Driving to and through the countryside is an important feature of passive countryside recreation. Often the drive is as important as the destination, which is frequently a general area rather than a specific site. The eventual destination is the site for relatively unstructured activities such as picnicking, sunbathing, listening to the (car) radio, sleeping, chatting, strolling, or watching children play. Table 2.5 indicates activities classified as 'passive' pursued by visitors to National Parks and recreational sites in England and Wales. Table 2.4 illustrates sites attracting passive recreationalists using road-side and lay-by parking as well as specially provided car parks, which lend themselves to activities listed in Table 2.5.

The term 'passive' countryside recreation is used to indicate that

Table 2.4 Brecon Beacons: informal countryside recreation attractions and facilities in a National Park.

Name of site	Attrraction	Facilities
A4069 Brynamman – Llangadog road	Open country, top of pass views, easy access	Car parks, toilets, ice-cream van(s)
Carreg Connan Castle Car park	Castle views	Car park, toilets
Cern Duon (Glyntawe Trecastle road)	Open country (one-side), streams, access to Carmarthen Fan and Hyn y Fan Fawr	Some lay-bys
Clyn Gwyn roadside parking	Access to falls, wooded valley, streams	Road verge parking, waymarked walk National Park walkers' way

(Source: data from Brecon Beacons National Park: *Informal Countryside Recreation: Discussion Paper* January 1976.)

participants are involved more in the consumption of experiences rather than in their production (*see* Table 2.5 and Figure 2.5). It is possible to argue of course that recreational driving, picnicking, sunbathing, strolling, watching the children play, do involve production, and that caving, climbing and rambling are examples of consumption as well as the production of experiences.

Other attempts to categorise and make sense of the term 'countryside recreation' make a distinction between formal and informal recreations. Thus the Northumberland National Park Plan (1977) states:

Most visitors to the Park are engaged in some informal recreational activity which may be pleasure motoring, finding somewhere convenient to park for a picnic, a casual walk or simple enjoyment of the relative peace and quiet of the countryside as a change from more urban surroundings.

Here informal and passive are synonymous. The passive or informal recreationalist values the environmental 'bubble' of the car which serves as a comfortable, mobile home: 'a travelling lounge with windscreen replacing TV and familiar defensible space' (Patmore, 1983). The car remains a central location for the activities listed in Figure 2.6.

Nevertheless as noted in the section on sports, active countryside or 'environmental' sports might usefully be characterised as informal (e.g. rambling, cycling) inasmuch as there is no competitive framework, and participants determine for themselves how the activity is to be structured. These loosely organised countryside recreations have different resource requirements from structured competitive sports which might demand specific land management (e.g. game sports) or specially constructed facilities (e.g. motor cycle scrambling, golf).

The Countryside Commission (1986) has acknowledged the definitional difficulties in countryside recreation and has used the term 'recreationist' to refer to all sports and recreation participants, contrasting these with

Table 2.5 Active-passive classification of countryside recreation

Passive	Active
Consumption of countryside experience	Production of experience in countryside
Typical pursuits:	*Typical pursuits:*
Recreational or pleasure driving	Sports (water sports, skiing,
Picnicking	caving, climbing)
Sunbathing	Rambling, hiking, cycling
Strolling/casual walking	

other land users or land managers. The 1986 study distinguishes between 'informal recreationists' (those whose enjoyment of the countryside does not include a specific sporting activity) and 'sporting activists' (who do take part in specific sporting activity). The latter group is further divided on the basis of participation through club membership or on a more casual basis; and between those seeking competition and those who pursue an activity for more generalised recreational benefits.

In summary, there are a variety of ways of classifying countryside recreation along dimensions of passivity and activity; informality and formality; resource and demand-bases. No one classification can unambiguously embrace all activities which are labelled 'countryside recreations'. Similarly, 'countryside' is a term capable of a variety of connotations and meanings from the aesthetic to the functional. These have become increasingly important as changing agricultural practices have threatened the town-dwellers' vision of rural paradise.

Provision for countryside recreation

Countryside recreation is characterised by concentration of demand in terms of time and space. Temporally, daily, weekly and annual patterns show concentrations of demand, with acute peaks reached for only very short lengths of time. Such concentration poses problems for planners of what level of demand to accommodate. Spatially, patterns of demand suggest that very few of the activities subsumed under the heading 'countryside recreation' require wide expanses of land. Much of the concentration is linear (along roads, rivers, canals) or at nodes (lakes, gravel pits, beauty spots, sites of specific interest or managed facilities). Even though it is estimated (CC:NCRS 1984) that some 44% of trip destinations in 1984 were to farmland, woodland, inland or coastal areas *not* primarily managed for recreation, the spatial concentration hardly supports the notion of a leisure wave of urban-dwellers sweeping across the countryside.

A multiplicity of agencies is directly or indirectly involved in countryside recreation. Nationally, agencies such as Tourist Boards, the Countryside Commission, National Parks Authorities, Forestry Commission, British Waterways Board, and the Sports Council provide opportunities and facilities for both informal and active/organised recreations. Other national agencies are more indirectly involved. The Ministry of Defence is by virtue of its ownership of wilderness land able to restrict recreational use of large areas of countryside. The Ministry of Agriculture, Fisheries and Food can and does promulgate policies which are inimical to access to countryside and which can affect the quality of the landscape in which recreation takes place. The Nature Conservancy Council is also able to affect recreational use of areas of countryside by declaring Sites of Special Scientific Interest and Nature Reserves.

Dartmoor (1975)

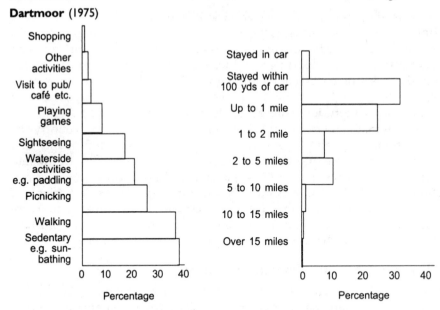

Visitor pursuits and distance travelled from the car, Sunday, summer, 1975
(Source: Data from *Dartmoor National Park Plan* (Dartmoor National Park Authority, 1977)

North York Moors (1976–77)

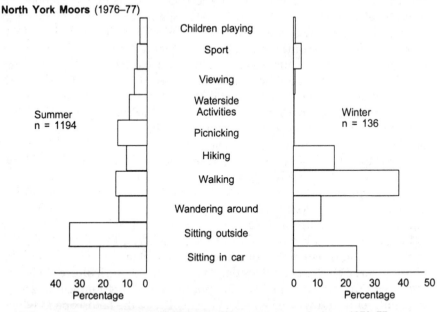

Visitor pursuits observed in North Yorkshire Moors summer and winter, 1976–77
(Source: Data from D. Haffey, 'Recreational activity patterns on the uplands of an English National Park', *Environmental Conservation*)

Figure 2.6   Surveys of recreational activity in the countryside

Lake District (1975)

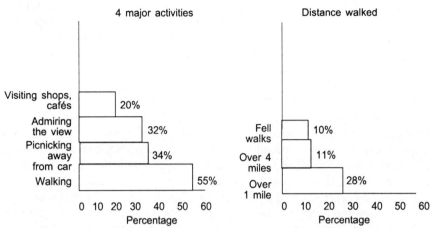

Visitor pursuits and distances walked from the car in the Lake District National Park during the summer of 1975. Visitor questionnaire survey of 77 car parks

(Source: Data from *Lake District National Park Plan*, Lake District Special Planning Board, 1978)

Figure 2.6 (continued)

At a local level, Local Authorities, usually in conjunction with National Agencies, also provide facilities and opportunities for informal and active/organised countryside recreation. The development and maintenance of footpaths and the creation of country parks exemplifies Local Authority and National Agency (in this case the Countryside Commission) working together, often in country areas in the urban-rural fringe.

A wide variety of voluntary groups are also involved in providing recreational opportunities in the countryside. These include organisations such as the Trail Riders' Fellowship, the Ramblers' Association, The Royal Society for the Protection of Birds, The Caravanning and Camping Club, and The National Trust. Often these groups have competing and conflicting interests.

The commercial sector is another vast area of countryside recreation provision. The range extends from the exploitation of natural features (caves, riverside walks to spectacular waterfalls, and parkland) to stately homes and other attractions such as safari parks, zoos, museums, and art galleries. Frequently the attraction becomes more important than the setting and the emphasis shifts from countryside experience to entertainment in the countryside.

Issues

Increase in recreational use
The countryside has always been used for recreational purposes.

Enclosure of open spaces in the eighteenth and nineteenth centuries was resisted in part because of the restrictions placed upon recreational opportunities. The last 25 years have, however, seen an enormous growth in both passive and active countryside recreation. This has placed enormous pressure on resources, increasing conflicts between recreational users (mainly town-dwellers) and landowners, farmers and countryside dwellers.

Differences between the two groups arise from different perceptions of the countryside referred to earlier. For one group the countryside is primarily a site for recreation; for the other a site for work. While the two are not always and inevitably incompatible (camping and caravanning are developed by farmers/landowners to supplement income), increased and uncontrolled invasion of the countryside for recreation by town-dwellers has been resisted by farmers and landowners. There has always been a siege mentality in the farming/landowning community, and this is reflected in legislation. The National Parks and Access to the Countryside Act 1949 was based on the Hobhouse and Dower reports. The latter defined one of the functions of a National Park ensuring that 'established farming use is effectively maintained', the former referring to the need 'to ensure that the peace and beauty of the countryside and the rightful interests of the resident population, are not menaced by an excessive concentration of visitors, or disturbed by incongruous pursuits'. The Countryside Act 1968 similarly responded to increased pressure for recreational use of the countryside by providing country parks as a means of reducing congestion on roads, easing pressure on 'remote and solitary places' and 'reducing the risk of damage to the countryside'. Country parks were thus conceived as a means whereby the town-dwellers might be directed for 'countryside recreation' into urban-fringe locations. The variety of country parks which emerged after 1968 illustrate the difficulties planners had in deciding exactly what 'countryside' was, and what countryside recreation meant. Some parks, therefore, have the minimum facilities and are designed for informal passive activities. Other parks provide 'attractions' and are indistinguishable from urban parks. Still others provide space for active, organised recreations.

Although the two acts were responding to different kinds of pressure (the 1949 Act was a response to demand for access to open country by a relatively small group of walkers, hikers, and ramblers, while the 1968 Act was a response to the car-borne passive recreational user of the countryside), both illustrate concern for containing the multitudes from the towns.

Increase in industrial use
Differences also arise out of the aesthetic and functional perspectives held

by different groups. Those who seek to extend use of the countryside for farming, mineral extraction, defence exercises, water collection, and forestry, have during the last 25 years come under increasing pressure from the recreation lobby who wish to maintain what are regarded as traditional features. For example, the Forestry Commission and the various water companies are constrained to respect the quality of the environment and to retain access to publicly owned land; the Forestry Act (1967) and the water companies (1973) are illustrative of these pressures.

Aesthetic and functional perspectives are blurred when one considers that increased recreational use of countryside is a contributory factor to destruction of the resource itself. Erosion of paths, litter, congestion, overcrowding, destruction of flora and fauna can lead to damage as serious as that produced by changes in agricultural practices. The Wildlife and Countryside Act 1981 was a reaction to the growing concern about increased recreational use, as well as changes in agricultural practices.

Access and accessibility
The term 'access' is ambiguous since it may include two quite separate issues:

● the legal right of entry to the countryside;
● the ability to exercise such a right.

Access in the former sense refers, according to Collins (1984), to legal or customarily defined rights of entry or use. In its latter sense, access refers to accessibility which includes factors contributing to the exercise of legal or customarily defined rights. Accessibility thus involves consideration of a whole range of socio-economic and cultural influences which may or may not facilitate the exercise of legal rights Thus, for instance, legal right of access to Forestry Commission land does not mean that the resource will be accessible to everyone. Some will be unable to afford the cost of travel, others will be unaware of the resource's availability others such as the disabled, may find facilities inappropriate inadequate or non-existent.

Conflicts over legal rights of entry to land for recreational purposes are a reflection of a fundamental division between those who own and those who do not own the land; between those who seek 'freedom to roam' and those who regard that land as 'their' property.

Most land in the UK is in private hands and this ownership is increasing as public bodies such as British Rail, and Forestry Commission, sell off land. Shoard (1987) indicates that some 13% of the surface of the UK is owned by public bodies; 87% is in private hands. Access raises questions about the rights of one group of people (landowners), to restrict recreational opportunities for others, and about how far those who own land can use it as they think fit.

Clashes over ownership are not new. Enclosure, particularly as it gathered momentum in the eighteenth and nineteenth centuries, led to the formation of various societies preserving the use of the countryside for recreational purposes. The history of this struggle is dealt with in various texts (Hill, 1980; Rothman, 1982; Shoard, 1987; Spink, 1994). In the 1970s the growth of groups concerned with the environment (Friends of the Earth, The Farming and Wildlife Advisory Group, The Tree Council) and 'amenity' indicates a different challenge to the right of landowners to do as they like with land in their ownership. Public bodies have had to face a similar challenge.

Conflicts amongst recreationists
Other issues centre around the differing demands of recreational groups. Anglers stress peace and tranquillity to win support for the exclusion of other water-based activities such as canoeing and pleasure cruising. The British Mountaineering Council attempting to preserve the natural challenge of an environment for climbers may oppose measures taken to way-mark and improve footpaths for the use of walkers. The walker anxious to preserve peace and solitude will seek to prevent activities such as trail riding. New recreations like hang-gliding, land-yachting or splash-zone traversing emerge and conflict with established sports and recreations. Groups will defend their interests against other recreational users of the countryside particularly when incompatible with their own pursuits. The resolution of such conflicts (e.g. over the use of a reservoir) often demands scheduling of activities at particular times of the day, week or year. Such conflicts provide further illustration of the varied nature of countryside recreations.

Agricultural policies
The complex and dynamic relationship between competing uses of land is clearly illustrated by recent developments in agricultural policy. Growing concern amongst politicians and members of the public about subsidies to wasteful overproduction has led to reductions in quotas for milk and reductions in intervention spending. Farming is under pressure from reduced incomes and profits, which in turn have forced land values down. It seems highly likely that some farmers will go out of business, and farm sizes will increase. Inevitably some land will come out of agricultural production.

How this land is to be used raises new issues, particularly since recreation is one of the alternatives to be considered. As yet, no clear trends may be discerned. Farmers are often reluctant to part with inherited land and lacking capital to develop recreational projects themselves, may allow land to return to wilderness. Even this alternative has implications for the type of landscape which may be created.

Farmers themselves are having to re-think their attitudes to recreational land uses. Early indications suggest a strong emphasis on developing 'traditional' country sports: hunting, shooting, fishing. Other recreational uses of land – golf courses, hang-gliding, motor cycle scrambling, tourism are also being considered. With forecasts from the Countryside Commission Review Panel (Countryside Commission, 1987) of increases in the total volume of trips to the countryside and continued growth in the use of rural areas for active sports, opportunities for farmers to diversify seem plentiful.

The Countryside Commission Review Panel set up in May 1986 made a total of 57 recommendations which included:

1 Land diversification, including the transfer of land for uses such as wildlife reserves, new woodlands and public recreation;
2 Promotion of multi-purpose forestry with the aim of growing trees for timber but also for improving landscape, creating wildlife habitats and providing better recreation facilities;
3 Encouraging 'environmental friendly' farming and developing environmentally sensitive areas to provide for public recreation and improved access to the countryside;
4 Create new recreation sites and maintain rights of way;
5 Encouragement of new non-farming enterprises;
6 Conservation grants;
7 Encouraging countryside management schemes.

How far a new landscape of leisure will emerge is a matter of conjecture. Elson (1987) offers a number of cautions. In the first instance the new leisure projects are likely to take place on the urban-rural fringe territory defended stoutly by ex-urban dwellers. Secondly, diversification by farmers is likely to be limited by factors such as location and available entrepreneurial skills. Thirdly, there are at present considerable doubts as to how important leisure and recreation use of land is regarded. Finally, green belt policies as presently framed are likely to place considerable restrictions on diversification. Squash courts, sports halls, golf-driving ranges have all been refused planning permission in the past. In the light of the above, it seems likely that the shift from agricultural to recreational use of land will be accompanied by a new set of conflicts, the resolution of which may have far-reaching consequences for those who live near green belt areas and for the future appearance of the wider countryside.

Conclusion

The future of the countryside is firmly on the political agenda. Proposals that 2 million acres of farmland should be taken out of agricultural production by the end of the century have prompted the Set Aside and Countryside Stewardship schemes initiated by the Countryside Commission. Both schemes have recreation and conservation as key elements and recreation is now seen as an important alternative land use on a list which includes rural enterprises, forestry and tourism. Planning and managing the countryside to ensure a balance between all land uses – but particularly between recreation and conservation – is likely to become vital during the next decade.

QUESTIONS AND EXERCISES

1 Attempt an observational site survey of the activities of visitors to a managed countryside recreational facility in your area. How many would you classify as active or passive recreationalists?

2 In what ways is countryside recreation influenced by wider socio-economic factors? Consider particular participation by:
   (a) women
   (b) ethnic groups
   (c) the disabled.

3 List areas/sites which are used for informal or passive countryside recreation within 15 miles of your home.

4 With reference to the typology of leisure activities (Table 2.1), list the ways in which the countryside provides a focus for different leisure experiences.

5 Which countryside recreation can be located within the typology of sports forms (Table 2.3), and which cannot?

6 What are the typical characteristics of participants in countryside recreation in terms of age, sex, social class and ethnicity?

Further reading

Two texts which focus specifically on countryside recreation and examine more closely issues raised in this section are: Sue Glyptis (1991) *Countryside Recreation*, Longman; and Carolyn Harrison (1991) *Countryside Recreation in a Changing Society*, The TMS Partnership Ltd. Both texts make excellent introductions to contemporary countryside recreation issues, which are also explored in John Spink (1994) *Leisure and the Environment*, Butterworth-Heinemann.

J. Allan Patmore (1983) *Recreation and Resources: Leisure Patterns and Leisure Places*, Basil Blackwell, examines the patterns of leisure and recreational activity in England and Wales, and the complexity of the demands on land and water resources generated by these patterns.

The Countryside Commission (1986) *Access to the Countryside for Recreation and Sport* (CCP 217), Countryside Commission, is largely a study of how access to the countryside for recreational purposes has developed. The book contains a useful brief survey of countryside recreation policy. Useful supplements to this text are: K. Bishop (ed.) (1992) *Off the Beaten Track: Access to Open Land in the UK*, Countryside Recreation Network, which gives reports of the proceedings of a conference on contemporary access issues; and H. Talbot (ed.) (1992) *Our Priceless Countryside: Should it be Priced?*, Countryside Recreation Network, which reports contemporary debates about the funding of countryside recreation.

Marion Shoard's book, *This Land is Our Land*, Paladin (1987), is an examination of the history of conflicts over land use and contains information on land ownership in Britain, the use of land by landowners and the effects of these uses on those who do not own land.

Two books by A. and M. MacEwen, *National Parks: conservation or cosmetics?*, George Allen and Unwin (1982), and *Greenprints for the Future?*, George Allen and Unwin (1987), provide a history of the National Parks in England and Wales and highlight conflicts which have arisen in and over the parks. The consequences of some of these conflicts may be gleaned from reading the report of the National Parks Review Panel chaired by Professor Ron Edwards, *Fit for the Future*, (CCP 335), Countryside Commission (1991).

The Countryside Commission's (1994) *Informal Recreation for Disabled People – a practical guide for countryside managers* (CCP 439), Countryside Commission, should be read in conjunction with Colin Barnes's *Disabled People in Britain and Discrimination: A case for Anti-Discrimination Legislation*, Hurst and Co. (1991), particularly Chapters 7 and 8. The Countryside Commission's *Tarn Hows: An Approach to the management of a popular beauty spot* (CCP 106), Countryside Commission (1978) is an early account of how problems of heavy use of a resource may be managed. The Countryside Commission booklet, *Countryside Stewardship: An Outline* (CCP 346), Countryside Commission (1992), describes how the scheme works.

Hobbies, crafts and education

Most leisure studies literature focuses *either* upon active recreations such as sports or arts, and issues related to encouraging participation; *or* upon the more consumer-oriented leisure activities and issues related to their licensing and control. But there are a range of leisure activities, broadly characterised as 'hobbies', 'crafts' and 'education' which are rarely the subject of sustained research, yet these activities comprise a major leisure interest for millions of people, who devote to them substantial personal resources of time, money, space, energy and skill. The nature and extent of these activities is vast. Some activities are conventionally called 'hobbies' or 'crafts', and some are provided through Adult or Further Education classes, others pursued only in domestic settings.

The nature of hobbies, crafts, education

Hobbies
These are primarily individual interests pursued at home, although they may be developed through more or less formally organised clubs and associations at local, national, and in some cases international level. They may be grouped broadly into either *collecting* products or found objects, or *nurturing* animals and plants. Usually, the overriding aim is to possess a complete 'set' of a product, or to procure objects which, because of their rarity, command high value. The motive for collecting would seem to be a combination of desire for personal possession and intrinsic interest in the objects themselves.

The breeding of different types of cats, dogs, fishes, hamsters, bees, hens, budgerigars, finches, pigeons, snakes, etc. is big business. Nevertheless, the caring, nurturing, and training of various animals, birds and fish is seldom motivated purely for the pursuit of profit. For each breed or variety there is a network of people who communicate through newsletters or specialised magazines, who form associations, and organise events, meets, and competitions, to exchange information, technical advice, and compare the 'products' of their activity. The comparison varies from dog shows for particular breeds, to the more exotic rat-fancying, mouse-fancying and ferreting competitions. The same applies to those who grow leeks, onions, bonsai trees, dahlias, and roses. Information and advice about different hybrids, and about optimum growing conditions are exchanged through various networks of information including TV and radio programmes.

Crafts
Words have inexact meanings, and the dividing line between 'hobbies' and 'crafts' is imprecise. Here crafts are designated as leisure activities which involve making things, i.e. converting various raw materials such as wood, clay, and wool into objects through the exercise of skills, typically requiring manual dexterity. This includes modelling activities, handicrafts such as macrame, tapestry, and knitting, furniture making

and upholstery, dressmaking, cookery, printing, and flower-arranging. Crafts can be valued for both their functional utility (e.g. making a child's toy out of wood) and for their form (e.g. sculpting an animal figure out of the same material). Craft-workers value the process and product in instrumental or intrinsic terms; as an artefact which has value or as a creative object with little utility. Knitting and dress-making, for example, can be seen as both domestic labour, therefore contributing to household finances, or as disinterested, creative leisure activity. Crafts are conventionally distinguished from 'arts' on the basis of the functional nature of the former and because crafts are primarily about reproducing or replicating particular objects. However, as discussed in the earlier section on 'arts', the division with 'crafts' is relatively arbitrary and has been sustained by particular interest groups who stress aesthetic criteria to the exclusion of functional significance.

Like hobbies, there are both informal and formal channels for exchanging information, displaying products and entering competitions, but communication networks tend to be more restricted in scope. Unlike most hobbies, because crafts involve the active and skilful production of artefacts, they are frequently provided by Adult Education programmes. The personal skill thresholds to activities are such that participants often depend on 'experts' to provide tuition. Nevertheless, the relationship between the 'teacher' and the 'class' varies from one adult education group to another, with some classes being formal whereas others are egalitarian and participatory. Table 2.6 presents a rough fourfold division of hobbies and crafts although students are encouraged to question some of the designations.

How does one set about coming to terms with the wide variety of hobbies and crafts, most of which are also taught in adult education classes? All occur in free time and are expressions of individual choice; all demand a productive use of free-time permitting individuals opportunities to be creative, develop skills of self-expression and self-organisation and to produce cultural artefacts of one sort or another. Many hobbies and craft clubs are locally based and are expressions of what Bishop and Hoggett term 'mutual aid in leisure'. People organise themselves, are productive and by and large consume what they produce. Such a view of leisure is clearly to be set aside from consuming dealt with later.

Bishop and Hoggett (1986) stress the point most forcibly:

In particular, collective leisure offers opportunities rare – if not unique – in our society to reassert values related not to passive consumerism but to production for one's own use and enjoyment.

Indeed, some argue that individuals are far more creative and productive in their leisure than they are at work, which is deskilled, repetitious and

Table 2.6 A typology of hobbies and crafts

Breeding	Growing	Collecting	Making
Caged birds	Allotments	Antiques – cars, bikes postcards, furniture	Models and modelling – boats, aeroplanes, railways, military
Rats	Gardens	Coins	Handicrafts – macrame, corndollies
Mice	Flower arranging	Clocks	Printing
Dogs	Railway/canal	Stamps	Upholstery
Cats	preservation	Stones	Dressmaking
Hens	Conservation	Metal detecting	Cookery
Bees		Family histories	
Fishes		Industrial archaeology	

driven by managerial discipline. Work in industrial society is driven by the dull compulsion of necessity and many radicals in the nineteenth century, such as William Morris, strove hard to retain craft-skills and control over the work process, emphasising design, aesthetics and taste.

Equally, futurists such as Gorz and Toffler stress that work will increasingly involve substantial periods of creativity. It is as if the fusion of production and consumption so effortlessly achieved in crafts and hobbies is the harbinger of future work and leisure. As has been suggested in Chapter 1, if individuals are in control of what is produced, the state is all the more likely to encourage such leisure forms. Education, crafts and hobbies are good examples of benign state encouragement not least because they encourage self-improvement and became, in the mid-nineteenth century, the hallmark of respectability. Many working men were willing participants in the 'cult of respectability' and were eager to join Mechanics Institutes, Education Classes, Temperance Movements and various religious denominations. Historians have remarked upon how the working class became divided into the 'respectable' working men who pursued 'useful knowledge' and the 'rough' who consumed popular culture in the public houses, music halls and brothels.

A survey, commissioned jointly by the ESRC/SC documented the substantial involvement of adults within what has been termed the voluntary sector. Particular attention was paid to comparing a part of Bristol (Kingswood) with a part of Leicester. Bishop and Hoggett discovered 300 groups in Kingswood, and assuming a membership of 90, this generated 28 000 people active in the area, has a total population of about 85 000. The research sampled 71 organisations in Kingswood and 63 in N.E.

N.E. Leicester. The explicit purpose of the groups is shown in Table 2.7

Table 2.7 is only the starting point for understanding the breadth of involvement and participation in self-organised leisure forms. It is essential to get behind these broad labels and explore the variety of meanings that people derive from their involvement, and the diverse contexts within which such involvement takes place. To enter the world of crafts and hobbies introduces a strange subcontinent of social networks, based on a common interest and characterised by mutual aid. These worlds are best understood as leisure subcultures, each of which has its own distinct language, significance and culture. Railway modelling is clearly different from rearing caged birds but each subculture has developed its own language, membership and patterns of involvement. Within each leisure subculture, clubs develop their own identity and style, marking themselves off from other clubs which are seen as being different in some way or another. Clubs generate a sense of identity and belonging, which is rarely experienced in other spheres of social life. Such clubs are not without conflicts as many secretaries bemoan the passivity of the bulk of members, who in their turn may cheerfully wish to assassinate committee members who run the club in Mafia fashion. Yet, such divisions pale into insignificance in the long term, as all are still members and experience a sense of solidarity for 'our' club.

Education

'Education' as a leisure activity has no element of compulsion. While school activities in the sports, arts and crafts areas might be termed recreational, lack of freedom of choice for children usually undermines their quality as leisure experiences. However, evening and day classes are freely chosen and the learning processes involved are diverse. They include arts and crafts but also studying foreign languages, local history, local geography and many others.

Table 2.7 Adult involvement in the voluntary sector

Area of interest	Kingswood		N.E. Leicester	
	no.	%	no.	%
Multi-functional*	20	28	21	33
Sports	26	37	22	35
Arts	9	13	11	17
Crafts/hobbies	16	23	8	13
Miscellaneous	2	3	1	2

*i.e. youth groups, women's institutes, OAP clubs, etc. (Bishop and Hoggett, 1986)

One in 25 adults attend night classes run by adult education centres throughout Britain. Such attendance far outnumbers the proportion of adults watching football. The variety of classes is extraordinary, as even a cursory glance at any local adult education prospectus will confirm. Perhaps the only common feature amongst the diverse courses is that people define 'education as leisure' and the 'ivory tower' of adult education for pleasure. People are drawn to education, and night classes in particular, for a bewildering number of reasons. Individuals choose to attend a class or a course simply because of interest in the subject matter or out of curiosity to discover what the subject is about and try it. Hence, an individual may choose a class which relates to a hobby, craft or handicraft in which he or she already has considerable expertise and consequently courses are often graded in terms of skill, expense and knowledge. Many choose to attend classes for self-improvement and the course, under the guidance of expert tuition, is expected to heighten one's performance and skill. All leisure forms may be seen in an educational context and consequently there are classes for sports, arts and country-side recreation, as well as courses related to tourism (e.g. language courses, cultural, history and architecture) and some to home-based consuming (e.g. cookery, woodworking, etc.).

People also attend adult education classes for reasons of self-improvement related to work and careers. Individuals may choose to attend daytime or evening classes in academic subjects to rebuild careers (e.g. women returning to study after child-care) to embark on new careers (e.g. Open University degrees and postgraduate qualifications) or to gain basic qualifications (e.g. day release/evening classes linked to industrial/ commercial training or management). For some people on academic or work-related courses, education may be seen not as leisure but more broadly linked with work-discipline and compulsion.

In contrast others may join education classes for more 'social' reasons, rather than individual concerns about performance and qualifications. Such people may be less interested in *doing* the activity but more interested in *being* there. Adult education classes provide an opportunity for 'going out', for sociability because friends have enrolled on the same course, to meet members of the opposite sex, to have a drink afterwards, to mix with people of similar educational class or social background. The more 'social' reasons for joining a class clearly are hard to separate from individual reasons of choice, related to intrinsic interest, performance and self-improvement. What is intriguing is the way in which both clubs organised around enthusiasms and adult education classes manage to fuse individual interests with networks of sociability. It is interesting that such organisations may not press members too hard on their motives for membership and thereby are able to accommodate a wide variety of people to participate in freely chosen leisure activity yet chosen for different reasons – some of which are not publicly voiced. It is no coincidence that women may regard evening classes as a good 'excuse' for getting out of the house and meeting people in a safe, interesting, public context. The men in their lives may accept domestic responsibilities for evening classes because they are distinctly timetabled, organised and improving, whereas forms of consuming (e.g. nightclubs, discos, pubs) would be discouraged.

As is clear from the analysis of women and bingo, certain leisure forms are acceptable to and for women. One therefore should not be surprised to learn that women outnumber men 2:1 on rates of attendance in adult education.

Issues in participation

Some hobbies, especially collecting, are identified more with children than adults, and there is an expectation that such activities will be abandoned as 'play' gives way to 'recreation'. Roberts, Sutton-Smith and Kozelka (1962) suggest that the continued obsessive pursuit of children's games into adulthood may reflect a failure to adapt to the values of adult society, and provides a secure alternative and compensatory world. More persuasive, perhaps, is the view of Caillois who sees hobbies – especially collecting, and puzzles and problems – as activities (*see* Chapter 1) which can be pursued individually, especially by children, but which await the opportunity to become social activities in order to develop into completely human play activities – or leisure forms in our terms. Evidence for this interpretation is provided by the fact that (even) children's hobbies are rarely solitary, but are subject to crazes when 'everyone at school' collects beermats, matchboxes or stickers. Equally, in adulthood most hobbyists and craft workers belong to clubs and societies, or to a wider community of participants who meet actively in adult education settings, or vicariously through the pages of interest magazines or books. Thus, it has been argued that hobbies must be seen as part of a mainstream leisure culture allowing the exercise of particular individual skills and interests in a social milieu, which in common with most forms is an important element in the leisure experience itself.

The social distribution of participation in these activities is poorly researched but some broad trends are discernible (see Leisure sections of the *General Household Survey* and *Social Trends*). For example, collecting objects (e.g. stamps) is more likely to be pursued by males than females and is predominantly a middle-class phenomenon in adulthood. Crafts related to household roles and activities, such as upholstery and embroidery, are largely the province of women. In both cases traditional gender roles learned in childhood explain some of these patterns. Recent initiatives in Adult Education have attempted to change these stereotypical behaviours by, for example, designating classes for women only in activities which they have not traditionally pursued – e.g. carpentry and joinery – albeit often with educational rather than leisure motives in mind. Some attempts have also been made to examine relationships between work and leisure lifestyles through the medium of involvement in hobbies and crafts, in order to test out work/leisure theories such as Parker's concepts of extension opposition, and neutrality which we considered in Chapter 1. Mott *et al.* (1974) identified possible 'opposition' patterns for heavy industrial workers in jobs such as mining and weaving whose work contrasted sharply in context with their leisure hobby, e.g. the pigeon fancier, when rough, gross-motor labour activity contrasted with delicate, caring, bird rearing. Bacon (1977) however, in his study of 'craft-workers' at evening classes found no consistent patterns in the motivation of these adult students of carpentry; they were not peopled solely by non-manual workers seeking a compensatory, skilful, manual leisure experience, but by a much broader spectrum of occupations. Bacon did, however, note that, in common with many other 'productive' leisure activities, carpentry classes were most likely to be pursued by men in higher non-manual employment and skilled manual workers.

In general terms our knowledge of participation in hobbies, crafts, and adult education classes is poorly developed as these activities have long been barely acknowledged as significant leisure forms. There is thus great scope for research and investigation by students into this group of activities. Much data is relatively accessible as well as being unexplored.

Policy issues

The public sector

Local authorities have two functions in provision for hobbies and crafts. One is to provide courses, tutors, equipment and spaces in order to foster and develop interests. The other is to provide premises for voluntary associations of hobbyists to use. Traditionally, adult education programmes have been limited to 'useful' forms of learning rather than mere recreations. More recently, this distinction has virtually disappeared and Adult Education programmes have expanded to cover a fuller range of productive recreations, hobbies, arts and crafts as well as more specifically educational activities. In addition to the organisation of leisure and education classes, the public sector presently has an important role to play in letting out premises for hobbies and crafts to flourish. This is confirmed in Bishop and Hoggett's survey in Kingswood and Leicester (Table 2.8).

Reliance upon the public sector for spaces has been further sustained in Leicester by the Urban Aid programme which recently created many new clubs around enthusiasms. Several issues arise from this dependence on the public sector. What type of clubs should receive state aid? What benefits do they generate? To what extent has public sector provision learnt from the 'Quality of Life Experiments' introduced in the 1970s? Will local authorities have to increase fees, rents etc. under pressure from local authority expenditure? If sports and leisure are run by private management what are the likely consequences for clubs using those facilities? Should traditional crafts and skills such as stained glass-making, copy writing, hand knitting, etc. be funded as part of a national, regional or local heritage or should they be left to fade away? What other crafts/ hobbies are likely to be 'rediscovered' in the future? What new ones will emerge? What evidence is there of cross-fertilisation between sports/ arts and education, if such leisure opportunities are provided on the same site or in the same building? Should such initiatives prioritise local people and participation? Do self-organised mutual-aid initiatives, by their very nature appeal to women and therefore should be encouraged? Are such clubs and networks useful for racial minorities to generate their distinct cultural identity, history and language?

The commercial sector
Participation in hobbies and crafts has been characterised above as particular subcultures. Their concerns, distinctive interests, values, knowledge, and organisational structures set them apart from mainstream culture. They are self-organised collective organisations which consume the leisure they produce, and within which transactions are essentially non-commercial.

Table 2.8 Hobbies and crafts premises

Premises	Kingswood	N.E. Leicester
Local authority centres	16	40
Passive schools	4	6
Active schools*	0	18
Church (+ church use)	9	6
Church (non-church use)	6	3
Private	18	9
Other institutions	31	2
Own premises	4	1
None	2	0
Other	0	2

*Denoted community development role rather than passively letting space.

However, this general characterisation needs modification. Collectors' items such as stamps, antiques, and coins have always been valued commodities to be bought and sold in the market place, with economic interests being one motive behind this set of hobbies. Many crafts and hobbies are dependent upon a specialised commercial sector for raw materials, tools and equipment to make the interest viable. Model railways are a good example of this reliance on commerce. Indeed, personnel working in retail outlets are likely to be enthusiasts themselves providing information and advice. Similarly, many arts and crafts rely heavily upon commercial outlets for raw materials and tools.

An indication of the vitality of hobbies and crafts is the development of specialist magazines catering for particular leisure interests. Published in glossy colour formats, and devoting much of their space to advertisements, they enjoy large circulations. Readership is composed not only of hobbyists themselves, but vicarious participants whose interest is to read about and discuss the hobbies of others! Colour supplements of Sunday newspapers exhort readers to collect reproductions or miniatures of porcelain, silverware, vintage cars, and other products. These are invariably marketed as 'limited editions', hence suggesting a return for investment.

The commercial sector provides an enabling and supportive role in the development of many hobbies and crafts. But such influence should not be treated as neutral since it may undermine the self-organised and self-determined nature of these activities. Does the commercial sector merely play a neutral role by enabling activities, or does it generate changes to their nature and form?

The precise relationship between the leisure subculture and the commercial sector depends upon a variety of factors. Bishop and Hoggett (1986) fear the intrusion of professionals from both the commercial and the public sector, though leisure subcultures may resist commercial pressures for ever newer and more expensive equipment

QUESTIONS AND EXERCISES

1 Contact the secretary of a club in your local community and find out about its history, finance, membership, organisation and events calendar.

2 Make a list of the 'voluntary organisations' in your neighbourhood/city. What percentage are sports/arts/ hobbies/crafts/multifunctional?

3 Visit a newsagent (or library) and examine the range of publications/magazines that relate to crafts/hobbies.

4 Find out about any/all of the following:
lapidary; war games; toy dogs; philately; aquarism; rat fancying; numismatism; aero modelling; lace making/macrame; beekeeping

5 Examine patterns of participation in Adult Education 'leisure classes' by such indicators as age, sex, occupation, ethnicity. Do particular hobbies and crafts attract specific social groupings?

6 Compare and contrast your own experiences of learning a hobby or craft for leisure reasons with your experiences of learning in educational or vocational settings.

7 How and why have your hobbies changed as you have moved through the life-cycle from childhood to present stage? What have you abandoned, and what maintained? Predict your hobbies 10, 20, 30 years into the future.

8 Attempt to discern the range of hobby and craft clubs and groups available locally (e.g. via advertisements in local libraries, craft and hobby shops). Visit one group and undertake a case study of local involvement.

Further reading

The most up-to-date and stimulating overview of 'hobbies and crafts' is to be found in P. Hoggett and J. Bishop (1986) *Organising Around Enthusiasms: mutual aid in leisure*, Comedia.

The following books address some of the policy issues surrounding provision, particularly with regard to Adult Education:

C. Smith, S. Parker and M. Smith (1974) *Leisure and Society in Britain*, Allen Lane.

M. Smith *et al.* (1977) *Leisure and Urban Society*, LSA.

B. Rees *et al.* (1979) *Community Arts and Leisure*, LSA.

Tourism

Tourism represents a significant, often prolonged, leisure activity. It has grown in importance as household real incomes have increased and has consistently been the second largest element of household leisure spending (*Social Trends*, 1987). In terms of leisure activities typology (Table 2.1), it can include both actively produced experiences largely devised by the participants, such as simple camping or walking expeditions or day trips; and much more elaborately constructed commercial ventures designed for package tourists or hotel guests. In both instances the experiences, and usually the context, are of prime importance in ensuring satisfaction for tourist or holidaymaker.

Tourism defined

Tourism may be conceptualised as an amalgam of several components: the act of travelling; a temporary stay; a particular destination; and activities undertaken at the destination. These components, present in both domestic and international tourism and holidaymaking, have as their central feature the tourist, although the term 'visitor' is the one most generally used by government agencies intent on measuring the various components. Thus the International Union of Travel Organisations (IUOTO) refers to visitors as 'any person visiting a country other than that in which he has his usual place of residence, for any reason other than following an occupation remunerated from within the country visited'. The definition, applicable to international tourism, can be adapted to include domestic tourism by adding 'or region' after 'country'. The term visitor has been further divided into two groups:

1 Tourists who are visitors making at least one overnight stop in a country or region and staying at least 24 hours
2 Excursionists (including day trippers and people on cruises), who are temporary visitors staying less than 24 hours in a country or region.

Tourism is frequently referred to as an industry. There are references to the tourist industry, to tourist demands, tourist resources, product and markets, tourist facilities and tourist services. There are two points to note about this terminology. The first is that it is not always clear if the term 'tourist' is being used in the precise sense suggested above. It would certainly seem more appropriate, consistent and less confusing to refer to tourism industry, visitor markets, visitor facilities etc. unless one wishes particularly to direct attention to those visitors who stay longer than 24 hours in a destination. The second point to note is that the designation of tourism as an industry is by no means uncontested (Chadwick, 1981) since there is no distinct product, but a combination of products from quite separate industries (transport, accommodation, entertainment) which do not cater exclusively for visitors but also for members of local communities.

Nevertheless others have argued that tourism does have characteristics which justify its being designated an industry. The summaries of research in Mathieson and Wall (1981) and Murphy (1985) include the following points:

1 *Tourism has a distinct product*: the experience, discussed in the introduction to this chapter. This product is unusual in that it is often located at a distant destination to which customers have to travel in order to consume the product. The context may well be of prime significance to consumers, who pay for the product before seeing/experiencing it and have to rely largely on information provided by the travel agent (and perhaps a little on previous experience and information from other consumers). The product is an amalgam of activities available and undertaken at a destination and of the services which make the destination and activities accessible. Each destination will have its own appeal which may develop without conscious effort or may be developed consciously to suit particular client groups. The identity and image of a destination are thus a vital part of the activity. Tourism's products are diverse and complex and this has important consequences for marketing. The combination, for example, of airline ticket, hotel accommodation and entertainment, as part of a deal, means that airlines are not just involved in selling travel, or hotels in selling accommodation. The one is dependent on the other. Co-ordination of the various industries at a variety of levels is essential in the creation of a tourism product.

2 *Tourism is a resource-based industry.* In this respect tourism has been likened (Dearden, 1983) to fishing and forestry. Resources may be distinguished as follows:

   (a) *Facilities*, including transport, infrastructure, superstructure (accommodation, catering, ancillary services, i.e. ski lifts, picnic sites). Transport services are vital since mobility is critical as it determines access to the destination area and to attractions at the destination.

   (b) *Attractions*: these may be sub-divided as follows (Travis, 1982):

   - natural resources (specific scenery; Lake District, Swiss Alps, Niagara Falls; climate, sun, sea, sand);
   - man-made resources (event attractions such as Olympic Games, World Cup, International Soccer matches);
   - recreation opportunities; historial/archaeological attractions (Stonehenge, York Minster, historic cities);
   - cultural resources such as handicrafts, language traditions, gastronomy, art and music (including concerts, paintings and sculptures).

Attractions influence the choice of the visitor between one destination and another. All places are potential destinations if they have identifiable resources and if the host community manifests hospitality. The resources,

like those of fishing and forestry, are limited and can be depleted, de-
graded or destroyed by mis-use or over-use. Cultural and hospitality
resources are particularly fragile, therefore, and management to prevent
their destruction or degradation is vital if tourism is to survive. There has
to be an attractive product to sell or the industry fails.

3 *Tourism is an unstable industry* since:

   (a) it is seasonal;
   (b) it is highly susceptible to external influences (witness the cancella-
       tion of US package tours after the US raids on Libya and subsequent
       threats of retaliation; and the panic in the European tourism indus-
       try following Chernobyl (Kendall and McVey, 1986); changes in
       exchange rates (for instance Britain's currency restrictions in the
       1950s limited UK travellers to destinations within the sterling area);
       unusual climatic conditions (North American ski resorts faced ruin
       after the mild winter of 1980–1); energy crises (the oil price in-
       creases after 1973 had a particularly damaging effect on interna-
       tional tourism);
   (c) it is not easy to create 'product loyalty' because of the complexity,
       diversity and often incompatibility of visitor motivation;
   (d) it is greatly influenced by small changes in price and income. Re-
       ductions in price can increase the number travelling (witness the
       growth of international flights between North America and Europe,
       North America and Australasia, as a result of price reductions).

The nature of tourism

The designation of tourism as an industry is indicative of the economic
basis of much tourism research (see Fig. 2.7). It is worth noting too, that
the definitions given earlier have evolved largely in the interest of data
collection to facilitate international comparisons of tourism, its effects
national/regional economies, on balance of payments, and its contribution to component industries (hotel and catering, rail, air, shipping, car
hire) which depend on tourist traffic. The definitions serve to distinguish
visitors from migrants and seasonal workers, but lump together groups
of people (those engaged in education, business, sport, attending confer-
ences, visiting friends and relatives) who would not consider themselves
as tourists, and whose experiences are likely to differ greatly from the
experience of being on holiday. Indeed the terms 'going on holiday',
'going abroad for our holidays' are more accurate reflections of popular
understanding of what being a tourist is. The concern in most economic
based studies is likely to be with total visitor expenditure, income and job
generation, and multiplier effects, rather than with concern for the kinds

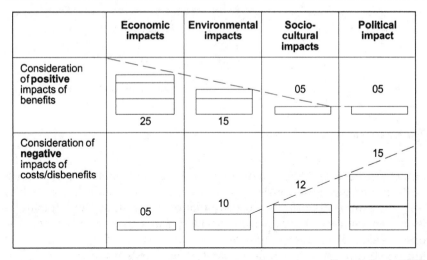

	Economic impacts	Environmental impacts	Socio-cultural impacts	Political impact
Consideration of **positive** impacts of benefits	25	15	05	05
Consideration of **negative** impacts of costs/disbenefits	05	10	12	15

(Source Travis: 1982)

Figure 2.7   Positive and negative impacts of tourism

of experiences visitors have in an area, their motivation and the quality of goods and services received. Holiday programmes and critical comments in magazines suggest that the experience of being a tourist involves feelings and memories, frustrations, embarrassments and disappointments. There are, of course, positive experiences as well.

Classification of tourism in terms of range of travel, distance travelled, length of stay, numbers travelling, travel arrangements, and type of accommodation, similarly tell us little about the experience of being a tourist. Classification in terms of visitor motivation (recreation, culture, ethnic, environmental, historical, sport, business, conference) perhaps contribute a little more to understanding the tourist experience, since such a classification focuses on expectations. Where these expectations are linked with particular destinations then some insight can be gained into tourist images of destinations. Nevertheless, tourist typologies based on motivation are fraught with difficulties. There are, for instance, particular problems associated with distinguishing between long, short term and intrinsic motivations, ascertaining multi-motive causes of behaviour and teasing out the differences between tourist perceptions of their own (usually laudable) motives and the researcher's often less charitable perceptions (Pearce, 1982).

The tourist

Jafari (1982) has posited a 'tourist culture' which refers to a way of life practised by tourists while travelling. This culture is quite distinct from

Non-institutionalised	Institutionalised
Explorer	Individual mass tourist
Drifter	Organised mass tourist

Figure 2.8 Tourist types (Cohen)

the host culture and the imported culture of the tourist. While from a tourist perspective the tourist culture involves a temporary way of life, from the perspective of the host population the tourists' way of life is permanent and has its own recognisable peculiarities of language, costume, places of residence, and leisure activities. Jafari claims that this 'tourist culture' is as yet little researched and little understood.

Cohen (1972; 1979) has developed tourist typologies which go some way to assisting an understanding of what it is to be a tourist and the possible impact on host populations. He distinguishes (Figure 2.8) four major types of tourist on the basis of the degree of willingness to experience the unfamiliar in the host society.

Two categories, the explorer and the drifter, are concerned to seek out the new, the unfamiliar, and the strange. They arrange their own travel, use local facilities and have a high level of contact with local residents. Since they are few in number the explorer and the drifter have little impact on the host society. Cohen labels these 'non-institutionalised' travellers. The other two categories, labelled 'institutionalised' travellers, consist of the individual mass and the organised mass tourist. Both categories arrange their travel and accommodation through travel agents and seek out popular resorts. The individual mass and organised mass tourists seek the familiar and are content to remain within the 'environmental bubble' of their own society which is recreated in the destination.

These two categories have a great effect on the destination. As demand grows there is increased commercialisation, development of artificial facilities, a growth of foreign investment and reduction in local control. A moment's thought about the type of accommodation and food provided for tourists from the prosperous industrialised nations will bring to mind illustrations of the environmental bubble. Accommodation resembles the familiar conditions of 'home' (i.e. in the prosperous industrialised nations), with air conditioning, private bathroom/shower, television, refrigerator, mixer taps. Food must not be (too) 'foreign', hence the fish-and-chips-on-the-Costa-Brava phenomenon. Recreation facilities (golf course, swimming pools, car hire, saunas), similarly replicate the familiar

Experience	Quest for a new spiritual centre	Experience: Quest for pleasure
Existential	Find a new spiritual centre	Diversionary
Experimental	Alternative lifestyle	Recreational
Experiential	Authenticity in experiences of life/culture of others	
[NON-INSTITUTIONALISED] Tourists as pilgrims		[INSTITUTIONALISED] Tourists as pleasure seekers

(Source: Cohen 1979)

Figure 2.9   Tourist motives (Cohen)

and the known, with the emphasis upon mass consumption of a commercially produced product.

Cohen's 1979 typology emphasises the way in which tourists relate to environments and seeks to explain why tourists travel (Figure 2.9).

The assumption is made that tourists travel because they believe that valuable experience can be found somewhere other than at home. Tourism is thus a quest, the nature of which will be determined by the extent to which the tourist identifies with the supreme and fundamental norms and values (the 'spiritual centre') of a society. For the tourist who identifies fully with their own society, its culture and values, then other cultures have no meaning or attraction For such people the holiday is a recreation – an entertainment and relaxation undertaken to recreate body and mind. Cohen's second category of tourist experience is the 'diversionary'. Here, the tourist is alienated from home society but does not wish to gain a new spiritual centre. The holiday is thus a diversion, an escape from the boredom and routine of everyday life. For both the recreational and diversionary tourist, pleasure is the experience sought.

Three other modes of tourist experience are distinguished In the experimental mode the visitor, alienated from home society, gains a valued experience by witnessing genuineness in the lives of others. The experimental mode sees the tourist experimenting with different and unfamiliar ways of life in the quest for a new spiritual centre. The tourist who finally acquires a new spiritual centre represents the existential mode. These three modes – experiential, experimental and existential are steps in the pilgrimage undertaken by modern men and women in their quest for identity, personal individuality and a new 'spiritual centre'. The modes can be identified with the explorer and drifter tourist types in the earlier typology in that the impacts on destinations are relatively slight. The recreational and diversionary modes with their concern for pleasure may be identified with mass-tourism in its demand for leisure and recreation facilities, its creation of contrived pleasure environments and its commercialisation.

Cohen's typologies are useful in illustrating the distinction, made in Chapter 1, between the nature and form of a particular leisure activity. In the case of tourism, the form (organised mass, individual mass, drifter, explorer) shapes the nature of the experience. And the experience sought (recreation, pleasure, quest for a new spiritual centre) determines the form of tourism undertaken. Thus organised mass tourists with their standardised Western-type accommodation, recreation facilities, services, food and travel arrangements have a different experience from the explorer absorb the host culture, use local facilities and make their own travel arrangements. The mass-tourism form will not provide experiences akin to those associated with finding a new 'spiritual centre' since mass-tourism does not allow tourists (even if they wish) to escape the environmental bubble of westernised comforts.

The tourist 'industry'

As has been indicated earlier tourism may be regarded as an industry and as such its development will have a variety of impacts. Since tourism was regarded as one of the UK's economic success stories in the 1980s, it would seem vital that those in positions to initiate tourism policies and plan development should be aware of the possible consequences of these policies.

The economic benefits of tourism are by no means as clear cut as central and local government, consultancy and tourist authorities' reports suggest. Optimism amongst these agencies seems to stem from the perceived potential of tourism to have favourable impact on economic features such as the balance of payments, employment, income generation, and entrepreneurial activity. There are, nevertheless, good reasons to advocate caution when reading over-optimistic accounts of the economic benefits which tourism can bring. Firstly, the undoubted bias towards economic factors usually benefits, has been accompanied by relative neglect of economic costs. Research into the social, physical/environmental and cultural costs (less easy topics on which to gather data) has been limited. Secondly, research is uneven in that more work is done on international tourism as it affects developing countries than on domestic tourism and its effects. Thirdly, while the amount of data on tourism has undoubtedly grown with more systematic collection, allowing for a greater degree of comparability between areas and countries, there still remains a wide variety of different uses and interpretations of terminologies, categories and methodologies. These differences are illustrated in the varying use of the concept of 'multiplier' in calculating income and jobs generated by tourism, and by the methods of calculating tourism's contribution to the balance of payments.

Calculation of economic benefits is thus not only difficult but likely to involve a considerable amount of 'guestimating'. Calculation of benefits in income generation and job creation is likely to depend on factors such as size of area under scrutiny, the type, diversity and self-sufficiency of an area's economy, patterns of local ownership and local trading, the amount of leakage into the study area from other areas, the type of 'community' studied, the type of visitor included in the study. Economic benefits which may emerge need then to be balanced against economic costs – less frequently researched and largely limited to studies of investment, infrastructure and service provision. Opportunity costs would also have to be taken into consideration, since alternatives to tourism might very well provide for the same or lower investment, greater income generation and more jobs.

At a time of massive unemployment with its consequent hardships and human suffering, job creation assumes considerable importance. The tourism industry's proponents highlight this factor when pressing the case for tourism development. It seems clear that tourism does create jobs and, under certain circumstances, a paid job is better than no job. However, where alternative industries exist or could be developed, then the type of job generated by tourism could well be perceived as a cost. Many jobs in the accommodation, catering and entertainment industries in the UK are low paid, low-status and low or no-skill jobs (Byrne, 1986). They tend to be dominated by women and are, in the main, non-unionised, a factor which makes the work-force susceptible to a variety of subtle and not so subtle pressures from employers. Tourism creates very few jobs at management and professional levels and where such jobs are created, labour is often imported into an area (TRRU, 1981; Getz, 1982). It is not just high status, higher paid jobs which are filled by imported labour. Since many of the jobs are part-time and seasonal they may be taken as second jobs by people already in work or by groups (such as students or housewives) who only want part-time jobs. Such jobs do not then automatically benefit a locality, nor do they necessarily contribute much to reducing unemployment. One thus needs to view critically statements which blandly announce job generation as a result of particular tourism related projects.

Table 2.9 Environmental impacts: costs and benefits

Costs	Benefits
1 Pollution: air, water, ground – by litter/wastes and noise pollution (loss of peace and quiet)	1 Environmental additions: development and realisation of infrastructure, superstructure, facilities, services.
2 Crowding and congestion: costs and damage of traffic congestion and crowding, accidents, effects of increased and excessive accessibility.	2 Heritage protection and management.
3 Damage to/destruction of heritage resources; degradation of heritage quality. Resource depletion of minerals and soils.	3 Pollution control.
4 Land-use loss from agriculture and pastoral use to built-up areas and so-called 'non-productive' uses. Impact of and damage to landscape by infrastructure development and from the scale of super-structure development.	4 Growth in water management, sewage disposal treatment, public health benefits.
5 Ecological impacts – damage to ecosystems – ripple effects on physical environments.	
6 Loss of fauna and flora: visitor numbers and visitor pressures displacing fauna/reducing coverage and types of residual flora.	

(Source: Travis, 1982)

Economic benefits have also to be calculated in the light of social, physical/environmental costs. These are summarised in Table 2.9 and while many of the studies used for this summary deal with tourism outside the UK there is a growing body of evidence from studies of UK destinations to indicate similar costs. Again, caution must be exercised in making sweeping statements about social and physical/environmental costs. The type and scale of physical impacts will depend very much on the type of development involved, the nature of a destination's attractions and resources, and the management. There are signs, for instance in the UK that the impact of tourism is increasingly being seen as too high a price to pay, and this attitude has led to an emphasis on conservation rather than an expansion of the industry (LDSPB, 1984; Yorkshire Dales NPC, 1984).

Social and cultural impacts (*see* Table 2.10) also need to be taken into account in calculating economic benefits. Research into socio-cultural impacts lags behind other areas of impact research, particularly in relation to UK destinations. Host–guest relationships have been generally under-researched but there are indications that the fragility of the hospitality resource is not given sufficient attention by those anxious to develop tourism in specific localities in the UK. More recently, Bradford Metropolitan District Council's successful promotion of 'Emmerdale Farm' tours as part of the Bradford package weekend has increased visitor numbers to the village where the TV series is filmed, an increase which has led to considerable disquiet and some hostility amongst residents.

It would seem clear that evaluation of the costs and benefits of tourism might be more rigorous and that present claims made by local and central government departments by private agencies and by tourist authorities, should be treated with caution. Those involved in the tourism industry and those involved in its development need to show themselves sensitive to the unique economic, physical environmental, social and cultural characteristics of an area and to the unique consequences for an area, arising out of the interaction between particular developments and areas.

QUESTIONS AND EXERCISES ————————————————

1 Examine a range of travel and holiday brochures and consider what kind of leisure experience is being presented by particular companies. Is passive consumption or active participation emphasised in creating holiday experiences?

2 Using brochures select the kinds of holidays you consider would appeal to each of Cohen's categories of tourists; the explorer, drifter, organised mass tourist and individual mass tourist.

3 Choose an example of tourism or holiday investment known to you. For the chosen scheme or project consider the type of client it appeals to, and the wider effects it has had on the local area – both positive and negative.

Table 2.10 Socio-cultural impacts of tourism: costs and benefits

Costs		*Benefits*
		Social
Host culture debasement. Unacceptable role and scale of cultural conflict and change.	Damage to cultural systems and to cultural resources. Minority languages at risk.	Increase knowledge of host cultures by visitors. Awareness of its music, cuisine and arts, and possibly language.
Rich visitors come to poor communities creating tension.	Cultural commercialisation and commodification of society.	Improved reputation and visibility of host community to outsiders.
Pressures to change social values, dress, mores, habits and behavioural norms.	Folk art becomes airport junk-art. Deeper values and ideals at risk.	Increased social contacts, new ideas, new values, new ways of life.
		Host Culture
Loss of original state and stability. Loss of cultural pride. Status relationship between host and guest cultures changes.	Consumption changes. Introduction or expansion of gambling, prostitution, drunkenness and other excesses; vice and drugs, theft and petty crime.	Develops because of demand for traditional entertainment, demand for traditional art, crafts and music.
		Enriching role of visitors
Increasingly mass-entry of visitors makes contact diminish and relationship meaningless.	No visitor understanding or knowledge of the hosts, their culture and language.	By provision of service amenities and facilities not otherwise available to hosts – and social and activity choices therefore arising. Education
		(continued)

Table 2.10 *continued*

Costs	Benefits
	and learning aided. Boost for heritage protection, interpretation and management. Increased social range and experience. Cultural interchange, peace and understanding. New experiences, new ideas, new cultures.

4 Examine the provision made by the tourist industry for:
  (a) pensioners
  (b) single-parent families
  (c) disabled groups.

5 What initiatives are being made to promote tourism in your area? In what ways do these initiatives reflect a concern for sustainable tourism and 'green' issues?

Further reading

A. J. Burkhart and S. Medlik (1982) *Tourism Past, Present and Future,* Heinemann (2nd ed.) analyses the theory and practice of tourism in the second half of the twentieth century. S. Medlik (1985). *Paying Guests: A Report on the Challenge and Opportunity of travel and tourism,* Confederation of British Industry, Centre Point, is designed to encourage the promotion of tourism in the UK. Although like the previously cited work it assumes that tourism is wholly beneficial. It contains relatively recent information on the tourism industry. A useful corrective to the generally optimistic tone of both the above texts is D. Byrne (ed.) (1986) *Waiting for Change? Working in hotel and catering,* Low Pay Unit/Hotel and Catering Workers' Union. This examines the conditions of employment of many employed in the hotel and catering section of the tourism industry. A. Mathieson and G. Wall (1981) *Tourism: economic, physical and social impacts*, Longman, reviews research on the effects of tourism on destination areas. P. E. Murphy (1985) *Tourism: A Community Approach*, Methuen, examines the problems of tourism and tourism development policies in the industrial nations of North America and Western Europe from the perspective of the destination communities. The Tourism and Research Unit (1981) *The Economy of Rural Communities in the National Parks of England and Wales*, TRRU, contains an informative chapter on tourism development in Exmoor National Park. J. Urry (1990) *The Tourist Gaze – Leisure and Travel in Contemporary Societies*, Sage, analyses tourism from a variety of perspectives – historical, economic, social, cultural – and relates tourism and its development to a range of cultural changes in contemporary societies. The English Tourist Board, the Rural Development Commission and the Countryside Commission have recently published (no date) *The Green Light: A Guide to Sustainable Tourism*, which outlines ways whereby tourism might be given a 'green overhaul' in line with other industries. R. Davidson (1992) *Tourism in Europe*, Pitman, gives a useful European dimension to various aspects of tourism including sections on theme parks, business tourism, social tourism and tourism in Eastern Europe. The same author's (1993) *Tourism*, Pitman is a more general look at the tourism industry with useful sections on the economic, social and environmental impacts tourism can have. Both of the texts contain contemporary case study material.

Consuming

This section explores a variety of leisure forms and experiences which we have chosen to define broadly as 'consuming'. Unlike other leisure forms included in this chapter the term 'consuming' is not in common usage in our language. This is a peculiar irony in that one of the central arguments of this section is that consuming is more commonplace and popular than other leisure forms. The three main aspects of consuming explored in this section are: entertainments, commodities/retailing, and gambling/gaming although they often overlap.

Generally these leisure activities involve consumption of goods, services and miscellaneous products created commercially, usually for profit. Although individuals are involved in an active search for pleasurable experiences in such places as cinemas, theatres, pubs, pizzerias, shopping centres and casinos, these leisure forms mostly encourage passive consumption of mass-produced goods. As well as being commonplace and popular, 'consuming' is central to increasing numbers of life-styles, and plays a growing role in the commercial and service sectors of the

economy. Its influence on individuals and national economic well-being
is considerable and probably includes the majority of leisure experiences
in contemporary society.

'Entertainments'

Is wrestling entertainment or sport? What if the participants are women
and the sporting arena covered in mud? Is jazz played in a pub 'entertainment' whereas a jazz concert at the Albert Hall is music and should
be thought of as belonging to the arts? What if the concert is televised or
broadcast on the radio? Is the televised 'Last Night of the Proms' entertainment and how much should audiences participate in the performance? Why are family quiz shows, videos and chat-shows so popular on
television and radio? Why should it be acceptable for young people to
drink alcohol socially but unacceptable to smoke cannabis at home or use
drugs at 'raves' and parties? Why do advertisers use 'personalities' to sell
cereals, cars and condoms? Why do so many people spend 2–3 hours a
night on average watching British serials like Coronation Street and East
Enders not to mention Neighbours and other 'soaps'? Why do certain
characters, even monarchs, become newsworthy, household names
whose private lives are fused with the parts they play and are subject to
such newspaper coverage and scrutiny?

All the above questions say a great deal about the entertainments
industry and its capacity to win mass audiences. The term 'entertainments' properly describes particular leisure forms that developed mass
audiences towards the end of the nineteenth and twentieth centuries.
Many leisure forms such as sports, arts and recreation involve only a
minority of people and none can realistically claim mass popularity and
involvement (*see* Chapter 3).

Throughout the nineteenth century traditional popular forms of entertainment proved to be quite persistent and resilient (e.g. public houses,
fairs, horse racing, boxing, etc.) as new leisure forms emerged with
advances in technology (e.g. music halls, radio, cinema and television). It
seemed that capitalism was now firmly established in the hearts and
minds of ordinary working people, whom Marx supposed to be its grave-
diggers. By the twentieth century the only thing that was worth 'digging'
seemed to be rock 'n' roll. Affluent 'classless' youth seemed to be more
tuned into the variety of consumption styles and pop music of
capitalism than they were to the five hour television speeches by Fidel
Castro on Cuban socialism. Some historians refer to this long-term
consolidation of commercial leisure and entertainment as developing a
'culture of consolation' amongst ordinary people. The commercial sector
via the music hall, the pub, the cinema and the television, binds mass
audiences into a shared popular culture which values humour,

amusement, and diversion which broadly can be conceived as 'having a good time'.

Such a view of leisure assumes that leisure, and entertainment in particular, serve to make up for inequalities in power, wealth and life-chances in the serious worlds of politics, economics or religion. Unlike other leisure forms, such as sports, the arts and hobbies, entertainments are passive, inferior and proletarian; unwelcome leisure forms which appeal to the debased (and sometimes depraved) tastes of the people. Whereas popular culture seeks relaxation, amusement, diversion and pleasure, its critics fear such activities and such idleness. As a result the state has often been drawn into censoring and controlling entertainment in a variety of ways, as well as literally policing the leisure forms that take place. Chapter 5 will explore more fully the historical and changing relationships between the state, national culture and popular leisure forms.

Entertainments are best understood as consuming activities which are provided by the commercial sector and are appropriated by mass audiences. Historically mass audiences were an important dimension of the leisure experience; huge crowds travelled to and watched sporting contests, listened to music-hall songs or watched films in the cinema. Seaside resorts were full of circuses, holiday shows and diversions as packaged holidays became possible for more individuals and families during the twentieth century. With radio, television, and video the penetration of markets by the entertainments industries has grown, although the site of consumption is now more likely to be individualised, privatised and home-based. Yet the entertainments industries, through newspapers, radio, television and advertising are capable of generating mass audiences which over-ride differences in age, locality, gender, race and class. Like the weather, talking about television programmes is a safe, shared topic of conversation. It is therefore only possible in the twentieth century to talk of a 'national' popular culture, which may be further strengthened by patriotism in national sporting teams.

If entertainment means mass audiences, it also carries strong undercurrents of passivity, i.e. of 'being entertained'. It is someone else who provides the hospitality, the humour, the diversions and amusement and most frequently these require specialist skills, resources and finance. Bailey's (1978; 1986) analysis of the capital investment in music halls and professional performers, documents the gradual shift away from coarse alcoholic 'free and easies' where audiences and prostitutes 'sang along' and 'did turns' towards drier, managed, music hall entertainment which was more carefully licensed and policed, although not intensively so. Historically, ordinary people welcomed being entertained.

Current feminist analysis stresses 'entertaining at home' actually means substantial domestic labour in shopping, house-cleaning, dressing up, providing the meal, conversation and washing-up on the part of women. Male guests in particular restrict themselves to an unproductive consuming. It is perhaps no historical accident that the bulk of male leisure expenditure is directed to buying alcohol and consuming it in public houses, restaurants, winebars, discos and clubs. Taking cans home from the off-licence or supermarket or drinking 'home-brew' is not quite the same. Throughout the past few hundred years, the public house has served a variety of functions – a local meeting place, sports centre, a business and banking facility, a convivial world to pursue relationships (of whatever nature), a hotel and so on. It has been a popular and ubiquitous locale for male leisure and entertainment and conversely an uncomfortable place for unaccompanied women to be.

For many adults entertainment means 'going out' to the pub, restaurant, films or visiting friends and neighbours. For many more, entertainment is home-based, often constrained by income, time and domestic labour, and provided by the mass media with the consumption of popular culture provided by the television, radio or videos. Because households are dominated by family relationships, young people seek entertainment outside the home and beyond parental influence. Youth too 'goes out' but often finds itself with nowhere to go or nothing to do. Such 'hanging around' talking to friends and being on the margins of delinquency has often meant substantial entertainment or 'having a laff' with resultant concern from parents, youth workers and the police that young people should fill their leisure time more productively.

Since World War II there has been substantial discussion by academics, experts and journalists about the youth revolution in tastes and 'style'. Much of the debate has concentrated on the affluence of youth and developing forms of youth style. During the 1950s, 1960s and 1970s successive waves of fads and fashions have emerged producing distinct styles or subcultures, e.g. Teds, Mods, Rockers, Hippies, Skins, Punks, New Wave and so on. These spectacular youth styles have been amplified and sensationalised by popular newspapers. Bernice Martin provides an interesting account on the 'expressive' cultural revolution of youth in the 1960s and emphasises the youth drive towards 'liminality', i.e. pushing social rules to their limits and hence offending the 'respectability' of parental culture. Whether in humour, art, dress sense, sexual relationships, drug use or everyday social manners and language, the 1960s witnessed a redrawing of cultural boundaries with the entertainment industries at their cutting edge.

Many of the studies of these youth styles stress the resistance of young people to wider society, symbolised by authority figures, the Establishment and parents. What has emerged is a complicated interaction of youth style; its choice of music, language, transport, places to meet, drugs (legal and illegal) with a swift response from mass media industries to develop and to commodify a particular style. Fashionable styles in clothes, shoes, music, drinks, transport, etc. which were a distinctive mixture of previous styles become copied by others and available to a wider mass audience. For example, distinctive 'live' music becomes transformed into managed concerts or shows with backing tracks, laser lights, film clips and events, all of which are also available on video. But novelty always waits in the wings of the entertainment industry.

According to Phil Cohen such youth styles are 'magical' to the problems of being adolescent in a class society and having to face up to the demands of work, unemployment, education, living at home with one's parents and having limited choices because of low income and little geographical mobility. Being a hooligan/a mod/a punk/a raver permits one to consume 'Saturday Night Fever' and escape into the world of romance, excitement, amusement and diversion. Many factions of youth (although divided by class, gender and race) have (or at least hope for) a 'good time'. It is a hopeful vision that the commercial sector serves with fashion clothes, pop music, alcohol, dancing, atmosphere and so on. It is in this space that individuals can be themselves – free from the constraints of school, work, unemployment, and family, allowing them to develop themselves and their own particular cultural identity. Such self-expressions are clear statements about masculinity and femininity and vary with class and racial background. Equally, there can be conflicts as to whose leisure interests dominate. For example, at clubs and discos, girls may be more interested in performing and dancing to the music, whereas boys appear towards pub closing-times and favour 'picking up' girls to which end dancing is simply a means.

For adults and youth alike entertainment is synonymous with 'having a good time' and spending money in the commercial sector. It is this sector that seems to have the entrepreneurial spirit to meet and develop popular tastes. Somehow, when public sector or voluntary organisations attempt to entertain they do not offer the egalitarianism, or the freedom, open to the consumer who has 'paid at the door'. Public authorities seem to be providers who know best, and therefore, a discreet paternalism sets in and is ever-present. The youth club disco is not quite the same as commercial ones, and youth workers may feel that there is more to youth work than being an entertainer; swimming in the local pool is not the same experience as a leisure pool with saunas, restaurants, wave machines, water splashes etc. If public sector organisations attempt to break into leisure markets they often do so in a tired jaded way, which appears a pale reflection of the 'real thing' provided exclusively in the commercial sector. The public sector seems to operate with constraining values which often filter out 'fun' – there is always the 'parkie' to stop ball games or worry about litter or the swimming-bath attendant to stop people 'bombing' off the top board. With commercial sector provision, entertainment is second nature and there is more licence to have a good time. It does mean however that in the process things may go 'too far' when people consume alcohol to excess, make too much noise or harass other members hoping to be entertained. Consequently, commercial entertainment palaces may be 'no-go' areas for the very young, single women, some racial minorities, the middle aged, the disabled and the elderly.

QUESTIONS AND EXERCISES ————————————————

1 Why is it that 'entertainment' is most usually supplied by the commercial sector?

2 What kind of influence do American leisure corporations have in UK markets for entertainment?

3 List ten top TV or sports personalities? What makes them popular?

4 What impact does TV have upon sport; people's leisure lifestyles; shopping?

5 Why should 'having a good time' on holiday be closely associated with spending money?

6 Are mass audiences passive consumers of the spectacle or entertainment they attend?

Commodities and life styles

In the last 25 years the British public has come to expect a growth in real incomes and increased opportunities for personal acquisition of goods and services (disposable incomes increased 71% between 1971 and 1991, *Social Trends* 1993). Consumer durables of all kinds have become commonplace (e.g. televisions in 99% of households, refrigerators 94%, washing machines 87%, telephones 88% by 1991; *General Household Survey*).

Much of people's leisure time in both public and private involves the largely passive consumption of a wide range of products. Many, like video films or restaurant meals, are provided by businesses and are purchased by individuals for their own consumption. Others, like public parks or operatic performances, are supplied collectively with either total or partial subsidy from local or central government. Some, like allotment gardens or country walks, are produced and used on a self-sufficient basis.

This broad leisure category encompasses activities involving various degrees of control exercised by individuals and by government. Increased consumer passivity is reflected within the growing sphere of commercial leisure enterprise. The miscellaneous activities outlined here represent the bulk of household spending on leisure. Consumption of alcoholic drink away from home remained until recently the single greatest item of household leisure expenditure, even surpassing spending on holidays and tourism. Although consumption is officially designated in 'household' terms, the pre-eminence of drinking reflects inequalities in spending within households and the gender dominance in traditional patterns of leisure consumption (Delphy, 1984). Increasingly, however, all sectors in society are likely to purchase leisure opportunities as commodities supplied by commercial interests. This process will be speeded if local public subsidies are reduced and a materialist spirit assumes wider social acceptance.

Growth in incomes and free time has led to increasing commercial interest in the production, distribution and sale of leisure experiences and goods. With the decline in manufacturing industry, leisure has become a suitable vehicle for investment, along with other service sectors of the economy and has been developed accordingly. Both individuals and households form suitable targets for the producers' leisure commodities. Packaged entertainment, holidays, sports-wear, food, and drink have been specially developed and directed at an affluent public.

People's concern for social status and individual identity has been reflected in the advertising of leisure commodities. Selling involves not simply the goods and services to be consumed, but represents a particular image and lifestyle. A largely illusory individualism based upon choice of particular products and styles has been created, disseminated and accepted. Some consumers seek high technology, associated with the latest audio systems, micro-technology and fast cars, while others adopt peasant styles of stripped pine, Arts and Crafts wallpaper, macrame hangings and craft pottery.

The diversity of available, but commodified, lifestyles is represented in shopping centres where units range from those catering for macrobiotic vegetarian health nuts, to supersaturated fatty fast food, dairy product and white sugar consumers. Despite this apparent diversity, what is being sold can be seen as part of a subcultural image with its own leisure styles and forms. The only constraint on the range of products and styles available commercially is that of profitable production and marketing.

New and divergent patterns may soon become incorporated within the 'goods' on offer commercially. Individual, amateur and distinctive subcultural forms quickly become appropriated, provided they can be adopted profitably. Before long, designer 'punk rock' clothes, suitably ripped and slashed are available 'off the peg' in retail multiple stores. The pace at which the industry changes seems to resolve some of the issue of whether young people determine their own fashions or whether manufacturers determine what is worn. For most of the population, lacking the imagination or ingenuity of the few, conformity to what is being commercially reproduced, advertised and distributed, tends to dominate, while the diversity of available modes promises a currently stylish identity of spurious individuality.

Most people derive satisfaction and security from the reassurance of social status which consumption of particular leisure experiences or goods brings. Acquisition of named brands, major household items or the conspicuous consumption of services, represents a celebration of individual affluence aided by large scale suppliers.

A nation of increasing owner occupation (over 69% of households in England and Wales) ensures that much consumption takes place within the private sphere of home. The link between income, status and neighbourhood is a real one and gives a solidarity to the growing 'middle mass' (Pahl, 1984) which may replace traditional community links. The growth of home-based leisure pursuits like do-it-yourself repairs and decorating, gardening and needle skills, are testimony to the close links between consumption, investment of free time and leisure life-styles.

The dominance of television as a packaged entertainment is symptomatic of household-based leisure and by its very nature pre-supposes consumption of electrical goods, durables like furniture, and housing. The social relations of consumption represented by such a leisure mode reveal much of the patterns of inequality and opportunity in contemporary Britain. It is the preserve of 'people like us' who can afford a particular lifestyle and neighbourhood, and may well serve to separate suburbanites from an increasingly marginalised and residual 'underclass', unable to afford consumption of vehicles, goods and housing which forms the key to this particular leisure style.

Home ownership and its attendant trappings does not come cheaply and is purchased for many households only by the incorporation of women into paid employment. By their involvement the cost of maintaining many households has been broadened, and increased income has for many facilitated and encouraged further purchase of commodities. Increased female employment has begun to change the nature of household relations and can be expected to have a growing impact on the nature of female and family leisure forms (*see* Chapters 3 and 7).

Along with home ownership, car ownership has brought enormous change to leisure opportunities and activity patterns. It has freed the majority of households from the constraints of their locality and local facilities (*see* Chapter 4) and opened up a whole new range of publicly and privately provided goods and experiences. In addition to individual recreational activity like gardening, angling, personal stereos, and jogging, car use has led to growth in family-based outings for outdoor recreation, commercial events, tourist trips and shopping.

Brent Cross, Meadowhall and Metro Centre Gateshead may not sound like leisure centres, but in a real sense of where people choose to spend large amounts of pleasurable 'free time' they are. They represent the growing links between the purchase and consumption of commodities in this rapidly growing sector of the leisure industry.

QUESTIONS AND EXERCISES

1 Consider your own leisure time and general life-style. How far does it depend on commercially produced experiences and manufactured goods? How many are strictly necessary, and how many might formerly have been considered 'luxury' items?

2 How much of your own leisure-wear or sports equipment has a designer label or prestigious company 'logo'? Why have these become so much more important in the last decade? Why are they important to your own leisure image?

3 When watching an evening's television advertisements note how many references there are to leisure forms or leisured life-styles. Which products use which kinds of images to promote their goods?

Leisure shopping

What Napoleon called 'a nation of shopkeepers' appears to have become a nation of shoppers. Since World War II, 'shopkeeping', traditionally a small-scale service trade, has largely been replaced by 'retailing', a more cost effective and capitalised industry.

Growth in this sector has been accompanied by massive investment in retail management systems and presentation of goods to the public. Shopping has similarly changed from being a frequent, highly functional activity, mostly connected with purchases of daily necessities, into a less frequent and usually pleasurable event focused on desirable commodities. Grocery shopping for many has become a regular visit to a local superstore or hypermarket where bulk purchase of household goods for a week or longer is conducted under a single roof.

Changing social patterns have led to greater diversity among shoppers. Women's employment has encouraged male participation in household purchasing, and this formerly often solitary activity has increasingly become a family-centred event. With diversity has come both the need and potential for a broadening of focus of shopping expeditions. Families are attracted to shopping centres with an exciting range of facilities. The need to maximise the number of potential customers has influenced store and centre design accordingly.

Shopping precincts, malls and out-of-town centres compete with each other to attract households making weekly bulk purchases and allied spending on clothes, toys and consumer durables. The rising tide of consumption has been increasingly profitable for manufacturers and major retail chains, leading to massive investment during the last 20 years. Retailing became almost twice as profitable as manufacturing in the 1980s (manufacturing capital return for 1980–3 was at 9%; while retailing increased to 16%).

In an effort to retain the attractiveness of often congested city centres, expenditure on multi-storey car-parking facilities, re-vamped department stores, and pedestrianised thoroughfares has been initiated by businesses and local authorities. Similarly, in out-of-town centres there has been a recognition that a population of increasingly affluent consumers wishes to enjoy shopping as a pleasurable social activity.

The design of malls incorporates seats, weather protection, pleasant planting, water features, informal cafes, and glass-sided wall-clirnber lifts. Eye-catching visual effects, stimulating colours and layout all add to the impact and heighten excitement yet do so within a secure and managed environment. American malls pursue individual themes based on fantasy or adventure, and integrate active recreation features like swimming pools, splash areas, funfairs, and sports halls into their general design. In Britain the nature of shops in such precincts has changed to reflect a leisured society. An increasing proportion of units are devoted to sports goods, leisure wear, hobby photographic and electrical goods, and travel agencies, as well as specialised provision for health, fitness, cosmetics, clothes and furnishings.

The world of corner shops and small grocery stores has developed almost beyond recognition and changes encourage further public visits. Following the crowds on a Saturday afternoon is more likely to take you into the well lit promenades of a theme mall or 'consumption palace' than the cold and draughty terraces of conventional professional sports grounds.

The initial leisure shopping stage of acquisition is being made as pleasant and 'painless' as possible. Many retail giants are now as keen to issue plastic credit cards as to sell goods directly, since the interest rates on money borrowed to buy goods may well generate higher returns than the act of purchase itself. A limited number, no more than five multiple retailers, have come to control over 70% of grocery sales in some regions. Their investment in supermarkets and allied shopping centres represents a highly profitable component of the leisure industry.

Shopping as a leisure form reflects a society for which consumption of commercially produced commodities has assumed a central role in life-styles and popular expectations. Advertising, media and culture have supported and encouraged increased consumption as a way to high social status and self-fulfilment. Accordingly the act of acquiring goods and services has become seen as a pleasurable experience when individualism and preference can be indulged. Commerce encourages self-indulgence to ensure continuing and increasing profitability. A materialistic and instrumentally oriented society seems inevitably linked to growth of shopping time and consumption. Such activity is expensive and inevitably divisive. Not everyone can indulge in fantasy, using credit cards in futuristic shopping malls. Those locked out by increasing economic polarisation and the security staffs of centres cannot participate in this aspect of leisure in an affluent society.

Consumers themselves appear to have little similarity with the rational, sovereign and informed purchasers of classical economic theory, whose decisions on price and preference are directly influential on manufacturers. Current investment seems directed to ensure that the artificial environment and piped music of the mall is designed to lull participants into an unthinking pursuit of ever newer commodities. In an unequal world of limited resources such activities may well be profitable but may also present a threat to the very security and well-being of the affluent leisured society they represent (*see* Chapter 7 for debate on the nature of postmodern consumption theorised within Social Theory).

QUESTIONS AND EXERCISES

1 Note how much time in a normal week you and members of your household spend shopping. How do the individual patterns vary and how can you explain these variations? How much of the shopping is entirely purposeful and how much is leisure shopping?

2 Visit a shopping mall and note the features which encourage a 'leisure' approach to shopping and spending. What kinds of people visit particular types of shopping locations? Compare them for age, sex, and apparent affluence.

3 Consider the ways in which shops and shopping have changed in your lifetime. How have the changes reflected commercial pressures for productivity, large scale operations, return on capital, and meeting competition?

Further reading

G. Steadman-Jones (1983) *Languages of Class*, Oxford University Press, provides an accessible view of the historical development of popular culture, as do the Open University Course Units on *Popular Culture*, U203.

H. Cunningham (1980) *Leisure in the Industrial Revolution*, Croom Helm; Yeo and Yeo (1981) *Popular Culture and Class Conflict*, Harvester; and P. Bailey (1978) *Leisure and Class in Victorian England*, RKP; offer further evidence of the emergence of commercial markets in leisure.

P. Cohen's article, 'Subcultural Change in the East End of London', in E. Butterworth and D. Weir (1984) *A New Sociology of Modern Britain*, Fontana, analyses working-class youth styles, while B. Waites *et al.* (1981) *Popular Culture*, Batsford, provides a collection of articles by key writers.

Gaming and Gambling

Attitudes towards gambling expressed in both the contemporary moral climate and in state legislative control, represent a key indicator of tension between the values of hedonistic leisure and consumption, and those of the work ethic and production. Legislative changes since the 1960s have made gambling more easily available and have accompanied, and perhaps led, a move towards a less puritanical view. Certainly gambling represents an important element in the portfolios of the main commercial leisure providers who extended their operations across the whole field of leisure consuming during the 1980s. For example, Rank Leisure Services include bingo (Top Rank), Odeon cinemas and Butlins holidays amongst their interests; Ladbroke has betting shops, hotels and holiday villages, and Bass combines breweries and public houses with Coral Bingo, betting shops and Pontins Holidays. The recent acquisition of Nudge Bingo by First Leisure (1993) links gambling with sports (bowling), discos and resorts.

A characteristic feature of the approach of these providers to gambling, is the emphasis on developing it as a social leisure experience. They aim to change its image from that of a down market, somewhat disreputable activity, to that of a respectable and socially rewarding one. This is also reflected by recent changes in legislation, which allow betting shops to install more congenial facilities, providing televised horse racing in a leisure setting.

Until 1993, the only UK State gambling provision was the Premium Bond Draw – a mild form, and a pale shadow of State lotteries elsewhere in Europe. However, Parliament introduced a National Lottery in late 1994 with individual prizes of well over £1 million. Organised by Camelot (a commercial company), lottery profits are distributed by public agencies to the arts, National Heritage, sports, charities and the Millennium Celebration Fund. It appears that gambling is becoming a leisure activity which the State is now willing to promote, whereas a mere decade ago it was regarded as something to license rather than exploit.

Much of leisure literature is also ambivalent about gambling as a leisure activity, despite the fact that participation rates in some cases far outstrip those in more 'respectable' activities. Betting on football pools for example, consistently attracts around 40% of the adult population to invest on a weekly basis. No sport or art form approaches this figure. Some of the reasons for the wilful ignoring of gambling are undoubtedly moral, for it is still seen by some as an 'occasion of pure waste' (Caillois, 1958) and therefore scarcely worthy of recognition, or else too dangerous to highlight. However, some of the neglect may relate to uncertainty about the status of gambling as a leisure activity.

As the introduction to this chapter demonstrated, leisure activities can be analysed according to the degree of activity or passivity of participants, and to the extent to which chance or the player determines the outcome of action. Gaming and gambling is particularly amenable to such analysis; using three main categories:

1 Betting (judgement and chance)
Players have the opportunity to exercise some judgement implying knowledge or skill before placing their bet. This is normally the *active* phase, but once the bet is made participants become *passive* and await the outcome of the actions of others (usually footballers, horses or dogs) and there is no need to be present to watch the action unless the bet is on one's own performance. Some betting may be perfunctory involving little time or deliberation and simply requiring a cash outlay. Regular betting of fixed amounts weekly on the same numbers in a football pool is a case in point, and represents a minor leisure investment in activity terms, even if the fantasy potential is longer lasting. At the other extreme, on-course horse race betting is a lengthy process both in the active and passive phases and is thus more readily conceived as leisure activity. Furthermore, investment of time and energy in the active judgemental phase of betting provides opportunities for sociability in a discussion of 'form' aided by the publication of race cards, fixtures, results and records of

previous performances. For many punters such debates may bring leisure to work-places and invest other forms of leisure, notably drinking, with added significance.

2 *Gambling (pure chance)*

Players have no control over the outcome of pure forms of gambling. Chance is all, and players abandon themselves to fate and luck – the turn of a card, spin of a wheel, toss of a coin. Players in such activities are *passive* in their ability to influence the run of play. However, as with betting, the context in which this type of gaming takes place is a crucial determinant of its potential as a leisure form. Lotteries and raffles, for example, demand a minimum of time and no necessity for one's physical presence at the draw. Most of the other forms of gaming in this category however, demand the players' presence in social situations which offer opportunities for sociability, and hence have great leisure potential. Bingo, casino gaming such as roulette, and gaming machines (fruit machines, or in modern legal terminology 'Amusements with Prizes') all offer players extended periods of social activity. While passive in the sense of having no means of controlling the outcome of the game, players are frequently very active socially, and hence such games can be the site for important communal leisure experience – notably in the case of bingo as discussed below.

3 *Gaming (chance and skill)*

In most card games, and in dominoes and some board games, the reversal of the process found in betting occurs. Thus players are *passive* in the first stage of play, and rely on chance to deal their cards (and expect fair deals with no cheating), but then become *actively* involved in determining the outcome of the game. Such gaming is by nature social, and is therefore sufficiently engaging to stand as a major form of leisure in its own right, without the absolute necessity for gambling on the result. Many such games are played without stakes, or prizes, as private home-based or pub-based activity. However, more usually perhaps, gambling or prizes are an important element in playing, and in some such games, for example pontoon or poker, betting on the outcome of the turn of a card is intrinsic to the nature of playing. A certain generalisation is possible about these games: the greater the reliance on chance to determine outcome, the greater the need for betting to make the game interesting; and conversely, the greater the control exercised by players over outcome, the lower the necessity for gambling on that outcome. In other words, the more *active* the players, the more viable the game in its own right. The setting thus becomes important in determining the extent to which gambling accompanies these 'chance and skill' games. In casinos players expect to gamble, and most games are selected to emphasise chance

Table 2.11 A typology of gaming and gambling

	Betting		Gambling	Gaming
Characteristic features	Judgement and chance		Pure chance	Chance, strategy and skill
Process	Active then passive (mainly consumption)		Passive (consumption)	Passive then active (mainly production)
Context	Private	Public	Public	Private or public
Legal status	Licensed		Licensed	Lightly controlled
Social interaction	Solitary	Social	Social, gregarious	Social interaction necessary
Time span	Short sporadic	Extended continuous	Extended continuous	Extended continuous
Examples	Pools lotteries	On-course betting and betting shops	Bingo Casinos Fruit machines	Dominoes Cards Board games Pub games

above skill. In the home the reverse is probably true, and board games (e.g. Monopoly) and card games like whist and bridge are more common. In pubs and clubs, betting on 'chance-skill' games for small stakes is allowed by law and a variety of games are played on which betting may take place, depending on the culture of the context. Most pub games (typically dominoes, cribbage, darts and pool) do not require gambling, and of course the latter two are not 'chance' games; however, in some pub subcultures gambling is endemic in all games played, often with drinks being wagered on the results.

This analysis, summarised in Table 2.11, examines gambling as a range of distinct activities, linked by chance and monetary gain or loss, but differing in the manner and degree of control over outcome by participants, and the extent to which social interaction and sociability is available or necessary. Gambling then is not a unitary phenomenon, and this should be borne in mind in considering the patterns of participation in its different forms, and in the theories advanced to explain its social and economic significance.

Examples of participation in gaming and gambling

BETTING

1 Football pools are the most common form of betting in Britain. There are significant trends towards more regular betting, for example in 1950 23% did the pools weekly, increasing to 37% by 1976. Men are twice as likely to bet on the pools as women, and married men and women are both more likely to bet than their single or divorced counterparts. Social class (measured by occupation) is not, contrary to popular opinion, very strongly related to doing the pools. Skilled manual workers and their spouses are more likely to bet than any other occupational group; while proportionately fewer members of professional and managerial groups are betting than previously, and in general terms, working class punters bet more regularly than middle class ones. Among self-employed workers the sex difference in pools betting behaviour vanishes.

   Other social factors that appear to have some bearing on doing the pools are education (basically more education correlates with less betting), and religious affiliation (Non-Conformist churches actively and successfully discourage gambling). The nature of pools betting tends to make it a solitary event, and even when it is a shared activity as in pools syndicates, researchers have found little evidence of social involvement in the syndicate. Women are even more likely than men to do the pools alone, reflecting the male work-based nature of most syndicates.

   Football pools represent the promise of a fortune in return for relatively small stakes, and the player's main motivation is almost certainly economic. They offer few opportunities for sociability before the bet is laid, and no control over, or interaction with the outcome. The impact of football pools as a leisure activity is best seen in economic rather than social terms, and participation data should be considered in this light.

2 Off-course betting, largely on horses and dogs, is mainly channelled through betting shops, of which around 10 000 currently operate in the UK. Prior to their introduction in 1960, credit betting and postal betting were predominant, but now betting shops take over 90% of this business. This represents an important change in the nature of off-course betting as a leisure activity, for with betting shops, continuous betting became possible, and a site was provided offering opportunities for social interaction and discussion. Recent changes in the law permit betting shops to show live television coverage of races, and to make the physical surroundings of the shop less spartan, further encouraging the punter, and changing betting from a

spasmodic leisure event to an extended leisure activity. In many ways these changes will help off-course betting take on similar characteristics to on-course betting, providing 'continuous gambling in an atmosphere of excitement and spectacle' (Cornish, 1978). On-course betting attracts a regular clientele. Greyhound racing's audience is highly localised and working class and is much more likely to bet on-course than off; horse racing supporters are more mobile, and diverse in social class.

Major variations in betting behaviour relate to gender. Men outnumber women punters by a ratio of around 8:1, and they bet much more frequently and spend annually ten times as much as women. Women appear to trust to luck in choosing winners, while perhaps two-thirds of male punters claim to base their choices on skill, particularly semi- and un-skilled male workers. In general it is reasonable to characterise betting frequently and relatively heavily on horses and dogs as a lower working class activity. There may be some evidence to associate these forms of betting with dull and boring work (Downes *et al.*, 1976), but the evidence is uncertain.

There are indications of an overall decline in these forms of gambling since the mid-1970s. For example, the number of betting shops declined by 23% between 1976 and 1985, and attendances at greyhound racing halved from 8.8 million in 1971 to 4.4 million in 1985. There was only a slight fall in attendances at horse races over the same period, however. Taken together these trends may relate to inflation and economic recession, but they may also be associated with changes in the nature of work and the direction of the work–leisure relationship referred to in Chapter 1. Indeed as society becomes more leisure-centred, the need for activities oppositional to work and productivity, such as gambling, may decline in the same way that some 'industrial' sports have declined since the 1950s.

GAMBLING

1 Bingo has become a significant form of gambling only since 1960 (Betting and Gaming Act) and there are currently around 1200 major clubs in Britain, a reduction of around 30% from 1976. It is an activity in which players exercise no control over outcomes, but is essentially social in nature and since 1960 has become a major leisure activity for around 14–15% of the adult population. Bingo has been termed a 'predominantly female leisure activity' (Cornish, 1978) since as many as four-fifths of commercial bingo participants are women. It is much more a working class leisure activity than any other form of gambling – in the study of gambling in three British towns by Downes *et al.* (1976) they reported that 'not being working class was enough to predict virtually no bingo playing'. Bingo is also the province of the

middle aged and elderly, only around 10% of regular players being under 30.

It offers a completely chance-dominated gamble, in a communal atmosphere with relatively low admission prices and stake monies, both of which are limited by law. Working class women especially find this to be a safe and convivial environment, and the majority of women attend sessions with friends and relatives thus enhancing the communal element (Dixie and Talbot, 1982). Commercial providers have duly noted this trend and have improved the ambience of their clubs, highlighting the social and entertainment values on offer. These changes may explain a slight increase in younger and more affluent customers, observable in the early 1990s.

2 Casino gambling reveals an almost diametrically opposed participation profile to bingo. Players are more likely to be young, male, in upper middle class occupations or of an upwardly mobile disposition, and may well have been educated in private schools. The majority of the 115 or so casinos in Britain are situated in London and the South East, and in London as many as 40% of players may be foreigners. Some differences in the nature of gaming in casinos are discernible between the sexes; men are as likely to bet on cards (some degree of control over the outcome) as on roulette, while women are much more likely to opt for roulette (no control over the outcome).

Roulette is very like bingo – the only significant difference being the opportunity to choose a number or colour on which to gamble in the former, while in the latter, one's numbers are allocated randomly. Both games offer similar opportunities for social interaction and sociability before and during play, albeit on a different scale. The major difference between them is situational – the black-tie, plush and reverential atmosphere of the casino against the down-market 'game show' approach of the bingo parlour. The major class differences in participation may be much more to do with the image of the gaming context and the opportunities it offers for the exercise of certain styles of behaviour than with the nature of the gambling activity itself. This issue is discussed more fully in Chapter 3.

3 Machines, still colloquially referred to as one-armed bandits or fruit-machines, despite their changes of style and operation since their internal workings changed from mechanical to electronic, are a major form of 'pure-chance' gambling. Since the legalisation of these AWPs (amusements with prizes) in 1960, and the further loosening of their regulation in 1968, they have become a major feature of pubs, clubs and amusement arcades. By 1985 licensing records indicated that there were 177 000 machines operating in the UK, and it has been estimated that half a million customers play them each day, many in the 2000

amusement arcades which have become a feature in most British town centres since the late 1960s.

Recent developments in video games have increased the range of machines to be found in arcades, and not all of them give prizes, but reward players by the accumulation of points gained for simulating successfully the deeds of the racing driver, or for shooting down space invaders. More recently many of the latter games have become available in the home via the home-computer and TV screen. Most of this latter group of games require some skill and judgement and are not 'pure-chance'. In the 1990s home video and computer games have become a major leisure activity, especially for children. Amusement arcades now feature as many of these skill and judgement games as pure chance machines. The data which follow refer to gaming machines proper.

Age is strongly relateed to playing the machines – most players in Downes *et al.*'s research were in their 20s or 30s – and much of the recent concern about the dangers of amusement arcades, and consequent calls for their licensing are directly related to their use by youths and childrcn. There is some suggestion that most people 'grow out of' fruit machines because they quickly learn that control is minimal and percentage returns low, and this may explain the age relationship. Certainly manufacturers acknowledge the novelty factor and constantly seek new illusions and images – a leading British firm reckons on launching a new machine every 7–8 weeks: 'For an AWP machine in a pub a long life is 13 weeks. After that the punters get bored with it' (Harris, 1987).

Playing gaming machines regularly is predominantly a male leisure activity. Women are outnumbered by 5:1 but this is associated with opportunity as most machines are located in pubs, clubs and arcades which are 'no-go' areas for some women. Class does not feature strongly in relationship to fruit-machine use, although what data there are suggest a tendency towards greater working class involvement, in common with most other forms of pure chance gambling.

A popular image in fruit-machine playing is that of the obsessive loner, compulsively feeding his earnings to an insatiable bandit. However, research shows that most regulars play in company with others, frequently acting as a syndicate made up of friends or relatives. Many of these groups spend extended periods on the machines rendering the activity an extended social leisure experience, and not simply an economic transaction.

These examples of participation stress the need to focus on the characteristics of the *activity* (the extent to which either chance, or skill and judgement predominates); the *situation* in which it is set (its physical and symbolic environment); and the degree of social interaction which it permits or encourages. These factors interact to create significantly different experiences of gambling as a leisure activity, and the differential participation rates seem to be associated with these variations.

Theorising gaming and gambling

As noted in Chapter 1, Caillois (1958) identified chance-games (alea) as compensatory, in the sense that they offer a channel for the expression of self in a neutral world of luck and fate, which replaces a real world of unequally distributed skills and abilities. Caillois further argues that chance-games coexist in industrial societies alongside games of competition (agon) and that together these two types provide complementary and symbolic means of support and opposition to the established socio-economic order. Chance-games are thus functional for social structure; an explanation taken further by Devereux (1949) whose analysis examines their role in relation specifically to a capitalist society (the USA). He assigns particular importance to value-conflicts between the older work-centred Protestant ethic, with its emphasis on thriftiness and sobriety, and a modern consumption-centred, leisure oriented world. Thus the closer one is to the older core-culture the less likely one is to gamble heavily, when occasional flutters provide temporary relief from a predominant Puritanism. However, those distant from the core-culture, like the lower working class and some elements of the upper class, are more likely to gamble regularly and heavily. Allied to this explanation is the work of Goffman (1967) who focused on the opportunities which gambling allows for risk-taking in a relatively safe and conventional world, and in such risk-taking the opportunities to display character, style, skill, and knowledge uncalled for, or unwelcome in everyday life.

These socially based explanations of gambling underplay an economic motivation, which some writers (Cornish, 1978) believe to be of importance. Tec (1964) for example argues that in types of gambling such as football pools and state lotteries, economic motivation is central. Winning a large sum of money and thereby radically changing one's status in society is only possible for most people via the pools or premium bonds. This may explain why football pools are less clearly differentiated by class than other forms of betting, while being consistent with the fact that lower socio-economic groups are still the most avid pools gamblers.

The sociological explanations of Caillois and Devereux may help to explain the marked preferences of the lower working classes for games of pure chance such as bingo, the nature of which is furthest from the rational world of behaviour based on logic and control. Equally Goffman's description of the gambler seeking to display coolness and character in risky situations fits well with the popular image of the hustler, or in the glitzy casino setting, that of the socialite. These social theorists emphasise the personal and social significance of such leisure activities, stressing the importance of differences between forms of gambling and the situations in which it occurs.

QUESTIONS AND EXERCISES ─────────────────────────

1 Visit an amusement arcade and classify the machines into 'pure chance' and 'chance-strategy/skill'. Who plays what? Classify the clients by age, sex, ethnicity.

2 Play commercial bingo and
   (a) attempt to identify your own experiences of playing, e.g. excitement, confusion, boredom, etc.
   (b) classify your fellow players by age, gender, etc.
   What other facilities are provided besides bingo – e.g. social, music, other forms of gambling, alcohol?

3 Visit a betting shop. How is it furnished? Does it encourage extended betting in a social atmosphere, or a brief visit? What actually happens?

4 Using data from Social Trends, General Household Survey and other government statistics, examine trends in gambling since 1976, and suggest reasons for the changes which you observe.

───

Further reading

An informative source book is D. Cornish (1978) *Gambling: A Review of the Literature*; while D. M. Downes *et al.* (1976) *Gambling, Work and Leisure*, Routledge and Kegan Paul, examines gambling both as an area of paid work and as a leisure activity.

LEISURE PARTICIPANTS

Introduction

In the previous chapter, it was emphasised that the nature and characteristics of leisure forms are diverse. In this chapter, the focus is upon *participants*, in order to understand the diversity of their leisure activity. Is this diversity to be explained merely as individual choice, or are there factors at work which effectively determine an individual's leisure? Are people free to choose or are leisure activities the outcome of constraints and opportunities over which people have no direct control? The answer, of course, is not simple. People do not have limitless choice in the ways they spend their leisure time, just as in other areas of life. Nor are people driven by outside forces which effectively deny any choice at all.

To examine the complexity of leisure participation, four propositions are made which, taken together, remain sensitive to both expressions of personal choice and also to constraints limiting that choice. On this basis, leisure participation is analysed with respect to social factors which constrain choices and are divisive in terms of leisure opportunity. The final section offers some suggestions and caveats which must be addressed in order to come to a fuller understanding of leisure participation.

The aim of this Chapter, therefore, is to consider participation in leisure within the broad context of people's lives, their experience of employment or lack of it, their age, sex, and family upbringing. Such factors have an important bearing on not only individual opportunities for leisure activity, but also people's perception and evaluation of those opportunities. Taken together these help to explain the diversity of leisure activity.

Four propositions about leisure participation

Some writers argue that there are fundamental social divisions in Britain which give rise not just to diversity in leisure activity but to inequality of opportunity which constrains leisure choice in a number of ways. Just as there are inequalities of opportunity in education, in employment, in housing, in income, so there are inequalities in leisure. An explanation of leisure activity cannot, therefore, be couched solely in terms of individual choice. Rather there are inter-related social divisions which pattern social life. These effectively limit choice of activity and affect people's perceptions of leisure opportunity.

The reader might regard this line of argument as misconceived. Surely, one's leisure activity and leisure time is the one area of life which is freely chosen? In Chapter 1 we noted that some conceptions or definitions of leisure support this view. Parker (1983) for example conceives leisure as time free from work and other obligations. Kaplan (1975) defines leisure as 'relatively self-determined activity – experience'. This seems to be borne out by everyday experience of leisure. We are neither compelled nor impelled to take part in any particular leisure activity; if we were, it would not be leisure. We can choose whether to watch TV, or the video, or listen to the radio, whether to play netball, soccer, volleyball, basketball . . . or none of these. Our interests in stamps, model railways, dog breeding, chess, music, books, films, bingo, motor sports, etc., are self-determined; we do not have to join any of the clubs and associations in our neighbourhood; and no one tells us where to go on holiday or whether to have a holiday at all. Leisure activity is clearly a matter of individual choice. After all, 'it's a free country isn't it?' Therefore the first proposition we can make about participation in leisure is as follows:

Proposition 1   People choose their leisure activities. Without this choice, the idea of 'leisure' would have no meaning.

This proposition, however, is not sufficient to account for participation in leisure, since there are various factors which circumscribe personal choice. These factors vary between individuals, and are dependent upon personal circumstances. One factor is the amount of time free from work and other obligations and how that time is spread across the day, week, or year. Another is where one lives in relation to the spatial distribution of leisure facilities, a theme which will be addressed in Chapter 4. Individuals vary in the amount of money they are either willing or able to spend on leisure, hence the cost of activities circumscribes choice. Finally, not all individuals have the same capabilities (physically and psychologically) and many leisure activities, such as sports and arts, demand particular skills and abilities.

These factors of time, space, money and individual capability constrain individual leisure and also begin to explain the diversity of activity. Further, individuals are generally aware of these limits and choose leisure activities accordingly. Hence, we can add a second proposition about leisure participation:

Proposition 2   People's choice of leisure is circumscribed by a number of *acknowledged* conditions. These reflect time, space, money, and individual capabilities and differ with personal circumstances.

Conditions vary with the individual. Some have an abundance of 'free-time' (such as the unemployed or the elderly) but have little disposable income, or in the case of the latter, reduced physical capacities. Conversely some individuals through onerous work and/or family commitments experience little free-time yet have the financial resources to engage in a wide range of activity. Similarly, the choice available to people living in rural areas might be circumscribed chiefly by the physical inaccessibility of many leisure pursuits, while the inhabitant of a decaying inner-city area will experience different, yet similarly critical, access problems, as many leisure facilities are located on the rural/urban fringe. The factors of time, space, money and capacity are different for the shift-worker, the working mother with dependent children, the young unemployed, the self-employed, the disabled and other identifiable groups.

Drawing these two propositions together, participation in leisure is conceived as the outcome of individual choice within a set of constraints of which individuals are aware. Choice is limited because some activities are perceived as costing too much, take up too much time, are not available in one's locality, or are beyond one's capabilities.

Much conventional recreational research focuses upon these issues. The reader should review user-surveys of leisure centres, arts facilities, libraries or community centres which present profiles of typical participants. For example, it is claimed that the use of many sports centres tends to be the preserve of the young, white, middle class male; therefore policies are pursued to broaden the appeal of centres, to minimise the constraints influencing non-participants. Such strategies are not confined to public sector provision. Professional football clubs, for example, have recently tried to broaden their appeal to families, to counteract the image of lawless terraces, and have increased their involvement with local communities. These initiatives are based upon a perceived need to improve the image of the game against a backcloth of hooliganism and falling attendance. In practical terms, the public sector devises various pricing policies, provides creche facilities, tempts the uninitiated with 'taster' sessions in various activities and acknowledges access problems by locating facilities near public transport networks. The overall aim of such policies is to minimise constraint, maximise opportunity, and thereby make activities less socially exclusive.

Influences upon leisure participation are extremely complex. Torkildsen (1985) lists no less than 46 factors which affect leisure choice. These are classified into three main categories:

(a) personal and family influences including age, stage in the family life-cycle, gender and educational level;
(b) social and situational circumstances in terms of income, occupation, social class;
(c) opportunity factors linked to perception, access, supply and management policies.

The *General Household Surveys* of 1987, 1989 and 1991 confirm this list by illustrating that leisure choice, and demand for facilities is the outcome of a complex matrix of inter-related individual and social influences.

The catalogue of influences upon leisure participation is extensive. But the reader must ask, which of these factors are most important, which are marginal? Roberts (1984) argues that leisure activity 'yields a plethora of data whose meaning baffles even its collectors'. He goes on to state that all leisure activities are delicately poised upon particular social, economic, and cultural circumstances. Roberts and other sociologists therefore suggest that an understanding of leisure participation can only be gained by focusing attention upon those factors in people's lives which both enable and restrict choice. Further, they recognise that society is not just a random conglomerate of individuals but is structured by social divisions, especially social class, gender, race and age. Each of these factors has a range of enabling and constraining influences and, therefore, provide the basis for explanations of diversity and inequalities in leisure activity.

Hence to adapt a phrase from Karl Marx, one must acknowledge that people choose their own leisure activities, but do not do so in circumstances of their own choosing. Such circumstances might be usefully described as an individual's 'condition of existence'. On a surface level, these conditions translate into restrictions on time, access, disposable income, and individual capacity. But this is only part of the explanation since such constraints are related to deeper social divisions. Therefore, a third proposition about leisure activity might be:

Proposition 3 People's leisure activity is related to the ways in which society is structured by social class, gender, age and race.

Proposition 2 emphasised constraints about which individuals are generally aware. In one sense, this third proposition identifies social divisions of which we are all obviously aware. But we do really acknowledge these social divisions since every one of us is born gendered, with a racial identity, and in particular social class circumstances? Together they represent conditions of existence which are omnipresent, experienced as 'natural', and therefore, in an important sense, are unacknowledged. But although experienced as 'natural' these divisions are social constructions. This leads to the fourth and final proposition about leisure participation.

Proposition 4 People's leisure activity is related to unacknowledged conditions of existence. They are the basis for attitudes, perceptions, and values which both facilitate and constrain leisure choice.

Support for these four propositions is provided by Rodgers (1977) who distinguishes between 'individual determinants of decision' and 'structural determinants of overall probability' about leisure choice. The former refers to pragmatic considerations about cost of activities, amount of free-time, awareness of facilities in one's locality, domestic responsibilities and transport availability (i.e proposition 2). The latter refers to age, sex, social class, upbringing and income (i.e. propositions 3 and 4). These four propositions about leisure participation account for both *individual's* relative freedom to choose and also the *structural* limits on their choice. These issues of individual action and social structure will be examined in more detail in the final chapter of this book, since they represent one of the fundamental problems in social theory.

In summary, an explanation of the range and diversity of leisure participation should be sensitive to these four propositions. People are instrumental in choosing their own leisure activity. Their choice is limited by an awareness of constraints which circumscribe the field of possibility. The range of opportunity is limited further by generally unacknowledged conditions of existence through which individuals act in the world.

Social divisions and leisure participation

In this section we address social divisions giving rise to differences and inequalities in leisure. These include material inequalities of income, availability of free time, access to leisure resources and cultural inequalities, in perceptions of appropriate behaviour and the meaning of activities for different participants. These differences and inequalities translate into a range of constraints and opportunities for leisure.

It is important to stress that these divisions are primarily *social*. One of the divisions is between men and women. Clearly there are also biological or sexual distinctions between men and women linked to reproductive function. In terms of anatomy and physiology, Weiss (1969) calls women 'fractional' men since they have smaller muscle mass, smaller lung capacities, and smaller skeletal structures. But the concern here is not with distinctions on the basis of sex but with gender divisions. Gender is a social construct and relates to society's conception of the attitudes, qualities and roles appropriate for men and women. These conceptions translate into and explain leisure activity. Similarly ageing is a biological process which affects us all, inevitably reducing our mental and physical capacities to participate in social life. Again, the issue is whether these physiological processes are sufficient to explain the leisure activity of individuals of different ages, or whether there are a range of connotations and perceptions about socially appropriate behaviour according to age which explain leisure activity. The term 'adolescence' for example, has a biological dimension but more importantly is a social construct, as is 'middle age' and 'old age'. There is also evidence of anatomical and physiological differences between ethnic groups, but none of this gives an adequate understanding of variations in leisure or any other activity.

The divisions discussed below are primarily social. They are the conditions of social existence through which people make choices about their leisure activity.

1 Social class

Social class is a 'slippery' concept having different connotations of power, prestige, linguistic codes, money and culture. But, in all social research, occupation is identified as the prime indicator of social class. Using the Registrar-General's classification of five occupational groups, evidence shows a relationship between leisure activity and social class membership. From Group A/B (Professional and Managerial) to Groups D/E (Semi and Unskilled Manual) there is an increase in television viewing, a decline in library membership and book-reading, a decline in membership of clubs and organisations, a decline in holiday-making, a decline in sports participation, a decline in countryside recreation, an increase in gambling activities. These statistical data suggest that the 'higher' occupational groups enjoy a more active and varied range of leisure activities.

The significance and accuracy of these data has been questioned. Based upon occupations, they relate mainly to males and only to those in paid employment. There are many families in which both husband and wife have paid occupations. In addition, the occupational classification is not sensitive to contemporary changes in the nature and availability of different types of work. Economic change has resulted in a decline of traditional 'working class' manual, relatively unskilled occupations; 'white-collar' work in technical and service industries has increased. Many writers have forecast the 'end of class' as a key social division. Increased affluence in post-war Britain has signalled the end of a society divided into sharply separated and antagonistic social classes. It is pertinent to note that the Registrar-General has in 1987, decided to dispense with the use of the term 'social class'. Distinctive cultures and lifestyles based upon class groupings have been eroded by the increased availability of consumer durables, especially television, and access to the products of mass culture. Access to leisure activities has widened so that in modern Britain, few are the sole prerogative of a discernible social class. Occasions such as polo at Windsor and the Henley Regatta might retain a social exclusivity (as might bingo and whippet racing), but in most leisure activities, participants are not drawn exclusively from any one social group.

However, even if one does acknowledge the explanatory power of social class, the statistical data produced by traditional recreation surveys give no explanation of *how* the range of constraints and opportunity translates into leisure choice. Statistics give a snap-shot view of who does what, but are silent about individual reasons, motives, perceptions and values in leisure activity. In short, such data give little explanation, and few insights into the complexity of leisure choice. A more thorough understanding of social class, and how social divisions impact upon leisure, requires an acknowledgement of two related dimensions. The more 'objective' dimension relates to position in the labour market, occupation and the correlates of education, income and housing. But there is a 'subjective' dimension termed 'class imagery'. This refers to individual perceptions or image of objective class structure. Class imagery (which is sustained through media representations) may be based upon individual accents or style of speech, residence, social networks, job, education, dress, car ownership, and money. Leisure activities also have class connotations. But class imagery does not solely distinguish *between* leisure activities but also *within* them – whether in publicly provided facilities, or private clubs, the people with whom one chooses to participate, and the 'style' adopted. The images and meanings of particular leisure activities might differ across the social classes.

Surveys of participation patterns in leisure map out the general distribution of preferences and interests according to social class membership (and other social divisions such as age or sex) but such research methods do not uncover the dynamics of choice and the complexity of perceptions, tastes, and meanings which underly these leisure choices.

Consider, for example, holiday-making. Survey data yield information about the frequency, length, and destinations of holidays, but why do people choose Benidorm, Blackpool, Brighton, Bournemouth, Bognor Regis, Biarritz, the Bahamas? On what basis do people choose camping, caravanning, self-catering cottages, adventure holidays, package holidays, holiday camps, coach tours? Similarly why do people choose golf or bowls, hockey or soccer, rugby league or rugby union, fox-hunting or ferreting?

Part of the answer is in the pragmatic constraints of time, money, space and individual capacities discussed earlier. These are the personal circumstances, of which people are clearly aware, which constrain leisure choice. Another dimension to leisure choice, however, is the 'class image' of these activities and holiday destinations. A French sociologist, Pierre Bourdieu (1985) has undertaken an extensive analysis of preferences and tastes in sports, arts, holidays, house decor, food and drink, clothes, and cars. Each of these, he argues, provide small numbers of distinctive features which allow fundamental social differences to be expressed. Bourdieu's analysis will be examined further in Chapter 7. For present purposes, however, he shows how the dynamics of leisure choice are related to images of activities and styles of participation or consumption which effectively exclude some social groups. To acknowledge the explanatory power of this class imagery, think of two leisure activities which are subject to similar constraints of time, space, money and individual capacity, yet have different participants. Hockey and soccer are good examples. In such cases, how does one explain differences in the characteristics of participants?

As already noted, most analysis of the influence of social class upon leisure activity uses occupation as the main indicator. But what of those without paid occupations, who are often called the 'under-class' of the unemployed? For unemployed people, leisure takes on new meaning and cannot be counterposed with paid work.

Unemployment is acknowledged as a key social problem in the 1990s and many leisure initiatives target this group in an effort to enhance unemployed people's quality of life. Those who have no income from an occupation are clearly restricted in disposable income available for leisure activity. On the other hand, they have an abundance of 'free time'. Individuals vary in their resourcefulness, but Stokes (1983), Marsden (1982) and Hayes and Nutman (1981) all explore the nature of leisure disadvantage experienced by unemployed people. Employment provides individuals with income, activity, and a source of social interaction. It also structures time (both on a daily basis but also in the longer term), providing individuals with a sense of purpose, and a sense of identity. All of this is denied to the unemployed, while the psychological impact of unemployment influences the way in which individuals spend their time. Note also that the impact of unemployment is uneven across occupational groups. The relative demise of manufacturing industries and the growth of the service sector affected working-class occupations far more than middle-class occupations in the 1980s. The 1990s is witnessing large-scale white-collar unemployment.

Unemployed people are often targeted by public sector providers of leisure for special consideration. Implicit in these initiatives is a conviction that 'leisure' activities might contribute to the quality of life for those who are denied the opportunity of paid employment. Sometimes targeting fails because it stigmatises the unemployed and therefore fails to attract individuals. A key issue, however, is whether leisure can provide, in the absence of paid employment, the same satisfactions or functions provided by work.

QUESTIONS FOR DISCUSSION ————————————————————————

1 What class connotations, if any, do the following have?
   (a) Greyhound racing, ferreting, fox-hunting, coarse fishing, fly-fishing.
   (b) Butlins, self-catering holidays, package holidays, adventure holidays, coach tours.
   (c) Squash, darts, archery, hockey, soccer, rowing, jogging, weight-lifting.
   (d) Football pools, betting on horses, bingo, casinos, stock market.
   (e) Beer, cider, dry/sweet wine, whiskey and . . . , gin and . . . , vermouth, rum and . . .

2 Can you think of elements of popular culture which transcend class distinctions:

3 Choose an activity with which you are well acquainted, and suggest how class distinctions are apparent, e.g. locations, public/private, equipment, choice of playing partners, dress codes, etiquette.

4 What are the arguments for and against singling out unemployed people for special consideration by leisure providers?

5 Why can unemployed people be termed an 'under-class'?

2 Gender

One of the primary relations between individuals in any society is based on gender, and many surveys in Britain indicate that gender is a crucial determinant of leisure choice and opportunity, with a relative imbalance in favour of men. But how far can this argument be sustained? Through the Equal Opportunities Act 1975 and the Sex Discrimination Act 1979 it is now illegal to discriminate between men and women, and 'watchdog' organisations such as the Equal Opportunities Commission aim to identify and redress discriminatory practices in both work and leisure contexts.

Young and Willmott (1973) argue that there is a general trend to balance domestic responsibilities more equally between the sexes. They suggest that the 'symmetrical' family is becoming the norm, characterised by shared housework, shared responsibilities for child care, shared decision-making about family leisure, shared control over family finances, and increasingly shared breadwinning. Increased sophistication and availability of consumer durables such as dishwashers, washing machines, freezers, and microwaves make domestic chores less time-consuming. Contraception devices mean that women can exercise control over reproduction and the size of the family. Small 'planned' families have become the norm, and the rearing of children is compressed into a shorter time-span. Moreover, surveys indicate that there are few differences between men and women in a range of leisure activities such as media (TV, cinema), informal outdoor recreations, holidays, home-based leisure. Early surveys by Groombridge (1964) and Mann (1969) illustrate that the imbalance works in favour of women with respect to library membership, patronage of the theatre, and other arts. Moreover, even in sports participation – a bastion of male privilege – women are increasingly involved. The Sports Council in its policy document 'The Next Ten Years' produces evidence to show that women's participation in both indoor and outdoor sports has increased over twice as much as men's since the mid-1970s.

One other argument is that social division on the basis of gender is too crude a classification to have any explanatory merit, separating individuals into two large categories. Women (and men) are not a homogeneous group with respect to relative constraints and opportunities for leisure activity. Compare, for example, middle and working class women, or women from different ethnic groups, or older and younger women, or women with dependent children and single women in paid employment. In each case, the differences between each of these sub-divisions in leisure opportunity might be greater than between men and women generally.

So how credible is the argument that 'gender' is an important determinant of leisure choice and opportunity? Clarke and Critcher (1985) argue (our italics):

Women have less leisure *time*, participate less in most leisure *activities* and draw on a narrower range of leisure options than men. They also spend most of their leisure in and around *home and family*.

The three key factors identified above are time, activity and space. In each case women, according to the authors, are disadvantaged. Time for leisure is restricted, the physical and social spaces within which leisure may be pursued are restricted, and the choice of activities is, in effect, restricted. These limits on opportunity and choice combine in different ways according to individual circumstances.

Time

Most women, although there are exceptions, have primary responsibility for household organisation and domestic work whether they are in paid work or not (Oakley, 1972; 1984). Unlike paid employment, such house-work does not have a precise line of demarcation. Deem (1982) argues that domestic responsibilities make it difficult to structure time, and delineate work from leisure, therefore leading to the 'fragmentation' of work and leisure. Consider the merging of work and leisure for women in activities such as ironing . . . and watching the television, or knitting and reading. Women have a primary role in childcare and the demands of children cannot be neatly allocated to particular periods during the day. Further, women often play a major supportive role in 'servicing' their children's leisure (Talbot 1979; 1980).

The definition of leisure as time free from the obligations of work has some credibility when work has definite boundaries both in time and in space. But for many women such boundaries cannot be easily drawn, hence the saying 'a woman's work is never done'. As McCabe (1981) argues, the notion of leisure as *free*-time is a male-oriented conception of leisure, foreign to most women's experience.

Spaces

Just as there is difficulty in separation of work and leisure in temporal terms many women use the same spaces for work and for leisure activity, notably the home. Hence, in contrast with men, many women's leisure is 'privatised' especially when there are dependent children. There are also far fewer institutional or public spaces where women feel they can go alone. Both Stanley (1980) and Gregory (1982) discuss the potential social stigma as well as the actual physical danger or fear of sexual harassment which restricts women's leisure space. Public houses, for example, are effectively 'no-go' areas for the unaccompanied woman, and many wom-en feel the same about other public spaces such as sports centres. Do women have the same range of choice as men of spaces for leisure activ-ity? Women also tend to experience spatial constraints through limited access to private transport. Note also that leisure spaces such as sports and recreational centres are typically controlled and administered by men. White and Brackenridge (1985) also point out, control over the national administrative structures of sports and arts is primarily in the hands of men.

Spatio-temporal restrictions on women's leisure results in a narrowed range of options for leisure activity. To this must be added the material factor of income. Women with no personal income are dependent on the husband for 'disposable' income over and above the household budget. But note also that most part-time and low-paid work in Britain is done by women. Hence, Deem (1986) and Chambers (1986), and the Equal Opportunities Commission (1984) indicate that women's position in the labour market also constrains leisure choice.

Activity
Statistical data on participation rates in leisure are presented in the *General Household Survey*, *Social Trends*, Arts Council, and Sports Council publications. Activities such as cinema going, theatre, amateur music and drama, leisure classes, outings to the country, to parks, and to the seaside, show little sex difference. In contrast, most sports surveyed with the exception of keep fit classes, yoga, and aerobics, are dominated by men. Britain has the lowest proportion of women taking part in sport in any country of similar economic status except for Italy. Spatio-temporal restrictions offer a partial explanation, but more crucially is the perception of sports by women themselves. There is incontrovertible evidence which demonstrates that decisions about whether to take part in sport or not, and which sports are chosen, are related to women's perception of appropriate 'feminine' behaviour (Scraton, 1986; Hargreaves, 1992), just as men's choice is influenced by perceptions of appropriate 'masculine' behaviour. One well researched example of the influence of gender on leisure activity is sports participation.

Gendered sports
Gender refers to socially prescribed patterns of behaviour attached to sex. It is culturally defined, as revealed by many cross-cultural analyses of male and female roles in different cultures. 'Femininity' and 'masculinity' refer to stereotypical attributes associated with a society's conception of gender. Sport is just one of the institutional settings where this is sustained or, in Clarke and Critcher's words 'celebrated'. Images of appropriate activity are inculcated through early child-rearing practices, different movement experiences in physical education, and media portrayals of femininity. Fashion, home, motherhood, and romance are the key themes of an idealised 'femininity' according to Hargreaves in her critical review of girls' magazines such as *Jackie*, *Just 17*, and *Photolove*. If

sports do appear, they are only those 'aesthetic' sports which do not contradict feminine imagery, e.g. swimming, dance, gymnastics. Sporting activities are therefore 'sex-typed' in gender suitability. Hackman (1978) points out that girls consistently under-achieve in sports since there is not the same social advantage within one's peer group as there is with boys. Note how the conventional image of femininity is exemplified in *Just 17*'s 'Self-improvement programme', the aim of which is:

Sporting a trimmer body, softer skin, pedicured feet, brighter make-up, and a nattier wardrobe.

If such images of femininity are promoted by the media, it is not surprising to note the massive drop-out rate from sports after full-time education ceases. Add to the observation that girls' leisure activities are often structured by their relationships with (primarily) boys (Hobson, 1981; McCabe, 1981), although in contrast Lees (1986) does produce some limited evidence of girls' independence from boys in their leisure activity. Girls tend, however, to drop their own leisure interests and adopt and service boys' leisure. This leads Rapoport (1975) to note the 'failure of young women to maintain adequate bases for the resumption of meaningful interests'.

Taking the restrictions in terms of space, time and activity into account Deem (1986) identifies four categories of constraint on women's participation in leisure:

1 Those inherent in society, its structures and power relationships perpetuated and promoted through education, socialisation practices and media representations.
2 Those inherent in the daily situations in which women find themselves (e.g. the home and family, peer group pressures, courtship practices).
3 Those inherent in the way leisure is organised and the attitude of the providers (most of whom are men).
4 Those imposed by women's perceptions of themselves and of the appropriateness of particular leisure activity (e.g. sports).

QUESTIONS FOR DISCUSSION ———————————————

1 Why is it difficult for women to make time for leisure?

2 Which sports are perceived to be appropriate/inappropriate for women?

3 Why are there few women snooker players, motor racers, jockeys, darts players?

4 Compare images of femininity and masculinity in
  (a) girls' and boys' magazines and comics
  (b) television advertisements.

---

3 The family

It has already been noted that the family is a key focus in analyses of women's leisure activity, because of the in which women's role in family life influences the experience and choice of leisure activity. In this section we note that such writers as Roberts, Sillitoe, Kelly, Fasting and most influentially the Rapoports, conceive the family as the cornerstone of individual leisure lifestyles, the major provider of leisure and therefore a major determinant of leisure participation. The Rapoports (1975) advance a model in which leisure, occupation, and family interact, i.e. each of these have effects on the other two factors. They identify four phases of the family life cycle (adolescence, young adulthood, family establishment phase, and the later years) each of which exhibit major preoccupations, which in turn have implications for leisure policy. For example the major preoccupations of 'adolescence' (the 13-19 year old group) are establishing a personal identity, an interest in new experiences, and experimentation with new activities. Hence leisure policy for this age group must be sufficiently flexible to allow the opportunity to generate and sustain new interests, without channelling adolescents in activities which constrain choice, and are adult-sponsored and adult-led. The 'establishment' phase (usually spanning the years from the mid-20s to the late-40s) is characterised, argue the Rapoports, by 'making satisfactory life investments'. Leisure interests tend to be more home and child-centred and the development of careers is a key motivating force. Leisure policy must be based upon a recognition of constraints especially those on women, and be designed to encourage leisure interests away from domicility. Kelly (1982) extending the Rapoports' work through case studies in Britain and the USA, emphasised the central importance of the family and the home as a focus for, and determinant of leisure choice and opportunity. In his analysis, Kelly found that 75% of leisure activities were family and home-based e.g. playing with children, day outings, DIY/home maintenance, gardening. One might question how many such activities are perceived as 'leisure' and how many as 'family obligations'. Clearly Kelly is operating with a residual definition of leisure as time free from paid employment. Nevertheless, what both the Rapoports and Kelly stress is that the family is by far the most influential *provider* for leisure.

Several criticisms can be levelled at these analyses. Firstly, the concept of family remains untheorised. Not all families are of the conventional nuclear type of husband, wife and children. Indeed most households in Britain (61%) are of only one or two individuals while the average size of household the 1990s is 2.5 people. Note also the increase in the number of one-parent families in contemporary Britain. Secondly, Kelly and the Rapoports ignore social class differences in family life, and clearly such a social division has an effect, upon leisure interests (e.g. occupation of husband/wife, the segregation or otherwise of responsibility for domestic chores including childcare, mobility through car ownership and the leisure interests and social backgrounds of husband and wife). The weakness of this analysis is that it obscures other crucial social divisions which cut across or modify such generalised assertions. Nevertheless, the Rapoports' analysis does recognise the importance of an individual's immediate social context as a powerful factor in leisure choice and opportunity, illustrating how constraints are relative to life-stage. Clarke and Critcher (1985) argue that the Rapoports' analysis tends to root itself in biology hence downplaying the fact that 'life-phases' are as much a social construction as a product of biological growth and degeneration. 'Age' is a social construction, e.g. in British society people tend to get labelled as 'old' once they have retired from full-time employment, but of course this is a variable division, illustrated by the increasing incidence of so-called 'early retirement'. Moreover, other life-events such as unemployment and divorce are not encompassed in the Rapoports' analysis.

We have already noted in our consideration of gender, that the role of women as wife and mother has a crucial influence on the time available for leisure activity Recent reports by the Family Policy Studies Centre (1987, 1993) suggests that, while the feminist movement and the rise in unemployment have begun to challenge traditional sex roles in family life, the 'symmetrical family' of shared family chores and responsibilities in Young and Willmott's analysis, remains very much the exception. Even in couples where the wife has paid work – either part-time or full-time – the division of household chores is unequal; as illustrated by Table 3.1.

Table 3.1 Gender divisions in domestic work: percentages of women in paid employment having major responsibility for domestic work

Domestic work	Part-time employment	Full-time employment
Cleaning	83	61
Washing and ironing	95	81
Cooking	79	61
Shopping	64	52

These reports also note that because of their greater responsibility for both household and childcare chores, women have less free-time than men. For women in full-time work, this was calculated as seven hours on weekend days, as compared with ten hours for their working husbands. Access to money is also unequal. Only about half of couples pool their income; and have equal access to resources. Moreover 25% of wives still depend on an allowance from their husband, therefore having no independent access to money.

Gender roles within the family therefore give variable constraints and opportunities in time for leisure, disposable income, and leisure activity. This, together with life-cycle analyses illustrates how family life has a considerable influence upon leisure opportunity and choice.

QUESTIONS FOR DISCUSSION _____

1 How crucial do you think the following might be in influencing leisure activity:
   (a) the birth of children?
   (b) retirement?
   (c) home ownership?

2 How much of your own leisure interest can be attributed to your family?

3 In your family, whose leisure interests predominate?

4 Do gender roles in family life vary with:
   (a) social class?
   (b) ethnic group?

_____

4 Age

Youth and leisure

Just as there is a social dimension to sexual differences, identified by the term 'gender', so there are social dimension to age and ageing which are more important than biological processes or chronological age in explaining participation in leisure. Clarke and Critcher (1985) emphasise this by stating that:

... society *constructs* age through its organisation of education housing, retirement and its images of youth and maturity ...

During the nineteenth century, three major institutional networks developed to both construct and manage youth – the family, education, and work. Changing family relations, the organisation of education, and the age of entering employment are significant demarcation lines for youth and adulthood. These three institutions are escalators upon which individuals reach maturity, and each reinforces the others. Consequently, an individual's personal biography is structured around and embedded in family, schooling and work. A substantial amount of research has focused upon the psychological stress facing adolescents as they move out of school and into the wider world of work. The existential question 'Who am I?' presses hardest at this time as youths seek to establish independence from parents, household arrangements and the constraints of childhood. According to conventional wisdom, youth is a time to experiment and to develop a confidence in one's own identity, one's own sexuality and relationships with others. Leisure is the key site where the young can find outlets to express their identity. It is therefore not surprising that the development of an identifiable youth culture is inter-related with the post-war growth of leisure. Youth is the time when people have few domestic obligations to fulfil yet begin to have some financial independence from their parents. As has been suggested commercial leisure industries have recognised youth as a distinct and expanding market.

The disjunctures between school and work, and the importance of youth leisure styles, have been subject to much academic debate and historical analysis. Throughout the nineteenth and twentieth centuries 'respectable' public opinion has been concerned about affluent working class youth, mainly boys, who engage in unruly leisure and develop a distinct and delinquent style of their own. Geoffrey Pearson's book *Hooligan* (1983) documents the parental fears that emerge every 30 years, about troublesome youth who seem to be resisting what society has to offer. Moral panics about drug abuse and AIDS in the 1980s are distant descendants of nineteenth century Victorian boys, Artful Chartist Dodgers and unruly apprentices. Throughout both the nineteenth and twentieth centuries, the state has been drawn in to 'do something about' youth. Historically, it has attempted to police and license youthful leisure while simultaneously providing more 'rational' improving and usually alcohol-free alternatives. Both the statutory and voluntary sector organisations have sought to guide individuals as they grow towards adulthood and leisure and leisure activities have been important meeting points and vehicles to such an end.

The fears of affluent youth have therefore been an important focus for both academic research and policy intervention. Yet what is often missed is that the vast majority of youths 'grow up ordinary' and manage the transition from family, to school, to work without too much trauma, although perhaps youths and parents may not agree this is so at the time. Recent research implies that only 1 in 7 belong to youth subcultural styles but nevertheless academic research has chartered the cartography of taste in post-war Britain (Hebdige, 1979) – Teds, hippies, skins, punks and so on. Such subcultural responses to the problems of growing up have been touched upon in Phil Cohen's article about class and community in the East End – the major argument of which are outlined in the section on entertainments. Pop music, clothes, language become resources for young people to display their resistance to parental culture. Perhaps the most distinct resistance and anger is to be found in male Afro-Caribbean youth which uses leisure and Rastafarianism to hit back at white Britain (viz. Hebdige, Gilroy). Listening to blues/reggae, going to parties, hanging-out in town centres, or being on the fringes of drugs and crime and prostitution represent a distinct threat to the white 'respectable' values of working police and perhaps it should be no surprise that relationships between black youth and the police are far from easy. The riots of 1981 and 1985 express the anger and tension experienced by both white and black youth in deprived inner-city areas with high unemployment. It is here that policy initiatives in sport and recreation have been chanelled through Urban Aid to deal with rising crime and unemployment. The causes of urban riots are complicated webs to unravel; some see them as radical protest whereas others see them as aggresive consumerism as gangs loot shops for goods they cannot afford to buy. It is no coincidence that the favourite items for theft relate to consuming – leisure clothes, videos, tapes, radios, TVs and the like.

In a variety of articles, Willis has argued that work and wage-earning are symbols of adulthood for young people. To be able to afford to buy leisure goods from the commercial sector signifies not only independence and maturity but also 'style'. The central question remains as what is to be done with youths who fail to gain employment, in regions where paid employment opportunities are absent? What happens when the escalator of work is missing and the transition from family to schooling leads nowhere? Bernard Davies in *Threatening Youth*, 1986, argues that the state has been forced to intervene and provide a national youth policy, orchestrated around work discipline and MSC training schemes. It is through cheap 'training' allowances that a youth income policy has emerged and that young people in the 1980s have insufficient income to buy into leisure and remain dependent upon their parents (both in the eyes of the DHSS, and for subsistence and housing). Clearly, youth un-employment affects young people in different ways; wider inequalities of class, race and gender reappear in youth unemployment. It is the case that white working class youths win places on employer-led YTS schemes leading, just as apprenticeships did in the past, to secure employment, whereas women and black groups find themselves on agency-led schemes that lead back to the Job Centre. Research into sports schemes for the unemployed suggests that leisure is no substitute for paid work for the vast majority of young people, some of whom see MSC and YTS schemes simply as slave labour.

Just as retirement is mediated by one's identity, social networks, and use of time and resources, so too are youth and adolescence. For some, youth is a period of constraint – with inadequate space, income and friendships to develop free-time into leisure and pleasure. Yet for others leisure is a celebration of being 'only young once', as licentiousness underpins many youthful leisure forms, and hence is of such concern to those in authority such as the police, teachers, youth workers and the like. The complexity of opportunity and constraint has to be worked out by individuals and their networks of friends – a process neatly captured in Sue Townsend's hero, Adrian Mole and his diary. As yet there is little in the way of social research that teases out the ironies of young people and the sometimes painful experience of leisure. The most comprehensive and lucid overview of the existing literature is in Kenneth Robert's *Youth and Leisure* (1983).

QUESTIONS FOR DISCUSSION ——————————————————

1 How do you explain the resilience of some fads and fashions? Why do you think that middle aged people prefer the musical tastes established during their youth?

2 What are the acknowledged and unacknowledged conditions affecting young people's leisure choices? (*See* Propositions 2–4, pp. 123–5.)

3 Do you agree with Chris Griffin's argument in *Typical Girls* that young women are confronted with two major tasks – 'getting a job' and 'getting a man'?

4 Compare and contrast the visions of youth offered by novels and by social scientists? Read for example Mike Brake's *A Sociology of Youth Culture and Subculture Styles* (1980) and compare it with Sue Townsend's *Growing Pains of Adrian Mole*.

5 'The leisure lifestyles of black youth in Britain inevitably lead to conflict with the forces of law and order'. Critically evaluate such an assertion.

The social construction of old age
Census data and publications such as *Social Trends* reveals that Britain, like most other Western nations, has an increasing proportion of elderly amongst its population. Part of this is due to progressive decline in birth rate, partly to increasing life-expectancy.

Sooner or later we all grow old. This ageing process involves an inevitable reduction in a person's physical and mental facilities and hence a decrease in capacities to participate in social life, including leisure activity. Hence, ageing imposes constraints upon leisure with a tendency to withdraw from more active production, if not from passive consumption, of leisure activities. Note, however, the recent growth of 'veteran' sports in western societies.

Ageing is one major determinant of patterns of participation, but how much of this is biological in origin and how much is social? Is leisure activity of the over-60s to be explained solely in terms of declining faculties, or are there social and economic factors at work which constrain leisure choice and opportunity? Who are labelled 'the elderly' in society? Is it just the infirm, those incapable of sustaining an independent lifestyle, those defined by public provision as a species of problem to be remedied by the social services?

The organisation of education, and the age of entering employment is a significant demarcation line for youth and adulthood. Similarly, the designation of 'elderly' is intimately related to the transition from paid employment to retirement.

However, it is clearly misconceived to equate retirement with old age in an economic climate which encourages people to give up paid employment at a comparatively young age. The last decade has witnessed a change in the retirement age from 65 years to 60 years in most occupations together with a high incidence of voluntary 'early' retirement – an unexpected, and for some welcome, gift from technological 'progress' – can be doubly attractive through the promise of guaranteed income (related to salary levels) offered in both the public and private sectors of industry. With later entry to employment and increasing longevity it is conceivable that in future the length of retirement will become as great as the length of one's working life. Therefore, leisure providers are becoming increasingly aware that the needs of retired people and the needs of elderly people are not necessarily synonymous.

RETIREMENT – A WELL EARNED REST?
For some people retirement seems to offer a relief from the iron necessity of oppressive and alienating work; a boundless and unqualified 'free time' for leisure. For others retirement might be experienced as a stagnation of boredom, idleness and loneliness. Surplus to requirement, one has

been thrown on the scrap heap, or in Grossin's (1986) words, 'parked in a siding'. However retirement is experienced, it represents an important life-event for most people. Some people make the transition in a well-prepared, happy manner, others do not. Clearly one element of social policy (of which leisure is but one aspect) is to make it possible for retirement to be an enriching, enlivening experience.

Most of the problems experienced in retirement relate to the contrast with a life which formerly had revolved around paid employment. Long (1985) identifies four potential difficulties experienced in the transition to retirement. They are:

(a) psychological values;
(b) the use of time;
(c) social contact;
(d) finance.

(a) Psychological values relate to the ways in which a person's identity and status are intimately connected with occupation. This is, of course, not always the case, since many people's self-esteem and their status in others' eyes revolves around their leisure activities. Nevertheless, a person's occupation is a crucial measure of worth in our society, and the retired are denied this. Compensatory strategies pursued by the retired include continuing in part-time work, increasing commitments to unpaid work like social and voluntary activities, and the elevating of work-like aspects of leisure activity.

(b) Employment also provides a structure for the day, week and year. Time is neatly compartmentalised into work-time and non-work time thus providing a reassuring framework within which particular activities have their designated place. Take this away, and the experience of leisure as rest, recuperation, as relaxation from toil loses its meaning.

(c) Another disjuncture at retirement is the loss of social contacts, reduced social interaction, the exclusion from a social milieu of shared interests which, for many, extends into leisure activity. This experience of retirement is, in part, what Cumming and Henry (1961) identified as ' disengagement'; the psychological withdrawal from a network of social roles which have previously sustained identity. This role-loss is a feature of ageing generally, rather than retirement specifically. However, it remains an important element of the voluntary or compulsory withdrawal from the social milieu of paid employment.

(d) The final disjuncture is that of finance. Despite state pension schemes, people enter retirement in different circumstances. Housing and health are variable, another is inequality in income. Lack of disposable income clearly imposes constraints upon leisure choice as noted earlier (see proposition 2). For some the absence of house mortgages, the maturing of life assurance policies and the financial inducements of early retirement might culminate in a well-heeled retirement replete with opportunities to participate in the leisure market. For others, however, income drops considerably, which is indicated by the relative neglect of the old by the commercial sector of leisure. It is significant that the old are conspicuously absent from much advertising imagery. Consumer products such as drinks, cars, washing powders, leisure wear, are marketed with reference to the young and the vigorous. Clearly the 'old' are not a significant target population and are of limited interest to commerce.

Taken together, these four factors contrast the experiences and circumstances of retirement with those of paid employment. Both Parker (1983) and Long (1985) suggest that, because of continued adherence to a work-ethic, leisure activities in retirement take on new significance, and new meaning. Since most people (58%) do not take up any new pursuits in retirement, the meaning of those activities which are sustained, change from being conceived as leisure (as a means of relaxation from work) to being more work-like and as a substitute for employment. Hence, common leisure activities such as gardening, DIY and voluntary-work structure time, are invested with new meanings, and are valued in new ways. Conversely gardening, experienced as a chore to be fitted in when other obligations permit, might now become a satisfying hobby. This shift of meaning of 'leisure' activities denotes the response of people faced with otherwise unstructured time in order to maintain a sense of purposeful activity.

ELDERLY PEOPLE

A distinction was made earlier between the experience of retirement and the experience of old age, a distinction made because of the incidence of early retirement. The 'elderly' old face similar problems of transition and 'low visibility' compounded by reduced faculties, increasingly onerous domestic chores, and decreasing access to family-based leisure. Children marry and move away in search of jobs, while widow(er)hood increases the isolation and 'privatisation' of the elderly.

Many old people therefore are faced with considerable constraints upon their leisure activity. These can be summarised as:

- decreasing economic, social and physical resources;
- increasing isolation from family and community;

● increasingly burdensome domestic chores and personal care concerns.

The Sports Council identified the over-50s as a target group for leisure provision in the Policy Document *The Next 10 Years*. Find out what provision there is for older people in your local sports centre. However, as Clarke and Critcher (1985) point out:

... the economic and social structuring of old age and the psychological consequences which follow, make it difficult to improve the access of the elderly to a meaningful range of leisure activities ...

It is generally acknowledged by both the public and voluntary sectors that the elderly are constrained in their leisure opportunities (propositions 2, 3 and 4) and therefore have limited choice (proposition 1). While it is important to emphasise the social structuring of age, it is interesting to note that much communal leisure activity of older people sustains cultural activity of a by-gone age. Step into these spaces and time seems to have stood still. The elderly rely on community support networks (churches, local societies, village institutes) for out-of-home leisure. In these locations are found residues of self-organised community activity which were dominant in the past, and which stand in sharp contrast to the consumer-oriented technology-based leisure pursuits of contemporary society (*see* Chapter 2). Activities such as whist-drives, community singing, poetry reading, talks by local experts, coach outings are organised by local groups such as Townswomen Guilds, Mothers' Unions, Women's Institutes, Darby and Joan Clubs. Here, people consume the leisure they produce in self-organised collectives. In the past, the absence of media alternatives meant that people had to make their own entertainment. The residues of this fast-disappearing leisure lifestyle are to be found in community groups predominantly peopled by older (mainly white) people.

5 Ethnicity

This term refers to a cluster of beliefs, attitudes and behaviour which distinguishes one social, racial or cultural group from others. Ethnic differences do not therefore necessarily have associations with skin colour. There are many ethnic groups that have emigrated to the UK, and to other western industrial societies, to find employment, a better quality of life or sanctuary from political, racial or religious persecution, e.g. Ukranians, Chinese, Latvians, Poles, Italians, Jews. Nevertheless, social policy in the leisure sphere focuses primarily upon ethnic groups of Afro-Caribbean and Indian/Pakistani origin (often lumped together as 'black') in an effort to combat racism.

The term 'racism' indicates the existence of power structures in society through which one 'racial' group is in a position of dominance over others. Racism equals power plus prejudice, i.e. power structures which support, or at least do not challenge, racist beliefs – ranging from biological theories of supremacy to unconscious assumptions of superiority. A critical issue for students and providers of leisure activities is to examine critically the ways in which policy and provision either perpetuate or combat racism.

Racism can operate on three inter-linked levels each of which is relevant to leisure practice and provision:

- *structural racism*: economic and social discrimination against black people embedded in the structure of society as evidenced in employment, education and housing;
- *institutional racism* whereby institutions (e.g. sports, arts) maintain practices, procedures and values which operate to perpetuate discrimination against black people;
- *individual racism* where the actions and (often unconscious, taken-for-granted) attitudes of individuals to black people support and reproduce discriminatory practices. Overt manifestations of this range from racist chants on football terraces to examples of 'paki-bashing'.

At a structural level, leisure professionals must find ways to address the inequalities of access to positions of power and responsibility in the leisure field. Differences in educational attainment between different ethnic groups translates to inequalities in career opportunities, an outcome being that few black people are in management positions in leisure organisations. At the institutional level, there is plenty of evidence in sports and arts organisations to indicate continued inequality. Funding for the Arts (*see* Chapter 2) favours established mainstream artistic practice with minimal funding directed at 'community' or 'ethnic' arts. Community arts is a political process, celebrating cultural diversity through dance, drama, poetry and other media, while also providing social commentary on inequality, discrimination and oppression. To facilitate this, some local authority leisure departments employ 'animateurs' to do outreach work, forge links with community groups, ascertain needs and provide opportunities for artistic expression.

Unlike art, sport does not seem to be an area of conspicuous ethnic disadvantage. Nevertheless, Afro-Caribbean people in the UK are under-represented in most sports (e.g. golf, tennis, swimming, outdoor pursuits) and over-represented in others, notably boxing, soccer and athletics. In soccer, for example, almost 10% of professional players are black British although comprising only 1.4% of the total population. Cashmore (1982) and Leamon and Carrington (1985) explain this over-representation as the outcome of 'channelling' in schools. Through teachers' high expectations of black athletic prowess, black children (especially boys) are channelled into sport and out of academic endeavour, facilitating the reproduction of the black worker as wage labour at the lower levels of the labour market. Without anti-racist intervention, black people will continue to function as the repository of menial labour and also as, what Cashmore terms, 'sporting gladiators' for British society. But for every successful 'gladiator' there are thousands of disempowered young black people. Sport is an avenue of upward social mobility, but only for a few.

There is also evidence to suggest that racist practices operate within different sports at the top levels. Analysis of position assignment in team games in the USA and the UK (American football, basketball, rugby union and league, soccer) reveals that black players typically occupy peripheral non-central positions, i.e. those which do not require qualities such as decision-making and intra-team co-ordination over team strategy (Coakley, 1979; Maguire, 1988; Kew, 1994). This phenomenon is known as 'stacking' – the over- or under-representation of black and white players in specific positions. A corollary to this is that black people tend to have foreshortened careers in sport, with few becoming coaches and administrators within the various national governing bodies for sport.

The specific research about sport and art underscores the need for 'positive action' – a term which appears in the Race Relations Act 1976 to describe policies which, acknowledging endemic racism, counter the effects of discrimination against ethnic minorities. (Positive action is not the same as positive discrimination which denotes a policy of reserving specific quotas of jobs, etc. for certain minority groups and which is illegal in Britain.)

One way forward is to raise consciousness among workers in the leisure field through race awareness training, equalising access to sport and providing opportunities for the expression of cultural diversity (e.g. Asian dance/theatre, kabbaddi, etc.). A more radical approach is to challenge the power structures of leisure institutions, e.g. decision-making, allocation of resources, control and appointment of staff. It is only through a radical appraisal of such power networks within leisure organisations that inequity can be addressed.

QUESTIONS FOR DISCUSSION ————————————————

1 Why do you think Afro-Caribbeans and Asians are over-represented in some sports and under-represented in others?

2 Compare the leisure activity of Afro-Caribbeans and Asian groups. Do the constraints and opportunities for leisure differ?

3 Re-read the section on institutional racism, and apply it to a leisure organisation of your choice.

---

6 *Disability*

What is meant by 'disability'? In an extended sense, we are all disabled in so far as individuals do not share all the capacities, resources and abilities required for participation in all leisure activities. A major thrust of current initiatives for and by disabled people is to dispense with the negative connotations of 'dis-ability' to focus on *abilities*, and the challenges which must be met for them to win control over their lives as far as is possible. The Ministry of Sport's *Building on Ability* (1991) acknowledges this with a series of recommendations (not statutory requirements) for the public, voluntary and private sectors of leisure provision.

It is estimated that there are some six million people who have some form of disabling condition. This includes paraplegics, blind and partially-sighted people, amputees, polio victims, those with cerebral palsy, people who are deaf, people who are dumb, people who are autistic, and people with a range of learning difficulties. The needs and abilities of each of these are very different and, consequently, disabled people should not be considered as an homogeneous group. Only 5% are wheelchair-bound, 55% have mental impairment, 20% have sensory impairment and 20% are ambulatory but with physical disabilities.

These are all descriptions of 'disability", but these medical divisions become crystallised into a social division with consequences for leisure choice and opportunity. The term 'handicap' relates to inequalities in the environmental and social conditions of a disabled person's life rather than to any specific psycho-motor impairment. This social division is manifest in different ways but primarily through inequality of access to leisure facilities and activities. Access and opportunity for leisure has different dimensions, namely:

- perceptual accessibility;
- physical accessibility;
- financial accessibility;
- accessibility of the leisure activity itself.

Perceptual accessibility
This refers to people's awareness of the existence of facilities, organisations, and also to an assessment of their own capabilities in relation to different recreation activities. Lack of previous experience often trans-

lates into low assessment of ability and consequently avoidance (e.g. of a sports challenge) through fear of failure.

Physical accessibility
This is perhaps the most common understanding of 'accessibility'. The Chronically Sick and Disabled Persons' Act 1970 and the Disabled Persons' Act 1981 made it a statutory obligation for local authorities to provide proper facilities for disabled people, including sports facilities. But there is a difference between 'proper' facilities and providing access on equal terms with able-bodied people.

It is often difficult to re-design or adapt older facilities (e.g. traditional swimming pools with vertical sides) and the design of user-friendly facilities for disabled people is expensive. Provision includes toilet and changing facilities, ramps, lifts, wide car-parking bays, hand rails on stair flights, lever taps on wash basins, automatic doors, non-slip floors, loop systems in meeting rooms, signs in braille, signs in a colour appropriate for those with a visual impairment, accessible shower controls, bar counters, lift control buttons, vending machines.

In practice, the design and adaptation of facilities inevitably has to balance the ideal of equal access with the realism of cost-benefits (e.g. a lift for disabled people to use the water slide might be as expensive as the water slide itself and it may be under-used). Sergeant (1987) argues that concerns about equity should outweigh concerns about cost. But in an era when public spending on all social services is under increasing constraints, inequality of access to leisure for disabled people is likely to continue.

Financial accessibility
According to *Building On Ability*, the incomes of non-pensioner disabled families are only 72% of the national average for other families. Many therefore do not have much disposable income for leisure. Consequently, pricing policies in the public sector are critical, as they are with all low-income groups. Grant-aid and interest-free loans are generally available to disability organisations from agencies such as the Sports Council and the Arts Council, who will consider applications for the adaptation of facilities, training of leisure and sport workers and the provision of equipment.

Accessibility of the leisure activity
The intellectual and motor abilities required of (some) leisure activities makes them a challenge to (some) disabled people. Activities need to be selected, adapted and modified to make them accessible. For sport, there are two elements to this, namely *task analysis* and *performer analysis*. Task analysis involves breaking down activities into component parts, analys-

ing and psycho-motor, social and cognitive requirements, and sequencing the learning process. Performer analysis involves assessing four sets of handicapping conditions relevant to a range of disabilities (*see* Brown, 1987). These are neuromuscular disorder, cardio-respiratory problems, progressive muscular weakness, loss of function or paralysis. Each of these present major problems that interfere with performance. Through this type of analysis, disabled sports associations have developed learning strategies, designed equipment and adapted or modified games, sports and outdoor pursuits to make them accessible. Therapeutic Recreation, developed initially in the USA, adopts a similar approach of empowering people through assessment of an individual's capacities and leisure needs and a programme of activity to increase both self-advocacy and a person's quality of life.

There are a number of national sports organisations for disabled people. The British Sports Association for Disabled (BSAD) has a national and regional remit for developing both competitive and non-competitive sports and physical recreations for persons with physical disabilities, visual and/or hearing impairment. Separate associations for paraplegics, amputees, people with cerebral palsy, deaf and blind people operate under the umbrella of BSAD. The UK Sports Association for People with Mental Handicap has the national and regional remit for co-ordinating sport and leisure activities for people with learning disabilities. Their activities encompass arts and other leisure practice.

In addition there is a range of organisations who recognise that sport, art and other leisure activities have important curative, therapeutic, recreational and psychological values, increase a person's self-esteem and social skills, and are a powerful force for social integration of disabled people (e.g. Physically Handicapped and Able-bodied clubs (PHAB), the National Federation of Gateway Clubs, the Disabled Living Foundation, the Royal Association for Disability and Rehabilitation). Through this, the emphasis is on abilities rather than on disability, on integration rather than segregation, building bridges with the rest of the community and undermining divisive inequalities based on mental and physical capacities.

QUESTIONS FOR DISCUSSION/EXERCISES ─────────

1 What provisions are made for disabled people in the leisure facilities in your locality? Do these provisions allow equal access?

2 Disabled people have special needs. How far can these be met by integrating

their leisure activity with the able-bodied? When is it more appropriate to have segregated provision?

3 List the ways in which some disabled people might win control over their lives and their environment.

4 What measures might be adopted to enable disabled people to enjoy active leisure independent from clubs, groups or associations?

Making sense of the data

At the beginning of this chapter four propositions about leisure participation were given. Together, these attempt to account for individuals' experience of diversity and inequality in leisure activity, related to social divisions of class, gender, ethnicity, age, family circumstances and individual abilities.

The reader, must however, bear the following issues in mind in making sense of leisure participation. Simply stated these are:

1 Social divisions do not only impose constraints on choice but also provide opportunities for leisure.
2 Individuals make choices, and there are many examples of activity which contradict general analyses of constraints and opportunities in leisure.
3 Constraints and opportunities for leisure activity are not static but change over time.
4 The social-divisions of class, age, gender and ethnicity inter-relate with one another in leisure choice and opportunity.
5 The impact of class, or gender, or race, or age varies with different types of leisure activity.

1 Constraints and opportunity

People choose their own leisure activity but such choice is constrained by various factors. It is also useful to consider social divisions as not only constraining but enabling. Being an Asian in Britain for example, normally gives access to a range of cultural activities which non-Asians are not able to pursue. Similarly, the nature and demands of a person's occupation might place time limitations on leisure, but the experience of employment, the social interaction with colleagues might provide leisure opportunities which, in the absence of this social contact, would not be available. Similarly, having dependent children enables a number of social contacts to be fostered which are effectively denied to childless couples.

2 Exceptions to the 'rule'

The reader might refute an explanation of leisure activity based upon social divisions by indicating particular individuals whose leisure pursuits seem to confound the general 'rule'. There are mothers with dependent children who run marathons, there are black ballet dancers, there are individuals from working class backgrounds who shoot grouse there are young men and women who play bowls, and older men who play rugby, there are bricklayers who prefer Beethoven to the Beatles, and university lecturers who attend pop concerts. All of this demonstrates that individuals are not passive dupes, do make choices, develop interests and often overcome considerable constraints to leisure activity The power and resources of particular individuals in this respect qualifies but does not undermine a general explanation of leisure participation based on key social division in society.

3 Changes over time

Recent concern with 'leisure' and the development of a 'leisure industry' is a function of demographic, economic and social changes reviewed in Chapters 1 and 5. Patterns of employment change (e.g. numbers of un-employed, age of retirement, job sharing), as does the nature of work. The structure and size of families change (e.g. average number of de-pendent children, increase in single parent families, increase in divorce rate, and in 'second' families). Only a quarter of families in Britain are of the traditional husband, wife and dependent children variety. There is an increasingly 'old' population, more working mothers, changes in nurs-ery provision for pre-school children, increased car ownership, decreasing public transport networks, changes in youth sub-cultures. The outcome of such changes is that constraints and opportunities for leisure vary over time both for individuals and more generally for particular social groups. Leisure policies must be sensitive to such changes in peo-ple's circumstances if their aims are to be realised.

4 Social divisions inter-relate

Analyses of the influence of ethnicity upon leisure must acknowledge how gender cuts across or intermeshes with this social division. Asian women's leisure life-styles, for example, contrast sharply with Asian men's leisure. Similarly, the differences between middle and working class women's leisure may be just as stark as the difference between men and women's leisure more generally. Disparities related to class and ethnicity are also relevant to any consideration of family influence on leisure. There is also evidence that different youth subcultures over the last few decades (e.g. mods, punks, rockers, skinheads, beatniks, rastas, moshas, ravers) are controlled by social class and race as well as by more obvious signifiers such as music, style and dress codes. Some theorists argue that, because we live in a *capitalist* society in which some social groups have control or ownership of the means of production, social class is the key social division. Others argue that, because we live in a *patriarchal* society, power and resources are inequitably distributed between men and women. Others indicate there is *'structural racism'* operating in society which effectively disadvantages some racial groups in employment, education, and leisure. Each of these provide explanations of patterns of inequality in leisure activity, and the more thorough analyses indicate that social class, gender and race divisions cut across one another in different ways.

5 Leisure activities are different

In Chapter 2 we noted that the nature and dimensions of leisure activities are diverse. Similarly, the nature and dimensions of constraints and opportunities differ with respect to the type of leisure activity. Surveys show that the socio-economic characteristics of typical participants in sports differ considerably from the arts. Some leisure activities such as watching TV, gardening, playing with one's children or day trips are subject to constraints of time and perceptions of the relative worth of such activity. But other more formally organised activities have a different range of constraints related to equipment, skills, time, money, and car ownership. Therefore, an understanding of how participants are enabled and constrained in leisure choice must remain sensitive to differences between leisure activities.

Summary

This chapter has suggested ways in which the diversity of leisure activity can be explained. The principal concern has been to signify the complex social processes and divisions which influence, if not determine, leisure choice. Hence leisure activity cannot be seen merely as the outcome of individual tastes and preferences. Conversely, however, explanations of leisure participation cannot be wholly explained as a function of either social class, or age, or gender, or family circumstances. People do choose their own leisure activities if not in circumstances of their choice. Leisure providers, in order to encourage and enable participation in a range of leisure activities must, therefore, be sensitive to these social circumstances.

Further reading

Both J. Clarke and C. Critcher (1985) *The Devil Makes Work*, Macmillan, and K. Roberts (1984) *Youth and Leisure*, George Allen and Unwin provide excellent critical reviews of the literature on factors influencing leisure participation. A more descriptive treatment is provided by G. Torkildsen (1985) *Leisure and Recreation Management*, E. & F. N. Spon.

There is an extensive literature on gender divisions in leisure, the most recent being R. Deem (1986) *All Work and No Play*, Open University Press; E. Green, S. Hebron and D. Woodward (1990) *Women's Leisure: What Leisure?*, Macmillan; E. Wimbush and M. Talbot (1988) *Relative Freedoms*, Open University Press. D. Spender (1982) *Invisible Girls*, Writers and Readers Pub., presents a stark analysis of gender inequalities. The *General Household Survey* provides statistical information on participation rates in leisure activities according to gender and occupation. I. Reid (1981) *Social Class Differences in Britain*, Open Books, has a chapter specifically on leisure. Additional reading on class and gender analyses of leisure will be found in the final chapter of this text. Articles by Long (1987) and W. Grossin (1986) assess the impact of retirement on leisure activity. Other useful texts on social divisions in leisure include E. Cashmore (1990) *Making Sense of Sport*, Routledge; S. Parker (1983) *Leisure and Work*, George Allen and Unwin; J. Kelly (1982) *Leisure Identities and Interactions*, George Allen and Unwin. D. Hebdige (1979) *Sub-Culture: The Meaning of Style*, Methuen; B. Davies (1986) *Threatening Youth*, Open University; and G. Jarvie (1990) *Sport, Racism and Ethnicity*, Falmer Press.

The Ministry of Sport's Review Group has produced a set of recommendations to address inequalities of access, opportunity and power for disabled people in sport, to be found in *Building on Ability*, HMSO (1992). A. Brown (1987) *Active Games for Children with Movement Problems*, Harper Row, provides practical guidance on how to adapt games.

LEISURE SPACES

The environment within which leisure activities occur is for many leisure forms, like countryside recreation or tourism (discussed in Chapter 2), essential to the experience enjoyed. Even if not of paramount importance, the spatial context of every leisure activity serves to limit access for some participants and to provide local opportunities for others. The pattern of land use and the resulting distribution of leisure facilities in urban and rural areas are examined throughout this chapter. Understanding this pattern of leisure activities and facilities is necessary for a wider comprehension of the context of leisure provision within an urbanised society.

1 Leisure activity and opportunity

The diversity of activities, behaviour, and functions which can be regarded as 'leisure' presents problems when attempting to make sense of its spatial distribution. In addition to traditional venues like playing fields, sports centres or commercial theatres, a wide variety of types of locations and land uses needs to be examined, many of which do not clearly or solely reflect a single leisure function. The attractions of pedestrian streets in city centres, plane-spotting sites near major airports, or large do-it-yourself supermarkets out of town need to be considered, along with more traditional forms like city parks or bowling alleys. Many places represent a multiplicity of activities and, as the countryside recreation section of Chapter 2 noted, frequently these activities conflict.

Not all activities are equally accessible to individuals due to social divisions and inequalities. A fundamental issue when examining the spatial pattern of leisure activities is deciding whether they represent 'free' choice of individuals or are a reflection of what is effectively available to them, in the sense of being local, affordable, open, or within easy access (see also Chapters 2 and 3). The existing pattern of facilities can provide leisure opportunity, but may well act as an effective constraint, determining local leisure behaviour rather than freely reflecting it. The physical expression of leisure forms in the environment is, therefore, a significant factor in any review of activity or use of facilities.

In spite of these difficulties it is possible to predict a general pattern of leisure uses with particular forms, like shopping or theatre-going, well represented in urban areas, while others, like horse-riding or rambling, available in country districts. The diversity of provision reflects historic and contemporary variation in neighbourhood life-styles, life-stage, spending power and interests. These biases may become reinforced through time since many house-holders choose their locality on the basis of its recreational assets. Open space and greenery have long been significant aspirations for those who can afford to choose their neighbourhood or exercise some sort of preference. In this way the availability of leisure facilities needs to be seen as reflecting and reinforcing wider social patterns which form the context of social life generally.

Increasingly, leisure time is centred in the home, with television viewing as the greatest single domestic pastime. The quality, nature and distribution of residential areas thus forms the basic environment for any contemporary analysis of leisure activity (*see* Johnson, 1984, and Knox, 1987, for recent studies of social patterning of cities by class, ethnicity, lifestyle and life-stage).

The changing relationship between work and leisure explored earlier in this text has a parallel spatial aspect. Since the nineteenth century there has been a steady increase in the separation of home and workplace and this spatial distancing and increasing home-centred leisure needs to be taken into account. The increasing suburbanisation of both jobs and leisure opportunities and the potential of microtechnology for home-working have done nothing to simplify the patterns of work and leisure. Indeed, the variety of leisure forms and their intimate connection in an integrated multi-functional way with a range of allied residential and commercial uses, mean that it is necessary to examine leisure facilities in the context of general patterns of land use initially, rather than as a separate, isolated dimension of urban and regional land use.

2 *Urban land use processes and leisure uses*

Leisure in industrialised societies is increasingly being advertised, sold and packaged as a commodity. Like every other commercial product, leisure spaces have to compete against alternative land uses. This competition has generated the historic pattern of land uses in towns and

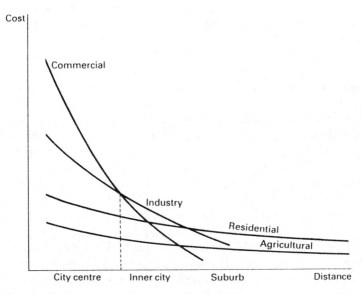

Figure 4.1   Generalised bid–rent curves (after Alonso)

cities. In general the most profitable activities occupy prime city-centre sites, while less intensively profitable activities are relegated to less advantaged, inaccessible, or less sought after locations, often towards the edges of town or city.

The concept of 'bid-rents', where different land users competitively attempt to rent space within city areas, is a useful way to begin thinking about leisure's place in the pattern of urban land use. In the model shown in Figure 4.1, developed by urban land economists like Alonso, activities are ranked largely in terms of profitability, which determines the amount they can afford to bid for advantageous sites. Commercial enterprises profit most from a prime central-city location, industrial users less so, and domestic or agricultural functions are less able to compete financially for space (Alonso, 1982; Johnson, 1984; Knox, 1987). The diverse nature of leisure activities means that these are spread throughout the city, occupying prime sites in the city centre if they are profitable enough, like bars, restaurants, or cinemas; and occupying peripheral suburban sites if, like sports pitches or golf courses, they require large amounts of less expensive land.

This simplified model begins to account for the general pattern of land uses in Western cities and is a useful starting point for any assessment of leisure provision. It makes several major assumptions about the accessibility of city-centre sites for the majority of citizens and the role of the profit motive as the prime factor in sorting land uses. These assumptions can be questioned given the changing nature of urban transport, as city-centre congestion becomes a disadvantage for individual car-users. Other criticisms focus on the fact that land is sold sequentially, rather than in a 'free' market, with only a few plots up for sale at any one time. In most cases it is buildings which are bought rather than land, and the bulk of costs reflects the nature of established real estate rather than theorised competition for empty sites (Harvey, 1973; Roweis and Scott, 1981).

Within established cities, historic patterns of development due to unique features of topography or routeways lead to a multiplicity of urban forms. However, there are enough regularities in competition to make some generalisation useful. The bid-rent model highlights the fact that within the urban setting, recreational spaces and facilities may be subject to commercial pressures, and that re-development when it occurs, will usually lead to a more profitable, often non-leisure, use. This is why many urban leisure-facilities are, in fact, residual features. They could not afford to continue to occupy that site if they had to compete within the contemporary land-market. It also emphasises the cycle of uses which many buildings represent. In British cities much of the investment in leisure infrastructure was established in the nineteenth century or earlier this century. Over time, music halls and theatres became cinemas, which evolved into bingo halls, and in some cases, have recently changed function yet again, for instance for retailing low-quality carpets or furniture. Some former industrial locations – mills, factories and even coal mines or slate quarries – have been redeveloped to serve a heritage tourism market as industrial museums or parts of 'folk' parks. The reuse of existing buildings and sites is another indication of the dynamics of postmodern economic change as service employment replaces manufacturing jobs, and commerce supplants industry. The physical expression of such changes can be seen within cities and regions as the built environment is adapted to mirror social and economic transformation (Spink, 1994).

The evolving use of leisure outlets reflects change in clientele. Facilities need to attract sufficient population or spending power to be viable, and as local people move or tastes change, established activities and their premises become vulnerable to redevelopment pressures. Changes in the potential users or 'catchment' areas of any facility are crucial for continuing usefulness and commercial viability. A minimum 'threshold' of population needs to be achieved, measured either as individual users or in spending power, in order for leisure facilities to be able to operate. Each requires a different number of users and hence a particular sized catchment area from which to draw its customers. Services used infrequently need larger potential populations than those used frequently. The more specialised the function, like race tracks, skating rinks, or water-sports centres, the fewer in number and more widely spaced the provision, as users are prepared to incur greater travel costs in order to avail themselves of the more specialised service offered.

The concept of viable catchment areas and minimum threshold populations applies to all leisure facilities; from out-of-town hypermarkets acting as major regional shopping-centres, down to branch libraries and sports halls serving individual localities. The potential of particular sites is of importance when leisure investment is being planned. An assessment of the possible number of users is vital for public utility or private profitability alike, and has been explored theoretically by geographical 'central place' theorists and by more practical operators (*see* Bateman, 1982; Torkildsen, 1986, ch 11; Cowling *et al.*, 1982).

The changing importance of particular premises and sites reflects changing patterns of lifestyles, population distribution and spending power, and facilities grow or decline accordingly. Continuing urban-renewal processes based on the search for profitability, investment in real estate, and the redevelopment of land and buildings, ensure that leisure takes its place in a dynamic setting, still reflecting historic land-use patterns but open to contemporary commercial pressures which combine to give the pattern of leisure uses found in modern towns, cities and regions.

3 *Patterns of leisure*

The historic social and economic processes previously described have created a changing yet regular structure of leisure provision within urban areas and surrounding countryside. Commercial competition, changing tastes, fashions and lifestyles, and the extent to which local authorities or central government subsidise particular uses, all combine to produce regularities in the distribution of leisure opportunities for resident populations. Some neighbourhoods are less well provided with public open space than others, some districts have a wider range of sports facilities and so on, but the general pattern can still be represented broadly as Table 4.1.

The impact of commercial competition for space is most obvious in the central areas of conurbations. Only intensively profitable users of space can survive here, unless receiving heavy subsidy from public authorities considering the maintenance of libraries, museums, galleries, or even opera companies, to be a necessary public service or tourist attraction. For many people traditional commercial functions, such as retailing, now constitute a major postmodern leisure activity. Huge expenditure by

Table 4.1 Leisure spaces

Location	Activities	Facilities	Pressures
Central areas	Shopping Evening out Eating out Promenading	**Commercial city core environment** 'Downtown' 'Bright Lights' Leisure uses – cinemas, theatres, galleries, museums, 'Fun Shops' – malls, plazas, and pedestrian streets Restaurants, cafes, pubs, and discos	Profitability Land used intensively High returns or Public subsidy
Inner Cities	Living Space Functional activities Spectator and indoor sports Selective activities (Gender/race/age)	**Deteriorating environment** Limited range of shops Residual leisure functions – bingo halls and cinemas Public parks, recreation grounds and allotment gardens Professional sports grounds Social clubs and pubs Swimming baths and sports centres	Limited profitability Disadvantaged local populations Competition from non-leisure uses; relatively high land values reflecting possible development potential
Residential districts and suburbs	Living space Home-based diy or gardening Shopping Evening out Eating out	**Popular environment** District shopping centres and parades Range of leisure	Residential uses dominant and protected Allied leisure and recreation spaces

(continued)

Table 4.1 (*continued*)

Location	Activities	Facilities	Pressures
	Outdoor and indoor sports Walking	functions – cinema, bingo, video shops Social clubs, pubs, wine bars, and restaurants Public parks, pitches, open spaces and allotment gardens Private sports clubs	maintained for/by affluent local populations More green spaces – lower housing density Sound profitability
Urban fringe and green belt	Commuting Car-borne shopping Outdoor sports, walking, golf, horse riding Day visits	**Prestigious environment** Shopping centres, hypermarkets and some scattered retail warehouses and smaller outlets Sports pitches, golf courses, stables, bridleways and footpaths Country parks and mansions Picnic spots	Development pressures – retail, residential and some industrial expansion. Local resistance powerful Agricultural and pollution conflicts Urban population use problems Leisure strong land user
Rural areas	Farming Retirement Tourism and day visits Outdoor and upland pursuits Naturalism	**Rural environment** Tourist facilities Countryside – green spaces and wildscape (National Parks, AONBs, SSSIs, etc.) Footpaths and bridleways Rural images – life and styles Villages and 'destinations'	Conflicting land users – agriculture, commerce, quarrying, tourism Resentful locals Urban swamping Private land and public access Second homes

retail chains and development companies, in partnership with local authorities create 'consumption palaces', malls, and pedestrian streets, which encourage congregations of people, particularly the young or more affluent. Fun shopping attracts leisured crowds and allied features, like busking, street entertainment, and mobile refreshment stands, generate still further participation. This multiplication of social attraction and the excitement of 'downtown', the 'bright lights', and the crowds themselves have become a significant feature of most Western cities, reflecting the commodification of leisure-time on a tide of consumption enjoyed by the affluent (*see* Chapters 2 and 7).

The attractions of historic city-cores have been enhanced through public investment and subsidy by local authorities keen to augment local economies by injections of spending from a growing tourist trade. Whether the focus is that of a medieval city core with town walls, castle or cathedral, or the nostalgic pursuit of a Victorian heritage in old mills, factories and shopping arcades, the general attractiveness of a 'heritage' environment and associated pedestrianised core as a focus for visitors and local residents has been well established and now represents a common feature of townscape.

Such attractive urban centres heighten commercial competition, pricing out those businesses unable to benefit from passing pedestrian trade and reinforcing the presence of highly profitable boutiques and fashion goods which the 'audience' considers attractive. Selection in turn reinforces the attraction of the centre for local residents and visiting tourists and for the commercial concerns able to profit from these groups. The major problem in many centres is simply that of policing the crowds, particularly in constricted shopping malls and shopping centres.

As Table 4.1 suggests, the growing popularity of 'fun retailing' in pedestrianised commercial centres can be contrasted with the situation in inner cities. These central districts just outside the city core of affluent commercialism provide living-space for considerable numbers of the less mobile and less favoured in modern society, in poor quality housing, developed in the nineteenth century and presenting a less than attractive environment today. Leisure facilities are limited by the extent of traditional provision of parks and play spaces, and the weaker economic circumstances of local residents limit the commercial viability of alternative uses. The impoverished nature of local populations has meant an inherited pattern of inadequate facilities, restricted in range and tending to diminish through time. Theatres, cinemas, open spaces and even sports clubs have tended to revert to other uses, unless supported by some form of subsidy. Local authorities may operate against the commercial tide by maintaining parks, and swimming baths, and by opening sports centres. Areas lacking this kind of public subsidy seem condemned to a residual leisure pattern of public houses and social clubs, few shops, and despoiled open spaces.

Diverse local populations within inner-city areas utilise a limited range of facilities which can only partially accommodate their needs. For households with children, likely to be either within or at the margins of poverty, the limited access to open space, play areas and cheap indoor facilities, close to home, presents a real difficulty. For ethnic groups, leisure activities may well be associated with centres of religious observance, having sports clubs and social events as complementary features. In many cases these will be linked to national networks of observance, kinship, 'brotherhood' and rites of passage ceremonies which come to dominate family leisure-time. For the elderly, restricted by income and by immobility, there is likely to be a continuing reliance on a traditional, but restricted and declining, range of leisure facilities provided by church, social clubs and public authorities.

The very diversity of inner 'urban populations; the poor, the immobile elderly, single parent families, single persons, and ethnic groups, suggests a heterogeneity in demand which is rarely met by deteriorating and limited facilities in reality. Additionally, for many 'trapped' within such environments fear may act as a significant constraint on personal 'action space', particularly during hours of darkness. Women and the elderly in such areas have leisure opportunities severely restricted by perceived risks, actual and potential, associated with venturing 'out', in addition to the limits enforced by economic circumstance (Spink, 1994).

Further from the urban centre, in more prosperous residential areas, a wider range of commercial facilities can be maintained, more appropriate to the age, gender and lifestyles of local populations. In these neighbourhoods, not only is there a broader range of shops and retail centres, but private sports clubs can afford to operate. In many cities such districts are attractive residentially because of nearness of parks, public sports pitches, and other open spaces. The greener environment encourages walking and outdoor sports, while larger houses facilitate more home-based recreations (Glyptis, 1987).

These neighbourhoods developed at much lower density than inner areas and hence gardening, do-it-yourself and other less formal leisure pursuits become available, alongside team sports occupying public and private pitches. The ambience, so important for outdoor leisure, is maintained through public subsidy and the protection of town planning zoning legislation, so that intrusive commerce and industry, found in inner areas, are far less of a problem. This prosperity and protection combine to maintain a broad range of leisure facilities, both public and private, in salubrious residential suburbs, with greater proportions of green space available towards the periphery of the built environment.

At the edges of conurbations, housing gives way to even more open land. Agricultural uses begin to compete commercially, so the 'rurban fringe' presents possibilities for walking on some of the 120 000 miles of footpaths and bridleways in Britain, and brings countryside recreation within fairly easy reach of town dwellers and suburbanites. Lower land prices and political intervention protecting 'green belt' areas permit more extensive land uses like golf courses or large parklands and country mansions to continue, and to act as major attractions for urban populations (41% of recreation trips are within 1 km of urban settlements, according to the Centre for Leisure Research, 1986).

Traditionally, urban-peripheral locations have afforded leisure for wealthy local residents and those travelling from the nearby centre. Most problems have arisen due to conflicts between recreational and agricultural uses of land and the pressure of residential development. Increasingly, peripheral 'green-field' sites are seen as ideal for commercial centres of hypermarket scale and for new industrial investment. Land with good vehicular access, particularly adjoining ring roads or motorway links, has been vulnerable to such pressures, and car-based shopping is increasing as a convenience and as a leisure pursuit around the edges of conurbations. The continuance of green-belt protection (now 14% of land in England) should ensure that leisure remains a relatively strong competitor in urban-fringe areas. The intermixture of high-class commuter housing and green spaces seems likely to be sustained in these districts (Elson, 1986) though as Table 4.1 suggests, conflicts due to expansionary pressures from retailing, housing and new industries are likely to continue.

Beyond the 'rurban fringe', the rural areas proper contain a range of functions described earlier in Chapter 2. In commercial land-use terms the dominance of agriculture, quarrying, or other primary industries is challenged in relatively few places and the image of rural life and styles has received political protection in areas of beauty or 'wildscape' through National Park, and Areas of Outstanding Natural Beauty legislation. The principal conflicts here arise through differences in forms of resource exploitation and the resentment held by local populations for tourists or day visitors. There also may be antagonism between urban users of such areas pursuing activities like rambling, nature study or landscape appreciation, when coming into contact with those indulging in noisy sports like trail biking or off-the-road motor rallying. In issues like second homes, traffic, or new building, the main dilemma is the potential of urban populations for destroying the very lifestyles, remoteness and isolation they ostensibly value. This destructive capacity of leisure use remains paradoxically the greatest potential threat to attractive rural areas (Gilg, 1978; Cloke, 1987) .

Thus the spatial pattern of leisure use can be established. The distribution of facilities reflects commercial pressures and political intervention with sufficient accuracy to be broadly identifiable in most urban areas. Specific localities present unique circumstances but the broad structuring by:

(a) social forces (spending power, lifestyles and life-stages, gender balance, ethnic preferences, etc);
(b) economic forces (competition for land and buildings based on profitability or utility); and
(c) political power (intervention to subsidise or protect valued uses or areas), provides a predictability in leisure use which can be observed in most areas.

4 *Spatial issues and policy responses*

The established pattern is not without problems. Commercial competition which underlies urban land use change ensures that some functions and facilities will disappear without protection or subsidy. Some areas are poorly endowed with open spaces or recreational facilities. The need to intervene in the market or to maintain public provision is a political issue which has been acted upon to differing extents, at different times, and by different authorities. Local authorities vary in their acceptance of the need to spend public funds on leisure facilities. Their attitude tends to reflect wider political philosophy on the role of public intervention in the provision of local services.

Some local authorities have accepted particular 'standards' of provision for leisure facilities and have attempted to bring non-market uniformity to the distribution of opportunities by opening swimming baths, sports centres and playing areas. This focus on a particular level of provision (e.g. National Playing Fields Association has a recommendation of six acres of open space per 1000 population, and the Sports Council suggests one indoor sports centre for 40 000 people) or the designation of particular areas or groups as 'deprived', using 'social indicators' drawn from the Census is essentially value laden. The extent of public investment and control varies according to the nature and opinions of central and local administrations. Local authorities can correct imbalance by using their own budgets to maintain or create facilities, and through local plans attempting to restructure land uses in their districts. Their effectiveness at resisting market pressures has varied according to the resources at their disposal. Current government attitudes and financial limits make market forces likely to dominate in allocating scarce resources.

Social change also affects the appropriateness and usefulness of existing facilities. Contemporary society has witnessed great changes in household composition with more divorce and single-parent families, more active and independent elderly, and smaller households with fewer children. Simple application of 'standard' provision to areas on a uniform basis will not reflect these changing patterns of need and demand.

Another change which has affected the established pattern of provision has been within modes of transport. With increasing car ownership (68% of households in 1991) distant and out of district facilities become accessible for many in society. Car use tends to reinforce existing social advantage and disadvantage, limiting participation for those restricted to a declining public transport service, and rewarding others with a complete range of motor-accessible facilities. Income levels, above all, determine accessibility unless there is considerable public subsidy.

Public attitudes, and those of politicians, about the supply of leisure opportunities are crucial to those who are weak competitors in the leisure market. Socio-economic inequalities are reinforced spatially in the pattern of resource distribution and access to facilities. Intervention through spending (on recreation grounds, leisure centres and public parks), or legislation (on urban land use zoning, green belts, conservation areas or national parks), are the principal means of supporting disadvantaged groups in society. The weaker the market competitor, the greater the reliance on public provision. This relationship is true both for individuals and for facilities. Playing fields, cinemas, parks, and evening classes are all vulnerable to commercial forces and spending pressures. The direction of market-based provision is clear from Section 3. It is a matter of political judgement to what extent that developing spatial pattern should be modified.

QUESTIONS AND EXERCISES

1 How does your town or city match the generalised spatial pattern of leisure facilities and functions outlined in Table 4.1?

2 Are there any local examples of conflicts between different users of the same area?

3 Can you think of local examples of a historic succession of uses occupying a single building or site and relate these to commercial pressures or public subsidy?

4 Can you identify local areas which are short of appropriate leisure facilities for local residents or particular groups?

5 Do more recent leisure developments – like out of town shopping complexes – appeal to particular groups in society and do they exclude others? How is their appeal and exclusivity achieved?

6 How is imbalance in leisure facilities perpetuated and reinforced? Is this inevitable, or should it be modified by public spending or legislation?

7 Is public subsidy the only way in which the imbalance in distribution of facilities can be corrected?

8 Can market forces in the environment only be modified for short periods?

Further reading

A comprehensive review of spatial aspects of leisure is J. A. Patmore (1983) *Recreation and Resources*, Basil Blackwell. This has been complemented more recently by J. Spink (1994) *Leisure and the Environment*, Butterworth-Heinemann. A useful introduction to rural leisure is S. Glyptis (1991) *Countryside Recreation*, Longman. For general issues of land use, A. S. Mather (1986) *Land Use*, Longman, provides specialised theory and evidence. Detailed research techniques for investigating spatial distributions of activities and participants are outlined in S. L. J. Smith (1983) *Recreation Geography*, Longman. For leisure forms, individual studies commissioned by national bodies are useful; Centre for Leisure Research (1986) *Access to the Countryside for Recreation and Sport*, Sports Council; or D. Cowling, M. Fitzjohn and M. Tungatt (1983) *Identifying the Market: Catchment Areas of Sports Centres and Swimming Pools*, Study No. 24, Sports Council.

LEISURE PROVISION

Introduction

This chapter examines the development, nature and structure of leisure provision in contemporary Britain in the commercial, public and voluntary sectors. The emphasis will not be on describing in detail the sectoral divisions, but rather on accounting for the development and form of the sectors. The intention is, therefore, to provide a framework within which to locate information and arguments.

Freedom and constraint in the sectors of leisure provision

The first point to note is that reference to each of the sectors will involve not simply analysis of the process of providing *opportunities* to participate in certain leisure forms, but will also involve consideration of the ways in which each of the sectors of leisure provision *constrains* the nature of leisure opportunities available.

1 The public sector

The state performs a dual function of licensing, controlling, or even prohibiting certain leisure forms; while on the other hand promoting, through tax concessions, grant-aid or direct provision, leisure forms which are regarded as desirable. Thus leisure behaviour which is regarded as dangerous (such as drug abuse, prize fighting) or as socially undesirable (such as prostitution) is actively suppressed or discouraged, while 'wholesome' leisure activities in the form of sport, cultural provision or certain informal recreations, are actively promoted.

2 The commercial sector

The commercial sector can be seen as both constraining and enabling choice in leisure activities. The notion of consumer sovereignty represents recognition that the market is likely to respond to the wishes of those in the market-place and cannot simply 'lead-demand'. The market may be even more effective in reaching some groups identified as priorities by the public sector, as in the case of commercial bingo, which provides social activities for working class groups, specifically women and the elderly. The consumption activities described in Chapter 2 have a mass-market appeal, and are provided largely by the commercial sector. However, the market operates on the basis of ability to pay, and thus constrains choice for those who lack the resources to influence commercial providers.

3 *The voluntary sector*

The voluntary sector can also be seen as having a dual role. Earlier discussion of hobbies and crafts in Chapter 2 suggested that voluntary organisations can serve as interest groups which have the potential to avoid problems of paternalism and bureaucratic organisation on the part of the public sector, and which are not tied to the commercial sector requirement of profitability. However, it should also be noted that the voluntary sector and its constituent organisations are arenas for the exercise of power. Thus where an individual organisation or a given segment of the voluntary sector is dominated by particular interests, which purport to speak for the organisation or segment as a whole, other interests may not receive consideration. A dissenting voice in such circumstances may be marginalised, or may not even be raised. Research on the relationship between local government and voluntary organisations, reveals that some groups are regarded positively by local government officials and councillors and regularly consulted about policy issues affecting them, while others are not consulted and remain ignorant of significant policy debates (viz. Dearlove, 1973; Newton, 1976; Limb, 1986). Similarly, the Quality of Life Experiments in the early 1970s (a piece of action-research in which small-scale voluntary bodies were funded to foster leisure provision in four areas) provides a good example of well-organised, articulate groups dominating resources in grant allocation. Thus the voluntary sector as a whole provides potential opportunities and constraints in representing its constituent interests.

The historical context of the leisure sectors

It is difficult to understand the nature of institutional arrangements in leisure or any other social sphere without gaining some insight into the forces which historically have shaped and continue to shape them. What is presented below, therefore, is an explanation of present sectoral arrangements and contemporary issues, by reference to key developments in the history of the leisure sectors. The division of chronology into 'significant periods' helps to organise the incremental development of leisure provision in each sector. An understanding of historical context is important in contemporary terms not simply because of the 'developmental' perspective it provides, but also because current debate on the role of the commercial, voluntary and state sectors in providing welfare services generally, is being couched in terms of a return to Victorian values of 'self-help', reliance on the individual or family, and reduction in levels of state intervention.

Within this analysis, five stages in the development of leisure opportunities are identified in the period from the end of the eighteenth century to the present day. The development of public sector leisure policy and of the commercial and voluntary sectors in the post-war period are discussed more fully later in the chapter.

1 The process of industrialisation and urbanisation, and the suppressions of popular recreation *c.* 1780–1840

Attitudes towards the state in this period are reflected in Adam Smith's liberal economic theory published in *The Wealth of Nations*, in 1776. Smith's economic philosophy provided a rationale for a non-interventionist approach by the state, arguing that the unfettered market would be the most efficient generator of public goods. Social policy was therefore to be minimal, restricted simply to easing any obstruction to market forces.

State intervention was rather less concerned with providing opportunities for recreation than it was with the control of leisure forms which had their origins in rural, agrarian communities but which were regarded as running counter to industrial interests in urban settings by undermining work-discipline. Animal blood-sports (except those like fox-hunting which were pursued by the emergent industrial middle-class and the aristocracy) were banned by force of law, while drinking, prize fighting and traditional fairs and wakes were also suppressed, though local policing-practices varied from one district to another (Yeo and Yeo, 1981). The concern of the legislature and the local magistracy with popular recreations was the result of three major concerns:

(a) The first was simply that many of the pursuits which had evolved in agrarian, rural society were 'inappropriate' in urban settings in that they were the occasion of much damage. Bull-running or mass football-games would result in considerable disruption in the streets of towns.
(b) The second major concern was with work discipline. While agrarian production relied on seasonal patterns of work with extended periods

of effort, particularly at harvest time, followed by traditional feasts and holiday periods, industrial production was ruled by the clock. In order to maximise production, machines had to be in operation as long as possible and this meant that workers had to be available for labour at the appointed hour. Absenteeism and drunkenness at work were seen as the result of uncontrolled revelry and resulted in loss of profit in factories which depended on a workforce to be regularly available, compliant, and alert. Thus, control of recreation was regarded as essential to the maintenance of production.

(c) The other concern of both the 'aristocracy' and the new industrial interests was social order. The American and French Revolutions provided evidence of the potential for insurrection. The establishment was, therefore, understandably nervous about gatherings of large, rowdy crowds among the lower orders for fairs, wakes, public hangings and other popular pastimes, seeing them as potential seedbeds for expressions of dissatisfaction with the existing order.

During this period there was an accelerating shift in population from rural to urban locations. One of the results of swift urban growth was that cramped insanitary housing conditions were experienced by the majority of new urban populations. The social focus of these new communities was the public house which provided relatively uncontaminated drink, together with heating and light as well as a medium for socialising. As historians, such as Cunningham (1980) have pointed out, although concerted efforts at suppression of recreation may have taken place, it seems likely that animal blood-sports, prize fighting, the 'worship of St Monday' (absenteeism from work after the weekend revelry) and other recreational forms survived throughout the period, often with the support of publicans whose patronage of such activities provided a substitute for the lost traditional patronage of the rural aristocracy.

2 The development and decline of the Rational Recreation Movement, mass leisure markets, and the erosion of *laissez-faire* government c. 1840–1900

As Britain became an increasingly urban and industrial nation so it became clear that industrialisation, if unchecked by the state, was likely to foster squalor and poverty among some of the workforce, and thus to militate against the need for a healthy, well-ordered populace, even breeding resentment and fostering social disorder. The Chartist movement of the 1840s and the early attempts at trades-union organisation appear to have stimulated concern about the reaction of working class groups to the excesses of free-market capitalism. Legislation was required to foster responsible behaviour, both among employers during working hours and among employees during non-work time. Thus the Factories Acts of 1847 and 1867 sought to protect children and women from an 'excessive' working week and dangerous or unhealthy working conditions.

During this period voluntary efforts, mainly on the part of middle class philanthropists, focused on providing opportunities for recreational activities. Where the Lord's Day Observance Society, the RSPCA and the Temperance League had sought to suppress leisure forms altogether, in the early part of the century, middle class reformers were now seeking to provide alternative and more wholesome activities to wean working people away from the temptations of dissolute and irresponsible recreations. The Church of England, for example, through Sunday School recreation programmes sought to provide alternative attractions to more dissolute leisure centred on the public house, with day trips, educational visits and other improving recreational forms. Similarly, some factory owners sought to control not only the work-lives of their employees, but also to provide organised leisure in the form of fêtes, trips, celebration of patriotic events and anniversaries. Provision of public parks, often on land donated by middle class benefactors, and the development of mechanics institutes, public libraries and museums, also constituted attempts by reformers to tame popular recreations by offering more acceptable alternatives. Those associated with the 'Muscular Christianity' movement promoted the newly codified games of football and rugby as a means of propagating appropriate values of self-discipline, teamwork, and subordination of individual interests to the greater good of the team. (Soccer clubs founded in this way included (Aston) Villa Cross Wesleyan Chapel, St Domingo's Church Sunday School (Everton), and Barnsley St Peter's). The 'rational recreation' movement sought to provide uplifting leisure forms for the working classes as, for example, when the Rev. Henry Solly helped to found Working Men's Clubs which he intended should remain free from the taint of alcohol.

This middle-class paternalism may be interpreted as an extension of the 'social control' attempted in the supression of popular recreations in the early part of the century. However, this fails to acknowledge that working class groups successfully resisted certain forms of paternalism. Football clubs which were originally founded in the context of religious groups, soon exerted their independence. Similarly, attempts to sustain teetotal Working Men's Clubs failed. Where attempts were made to exclude working class people from participation in sport, there could be resistance. The Amateur Athletics Association's exclusion from competition of those involved in physical labour (on the grounds that the nature of their work gave them an unfair physical advantage); and also Rugby Union's refusal to permit 'broken-time' payments proved ineffectual in the face of determined working class opposition. Organisations either gave way, as the Amateur Athletics Association did, or rival organisations were established, as was the breakaway Rugby League. Some exclusionary practices continued, but working people were able to assert their will in many instances. Finally, where middle class provision simply did not appeal to working class tastes (for example when the Mechanics' Institutes failed in Manchester, or the Temperance League experimented with alcohol-free pubs) this had to be modified or simply withered from underuse. The problem with claims of 'social control' is that they portray the working class population passively accepting the wishes of a dominant middle class, and fail to account for successful resistance to the imposition of unwelcome leisure forms.

More problematic than the issues of class control is the issue of gender, since the leisure needs of women, particularly working class women, are rarely evident in historical commentary. This is a function of the gender of those who recorded, or who now research, history, and also a reflection of the implicit and insidious means by which female recreations were controlled. As was noted in Chapter 2, the growing home-based consumption of leisure by the middle class male in this period was contingent upon the domestic labour of wives. The ideology of gender roles implied in 'a woman's place is in the home' has a considerable history, and does much to explain the invisibility of women in social history generally, and in leisure history in particular.

The role of government in this period of 'enlightened paternalism' is perhaps best described as one of fostering voluntary sector initiative. The Museums Act of 1849, the Public Libraries Act of 1850 and the Recreation Grounds Act of 1852, all attempted to provide public-sector resources which would allow local authorities to capitalise on gifts of land, exhibits, or books, from benefactors. The physical condition of the working class was also a concern of legislation. Insanitary conditions in the urban environment fostered disease, particularly cholera, which threatened all classes, and much of the rationale of the Public Health Act of 1848 was in evidence in the sponsoring of legislation for recreation. The Recreation Grounds Act promoted parks in the city as 'clean air' zones, and the Public Baths and Washrooms Act of 1846 was less concerned with fostering swimming than it was with encouraging working class people to bathe in disinfected water. Physical education was introduced into the curriculum in the Education Act 1870 but simply in the form of military drill. In summary, these health, discipline and cultural improvement initiatives were clearly related to thinking underpinning the 'rational recreation movement', as the movement to develop improving recreations for the working class was termed.

Although the government's role in leisure provision was only slowly evolving in this period, development of the commercial sector was proceeding apace and by the end of the century the development of mass markets in the leisure industries had begun. In the early part of the century the public house had become the venue of much leisure activity (legal and illegal) of the working class, generating income for the publican through increased liquor sales. However, in the same way as the small-scale entrepreneur in other areas of industry was beginning to disappear by the middle of the century, with the advent of large-scale capital investment, so the publican promoting animal sports, prize fights or entertainments, was giving way to the development of the music hall. Its large-scale capital investment and bigger halls were established from the middle of the century onwards (Bailey, 1986). This concentration of capital was evident also in other areas of industry associated with leisure, such as the railways, which by the 1870s were largely in the ownership of four major companies, providing excursions, transport for holidays, and facilitating the development of national sporting events. Other large-scale investments in leisure included the development of sports stadia, piers and steamship travel, and the factory production of leisure equipment such as the bicycle.

Concentration of capital in leisure industries was not universal. As Walton (1983) points out, domestic tourism in towns such as Blackpool was largely catered for by small-scale entrepreneurs, particularly those who provided accommodation for visitors. However, where the application of new technology necessitated large-scale investment, potential profits made such a scale of investment worthwhile. Despite continuing slumps and booms in trade, the working class experienced growing disposable income and increasing free-time, so that where an activity had mass appeal, potential for profit could be considerable and leisure was able to compete for capital investment with more traditional areas of industry.

Enfranchisement of the urban workforce in 1867 and rural workers in 1884, demonstrated acceptance by the establishment that working class radicalism had learnt the lessons inflicted by the collapse of Chartism, and that the working classes could be relied upon to act 'responsibly'. The need, therefore, to exert control over popular recreations, either directly through the state or indirectly through middle class paternalism and philanthropy, ceased to be an issue of major significance by the turn of the century.

3 Laying the foundations of the Welfare State 1900–39

Government intervention in the second half of the nineteenth century aimed to alleviate some of the worst effects of urban-industrial society.

However, further reforms were forthcoming when, after 20 years of Conservative Government, the Liberals assumed power in 1905, and embarked on a programme of social reform. The Unemployed Workman's Act of 1905, for example, represented a recognition that unemployment was not the result of individual inadequacies or fecklessness, and measures such as introduction of school meals in 1907 and old age pensions in 1908, demonstrated the state's willingness to provide (albeit in a relatively small way) for those least able to meet their own needs. The impetus for the introduction of school meals came from the Report of the Interdepartmental Committee on Physical Deterioration in 1904, which expressed concern about fitness for military service. The Boer War and a recognition of the need for readiness to defend the Empire did much to stimulate support for this apparently altruistic concern. However, despite the concern with extrinsic factors (rather than simply with promoting reform for its own sake) advances were made by this government which laid the foundations of the welfare state.

Within the increasing role of the state were policy innovations in the field of leisure. The Town Planning Act 1909, for example, listed recreation open-space as a category of land use to be recorded, while the Forestry Commission, set up in 1919, was the first governmental body to be given a statutory duty to provide for recreation. The Access to the Mountains Act 1939 also indicated government's willingness to become involved in legislation to enable recreational opportunities (though the Act required only voluntary agreements for access, with landowners to be compensated by amenity or recreation groups). However, perhaps the most far-reaching element of recreation legislation to be enacted before World War II was the Physical Training and Recreation Act 1937. While the Act appears to have been motivated largely by extrinsic concerns such as fear of the effects of unemployment, concern about fascist youth movements on the Continent, and about fitness for war, it also evoked support for recreation for its own sake. This legislation 'earmarked' £2 million to be spent on recreation initiatives which in real terms is the largest amount ever made available by government for such purposes.

The fostering of voluntary-sector initiatives in the late nineteenth century gave way during this period to the incorporation (into the ambit of government) of voluntary organisations, in legislation such as the National Trust Act of 1907, and the Physical Training and Recreation Act. In effect the voluntary sector co-operated in the development and implementation of government policies. Furthermore, prominent voluntary sector organisations such as the National Trust, the National Playing Fields Association, and the Central Council for Physical Recreation and Training were *national* in scope and in the movement for access to the countryside, the mass trespasses of the 1930s were national in impact, resulting in legislative reform. Thus voluntary-sector leisure pressure-groups were beginning to become sufficiently well organised to exert significant influence on national policy debates.

Though unemployment between the wars did not fall below the one million mark and peaked at over three million, it was not evenly spread across the nation. The unemployment was concentrated in the severely depressed areas of the North-West, the North-East, Scotland and Wales, while in the South-East and Midlands, economic growth and employment levels were sustained. Even at the deepest point in the recession, three quarters of the work force were in employment, and though prices rose faster than wages in real terms, there was an increasing prosperity for some groups, particularly white-collar workers. Among manual occupations work hours fell from 54 per week in 1900 to 46.5 in 1938. By 1939 paid holidays were enjoyed by more than 60% of the working population. In this context, investment by the commercial sector in leisure continued to grow. Spectator sport, particularly football, attracted considerable investment to build and extend stadia. The cinema became the natural extension of the music hall, replacing live entertainment with mass-produced, quality-controlled performances of enormous appeal. Walvin (1978) claims that by 1919 half the population visited the cinema at least twice a week.

Wireless also produced market opportunities in leisure. The sale of radios and other goods was accelerated by development of consumer credit. Hire purchase increased by 300% between the Wars and by 1938 it accounted for two thirds of all sales of mass-produced articles, including a whole range of leisure goods from sports equipment to pianos and bicycles. Broadcasting also provided another area of state involvement in leisure provision with the formation of the BBC, which under its first Director General, Lord Reith, adopted a paternalist stance, aiming not only to provide information for the British public, but also to educate and improve popular-cultural tastes. The culturally elitist tone of the BBC's initial policy stance is illustrated by the requirement that early radio announcers should wear evening dress while addressing listeners.

Motor transport provided opportunities not only for those who could afford to buy a car or motor cycle, but also for working class people who took coach-based holidays. Seaside holidays continued to attract public and private investment, with an average annual investment of £4 million nationally between the Wars. Thus the impetus gained by the commercial sector in the emergence of mass markets in the late nineteenth-century was sustained by further technological advances, availability of consumer credit, and the continued affluence of those in employment.

4 The growth and maturing of the welfare state 1945–76

The consequences of the war effort on post-war society were multiple and complex. Full employment for almost all those of working age was provided during the hostilities and in the industrial effort of the post-war recovery period. The conflict itself gave rise to what has become known as the 'inspection effect'. Having made sacrifices for the good of society as a whole, individuals were encouraged by the situation to take a critical look at the kind of society which they had fought to protect. The surprise defeat of the Conservatives under Winston Churchill in the post-war election is best understood as a reflection of the unwillingness of the electorate to fall back on the pre-war policies which had left a significant minority of the population in poverty. The 1945–51 Labour Government's programme of welfare policies which together constitute the backbone of the welfare state framework was signalled in their 1945 manifesto and had enormous electoral appeal. Wartime experience of centralised state control of the economy and social provisions, and the increased proportion of gross national product channelled through government spending, also fostered acceptance of greater state intervention in peacetime.

Along with fundamental social reforms associated with the founding of the welfare state in education, health, social security, unemployment assistance and so on, the post-war Labour Government also reinforced government involvement in leisure policy by the establishment of the Arts Council in 1947 and the National Parks Commission in 1949. However, though these initiatives were taken by a Labour administration, it seems likely that a Conservative government might have adopted a similar approach, at least to the arts. Indeed in the period to the early 1970s there seems to have been a consensus between the two major parties about the state's role in social and economic planning, with the Conservative Governments of 1951 and 1964 continuing to fund welfare policies established in the immediate post-war period.

This broad 'social democratic' consensus involving acceptance of a mixed economy can be traced in leisure policy documents. *Leisure for Living* (Labour Party 1959) and *The Challenge of Leisure* (Kerr *et al.*, 1959) were produced by the two major political parties in 1959 (the only time leisure seems to have become an election issue, albeit minor). Both these documents advocate greater state involvement for similar reasons. Concern centred on the problem of youth. Whereas in pre-war Britain unemployment among the young represented a major issue; in the post-war period with relatively full employment, concern related to the growing affluence of young people, and the use of increased discretionary time and income in 'unwholesome' leisure activities, particularly those associated with the emergence of youth sub-cultures. 'Teddy-boys' provided the focus of 'moral panic' of the 1950s which resulted in a major review, the Albemarle Report, and subsequent reorganisation of the youth service. The commissioning by the Central Council for Physical Recreation of the Wolfenden Report, *Sport in the Community*, in 1957, was prompted in part by worries about Britain's poor post-war Olympic record. In addition to dealing with issues of Britain's international prestige, the document focuses on the need to sustain youth involvement in sport beyond the years of formal schooling. Although the report stops short of arguing that participation in sport is 'character forming' it does argue that there are considerable gains to be made both for the individual and the community by participation in sporting activity.

A primary policy solution recommended by Wolfenden, to widen participation and promote excellence, was the founding of a Sports Advisory Council. Although both Conservative and Labour parties supported this recommendation initially, and the Conservative Government subsequently appointed as first Minister for Sport, Lord Hailsham, in 1963, it was only with the arrival of the new Labour Administration that in 1965 the Sports Council was established.

The Wilson Government of 1964–70 is particularly significant in the development of post-war leisure policy, not simply for founding the Sports Council as an advisory body, but also for publishing two White Papers on leisure topics, namely *A Policy for the Arts: the First Steps* and *Leisure and the Countryside*. The former, published in 1965, revised the charter of the Arts Council, and reviewed policy directions in the arts; the latter resulted in the establishment of the Countryside Commission to supersede the National Parks Commission. Both policy initiatives aimed at reducing inequalities in leisure opportunities. Jenny Lee was appointed Minister for the Arts in the new Wilson Government in 1964, and sought to foster access to the arts rather than simply protecting the 'high arts', by amending the constitution of the Arts Council and by promoting decentralisation of provision which had become concentrated in the London region. Establishment of the Countryside Commission and funding for countryside recreation sites outside the National Parks (most notably country parks), represented an effort to make countryside recreation accessible to a geographically and socially more diverse public than had been able to take advantage of National Parks. The Labour Government also established a Select Committee of the House of Lords to review *Sport and Leisure* though this reported in 1973 during the Heath Government.

The Sports Council was granted executive status in 1972 by the Conservative Government, giving it the status of a quasi-autonomous nongovernmental organisation (quango) similar to the Arts Council. The

Countryside Commission, by contrast, remained a government organisation funded directly by the Department of the Environment. Executive status allowed the Sports Council, in theory at least, freedom from direct state control so that the interests of sport might be isolated from party politics; keeping the government of the day at 'arms length' from decision-making on how funds should be allocated by the Sports Council.

The final element in the system of public sector provision was occasioned by reorganisation of local government which took place for most of Britain in 1974. Reorganisation established new, generally larger, local-government constituencies with comprehensive service departments. In many cases, particularly in metropolitan and larger urban non-metropolitan districts, local authorities unified many leisure functions of local government within a single leisure service or recreation department. This fostered the professionalisation of leisure services in the public sector with, for example, the emergence of undergraduate and postgraduate courses servicing this work. New and larger facilities were also planned and built by many new local authorities, or were inherited from predecessors, as public spending accelerated. The House of Lords Report advocated adoption of the slogan Recreation for All , and argued that inequalities in access to provision in the commercial sector should be compensated for by public sector investment. By the time the growth of public spending had been curbed after 1976, much of the organisational and facility infrastructure of public-sector leisure services was in place, and Labour's White Paper *Sport and Recreation*, was able to argue that sport was 'one of the community's everyday needs' and 'part of the general fabric of social services'.

The voluntary sector in leisure in the post-war period also grew in importance. Increasing affluence during the post-war boom fuelled membership of recreational organisations such as the National Trust (which grew from 23 403 in 1950 to 244 844 in 1976), the Caravan Club of Great Britain (whose membership grew from 87 992 to 237 108 in the ten-year period up to 1976), and the English Golf Union (1960 membership 131 208; 1976 membership 398 170). Voluntary sector membership in some traditional recreational forms went into decline, for example, membership of the British Cycling Federation fell from 66 528 in 1950 to 11 264 in 1976. As Sillitoe's (1969) study reveals, however, membership of voluntary leisure organisations, like voluntary organisation membership in general, was uneven. Professional and managerial groups which were more likely to move around the country in pursuit of career advancement, seemed more likely to seek membership of formal organisations, since they lacked the local informal support networks of extended family and friends available to those who had lived all their lives in one community. With the breaking up of traditional working class communities in post-war housing development, particularly in the inner cities, whether by rehousing in high rise, new town, or new council estates, such traditional informal networks were eroded in many locations. These networks, which had provided welfare support (usually through the unwaged labour of women) and also offered opportunities for socialising or learning recreational skills, were replaced for some by 'privatised' entertainment in the home or by the development of voluntary organisations with more than simply recreational goals. Some care has to be exercised in making general claims, since in some locations, working class communities had flourishing networks of voluntary organisations servicing local needs. Nevertheless, growing affluence, middle class mobility and the break-up of working class communities seem to have fuelled development of the voluntary sector in leisure.

The commercial sector also responded to the growth of consumer spending-power, providing hardware for the rapidly expanding home-centred leisure market. Over the 1970s, television rental and licence revenue more than doubled, while tape, record, television and radio purchases grew by more than 80% (Patmore, 1983). Meanwhile some traditional out-of-home regular mass entertainment in the form of football match or cinema attendances declined dramatically. A survey commissioned by the BBC reviewing the changing use of time, from 1961 to 1975, suggests that considerably more time was spent on leisure both inside and outside the home by the end of the period, and that time spent on work (both paid and domestic) declined significantly as had time spent on 'civic duties' (Gershuny, 1980). Thus, when investment in the traditional, manufacturing industries in Britain was becoming considerably less attractive, leisure provided a tempting alternative, particularly for multinational capital which, with the pound weakened by Britain's poor overall economic performance, was able to make business acquisitions in the UK relatively inexpensively.

5 The Welfare State under pressure – post-1976

In the period from the mid-1970s to the late 1980s, which provides the focus for the rest of this chapter, there has been a radical shift not simply in economic structure and levels of unemployment but also in political climate and social values. Starting at 1976 may be somewhat arbitrary, since some changes were already evident before this date. However, one of the reasons for adopting this date is that in 1976, following poor economic performance and serious alarm about the value of sterling, the Labour Government approached the International Monetary Fund to secure a large loan to avert economic crisis. The IMF placed conditions on the granting of this loan, the principal one being that public expenditure cuts should be implemented. Acceptance of this condition by a Labour government ushered in a new 'economic realism', that public expenditure levels should be tied to the overall performance of the economy. Expanding state spending in times of recession was seen as placing an intolerable burden on industry in increased taxation and spiralling levels of inflation. This change in thinking was symbolic of acceptance that economic recovery was not 'just around the corner' and that the post-war consensus that had seen welfare spending grow under both Conservative and Labour governments was likely to disappear.

Unemployment had been growing in this country and in other developed economies since the 1960s, but the rise was faster in Britain, particularly in the late 1970s. Concern about the inner cities had also been registered before 1976, with the introduction of Urban Aid by the Wilson Government in 1969, and a number of subsequent policy initiatives under both Labour and Conservative administrations. However, it was in the post-1976 period that the issue became central with the White Paper *A Policy for the Inner Cities*, published in 1977. A series of serious urban disorders, beginning with incidents in Brixton and Toxteth in 1981, resulted in a range of initiatives such as the establishment of urban development corporations and increased urban programme spending, as well as projects specifically aimed at leisure such as Action Sport, and pilot schemes for the unemployed.

Political change was also evident, with major internal battles within the two major parties. The evolution of the parties in the post-1976 period was one of polarisation, with the more radical 'New Right' brand of Conservatism gaining ascendancy in the Parliamentary party, while the radical left, or the New Urban Left in the Labour Party were mounting a strong challenge to the 'moderate' Labour Parliamentary group through 'grass roots' politics in local authorities such as the GLC, Liverpool and Sheffield. The resurfacing of ideology in British politics and the politicisation of local government represent major features of the post-1976 era.

Perhaps the most significant change in the post-1976 period, however, was the change in social values. Post-war consensus had been constructed on a shared acceptance by major parties of the need for a mixed economy, with growing state provision of social benefits and state control over service areas to reduce social and economic inequalities. In the period after 1976 the basis of this consensus had been successfully challenged by the newly dominant group in the Conservative Party. The values of the New Right imply an increase in the freedom of individuals to pursue their own interests through the market, a reduction of levels of state spending and the range of state services, an increased responsibility on the individual for personal well-being, and a commitment to law, order and discipline. Since local government is a major provider of many welfare services such as housing, personal social services, education and leisure, the Conservative programme has brought central government into direct conflict with local government and has led to attempts to curtail local powers of spending, to rate-cap high spenders, and to force local authorities to open many service areas to competitive tendering so that private sector companies may manage services paid for by local government.

This new commitment to reduced state spending and emphasis on law and order has clear implications for the leisure opportunities of certain groups. Policing of black youth and the discouragement of activities which attract official disapproval (such as 'hanging around' on street corners or in shopping arcades) or the suppression of illegal activities (such as the use of marijuana which has religious significance for Rastafarians) provide examples of ways in which the state closes certain leisure options.

Table 5.1 summarises the historical development of each of the sectors described, providing an important context for understanding contemporary institutional arrangements.

QUESTIONS AND EXERCISES _____

1 Trace the historical development of a leisure form (e.g. a sport; sea-side holidays; novels) and identify factors which have shaped or influenced development from the early 19th century to the present day.

2 Select either a local voluntary sports organisation, or a professional football club and discover what you can about its origins. Who were its founding members? Why has it been able to survive (and flourish) while other similar organisations were unable to survive? What roles have women played in such organisations?

Provision for leisure in contemporary Britain

1 The commercial sector

In the period since 1976, leisure has formed an increasingly significant sector of private investment, performing well against 'traditional' manufacturing in return on investment. There are four key aspects of development of the commercial sector in the 1970s and 1980s which help explain the structure of this sector. These are:

Table 5.1 Historical development of leisure provision

Chronology	Illustrative social and economic policies	Illustrative leisure policies
c. 1780 – c. 1840 Suppression of Popular Recreations	1834 Poor Law Amendment Act	1833 Suppression of Blood Sports, 1836 Enclosure Act
c. 1840 – c. 1900 Erosion of *Laissez-Faire* Approach to Social/Economic Policy	1847 and 1867 Factories Acts; 1870 Education Act	1846 Public Baths and Washhouses Act; 1849 Museums Act; 1850 Libraries Act; 1852 Recreation Grounds Act
c. 1900–39 Social Reforms – Laying the Foundations of the Welfare State	1902 Education Act; 1908 Old Age Pensions; 1911 National Health insurance; 1934 Unemployment Assistance	1907 National Trust Act; 1909 Town Planning Act; 1919 Forestry Commission founded with recreation role; 1937 Physical Recreation and Training Act; 1939 Access to the Mountains Act
1944–76 Growth and Maturing of the Welfare State	1944 Education Act; 1945 Family Allowances Act; 1945 Distribution of Industries Act; 1946 National Insurance Act; 1948 NHS launched	1947 Arts Council established; 1949 National Parks and Access to the Countryside Act; 1965 Sports Council founded; 1968 Countryside Commission founded; 1975 White Paper *Sport and Recreation*
c. 1976 – ? The Welfare State under Threat	1977 White Paper *A Policy for the Inner Cities*; 1980 Local Govt. Planning and Land Act (curbs spending); 1982 Local Govt. Finance (rate capping)	1977/8 introduction of Sports Council schemes for disadvantaged areas and groups; Arts Council funding reduced 1979/80 with cutting off of some clients; 1982 Countryside Commission given quango status

Table 5.1 continued

Emphasis in role of the leisure	Emphasis in role of commercial sector in leisure	Emphasis in role of state in voluntary sector in leisure
Attempts to control and suppress 'disruptive' leisure forms	Small-scale entrepreneurs (publicans) replace squirearchy as patrons of popular recreation	Formation of organisations to control working class leisure, e.g. RSPCA, Lord's Day Observance Society for Prevention of Vice, Temperance League
State support (particularly for voluntary effort) promoting 'improving' leisure forms	Increasing scale of capital investment, e.g. rail, larger music halls, sports stadia, mass production of leisure equipment	Sector reflects paternalism of middle classes but control of leisure orgs, eroded by working class e.g. Working Men's Clubs movement
Increasing recognition of leisure as a legitimate concern of government in its own right	Importation of leisure forms from U.S., cinema, music etc. New technology provides leisure equipment, radio, cinema, car and m'bike. New investment attracted by the discretionary income of those in work	Institutionalisation of the voluntary sector with establishment of national organisations and pressure groups, e.g. National Trust, Central Council for Physical Recreation and Training, National Playing Fields Association, mass-trespass movement
Leisure added to the portfolio of welfare services, recognised as one of the 'community's everyday needs'	Demise of traditional manufacturing industries, growth of service sector. Growth of multi-national investment in UK leisure industries.	Growth of voluntary leisure orgs, particularly for the higher socio-economic groups, Break-up of working class communities

continued

continued

Emphasis in role of the state in leisure	Emphasis in role of commercial sector in leisure	Emphasis in role of voluntary sector in leisure
	Leisure hardware for the home and tourism major growth areas	fuels need for formal organisation especially in 'new' communities
Leisure as a tool of inner city social policy, (tourism) of economic regeneration	Concentration of leisure investment in few multinationals, diversification of companies across leisure sector; vertical integration	'Voluntarism'; the use of voluntary groups and as deliverers of services previously supplied by the state

(a) The significance of multinationals in British leisure; and the 'diversification' of large-scale capital investment in leisure industries;
(b) processes of 'market concentration';
(c) vertical integration;
(d) the significance of tourism to the economy.

(a) Multinational interests in the leisure industries, and the process of diversification

In Chapter 2, the typology of activity forms (Table 2.1) noted that the major commercial sector effort was aimed at activities oriented towards 'consumption' or 'passive production'. These activities include *social entertainment* such as dancing, or *individual entertainment*, as in the cinema, theatre or reading; *tourism* and holidays; *gambling and gaming* and *consumption* of leisure goods as in drinking or eating out. A brief review of the profiles of some major business interests in leisure reveals both their multinational nature and the diversity of their leisure interests. Grand Met for example, with pre-tax profits in 1986 of £372.9 million, operate in brewing (with five breweries and 4700 pubs), hotels (100 hotels in six continents with 37 000 bed spaces in 47 countries), betting and gaming clubs, international wines and spirits trade and manufacturer of exercise and fitness products. Ladbrokes operate hotels and holidays (home and abroad), have interests in racing and betting, retail interests (the Texas Homecare DIY chain), property and financial services. Granada, in addition to television (programme production and broadcasting, and rental business), own 50 bingo social clubs, seven cinemas and various multi-activity leisure sites (including theme parks). Granada's pre-tax profits for 1986 were considerable at £92 million. Among many 'smaller' leisure companies is a similar pattern of diversification and transnational operation. Brent Walker with 1986 pre-tax profits of £7.1 million have interests in Britain, the United States, Canada and Australasia, owning hotels and leisure centres, gaming clubs and sports stadia, Brighton Marina, and a film, video and television production company. First Leisure, formed in 1982 to take over the leisure interests of Trust House Forte, own piers, holiday and leisure centres, discotheques, squash, snooker and health clubs, bowling alleys and theatres.

The multinational character of companies and the diverse holdings represent insurance against two kinds of uncertainty. The first is the volatility of leisure markets which may generate high levels of profit, but are often based on fads and fashions subject to changes of taste and therefore representing high risk investment. Investing a large proportion of a company's capital in a single kind of leisure facility such as casinos may be less attractive than spreading investment across pubs, discotheques, casinos, hotels and leisure travel, even if casinos provide the highest return on investment. The loss would be substantial if gambling tastes or legislation were to change suddenly and all investment was locked into facilities for gambling. By diversifying in a range of leisure markets, the company is protected against sudden, unforeseen shifts in demand. The second form of 'risk insurance' for multinationals allows companies the opportunity of disinvesting in one currency (which may be losing value). The UK-based company 'Pleasurama' provides a simple and relatively typical example of diversification to spread risk. In 1986 60% of the company's profits of £42 million came from casinos. However, with concern over the volatility of the Middle East (a major source of gambling income) the casino operation transformed itself into a broader leisure company, purchasing four hotels in Britain and one on the Continent, while also taking over President Entertainments, a theme-restaurant company, and purchasing four machine-hire businesses. Similarly, Brent Walker's purchase of leisure and property interests in the French racing and casino town of Le Touquet in 1987 was motivated by similar concern to profit from the buoyancy of the leisure market while spreading the financial risk.

The multinational nature of leisure investments in Britain is evident in growing interest in theme parks. In addition to the theme parks of UK based companies such as Granada, a number of significant investments have been made by overseas companies. Center Parcs of Holland opened their first UK site in 1987 with a holiday village in Nottinghamshire, while the two biggest projects currently being developed for opening in 1991 involve substantial overseas funding. A £170 million adaptation of

Battersea Power Station will be financed by funds from the Far East and British banks, while the even more expensive £190 million Wonderworld, a glass-covered complex planned for the Corby Steelworks site is currently being developed by Clubmed, a French holiday company. The reuse of old industrial sites for new service industries neatly illustrates the restructuring of the British economy.

(b) Market concentration
Leisure markets provide an increasingly attractive proposition for large-scale investors. Ownership in leisure industries has become increasingly concentrated in the hands of a few large conglomerates. Market concentration is not just a feature of the hotel, holiday or brewing industries (Gratton and Taylor, 1987) it has also greatly affected the cultural industries of publishing, television and music production and distribution. The most spectacular example is Rupert Murdoch's News International Company which, in addition to owning the *Sun*, the *News of the World*, the *Sunday Times*, having holdings in Reuters and owning a number of newspapers in other countries (including the *New York Post*), also owns Fontana, Collins, Angus and Robertson and Granada Publishing, as well as Satellite TV, European Sky Channel, and other media and non-media companies. Similarly, Thorne-EMI owns music publishing interests, EMI, Columbia, HMV, Capitol and World Records, ABC cinemas, TE Screen Entertainments, Elstree Studios, Columbia-EMI-Warner Distributors, Pathe-Marconi, Thames TV, Thames Cable and Satellite. As has been pointed out elsewhere (GLEB, 1985, quoted in Bennington and White, 1986), in the UK, five companies control 62.5% of the record market, nine companies control 95% of the British paperback market, six film distributors control 90% of film rental, Thorn-EMI and Rank control the majority of cinemas, and three groups control 74% of daily press readership. Similar patterns of market concentration are evident in the various segments of the gaming and gambling market, with Ladbrokes, Granada and Mecca prominent.

(c) Vertical integration
There is some evidence of a growing tendency towards vertical integration, with larger leisure concerns becoming interested in the acquisition and management of small-scale sales outlets such as health studios, theme restaurants, snooker clubs and similar businesses which had traditionally been the preserve of the local entrepreneur. Ladbrokes and First Leisure have purchased a number of such units. This may be the result of improved information systems which allow swifter, more effective control of geographically dispersed outlets, rendering them more attractive to big business, or it may simply be a recognition of the profit potential of such businesses. The successful stock market launch and

immediate growth of the Pineapple Studio Group demonstrated the market potential of such activities, though its subsequent decline also warns of the dangers of leisure fads and fashions.

(d) The significance of tourism in the commercial sector
Growth of the commercial leisure sector is significant as an earner of foreign currency; a so-called 'invisible' export. For the period 1974–85 expenditure by foreign visitors in Britain has exceeded British tourist expenditure abroad except for the period 1981–4. The surplus of income over expenditure for 1985 was £574 million. Indeed, the service sector generally provides a positive contribution to the balance of payments, unlike manufacturing which has remained a net loss since the late 1970s. However, recent history shows that the tourist trade is volatile and especially susceptible to fluctuations in interest rates.

QUESTIONS AND EXERCISES ———————————————————

1 Enquire at a local major library whether information is available concerning company records. (A number of services, such as Extel and McCarthy's, index the nature of activities of major quoted companies.) Select three leisure companies which are cited in the stock exchange data on the financial pages of daily newspapers, and examine their recent activities to establish whether there is any evidence of 'market concentration', 'vertical integration', 'multinational operations', or 'diversification'. Explain your findings.

2 Review the financial pages of a quality newspaper for the last three or four months. What news items are cited for leisure companies? What do these items suggest about the relative attractiveness of investment in particular sectors of the leisure industries?

2 The voluntary sector

The size of the commercial sector is difficult to gauge and estimates of the volume of business vary because of the complex nature and difficulty of classification of company investments. However, estimating the size of the voluntary sector provides an even more difficult task, given the paucity of data. Organisations may have short or intermittent histories, be only semi-formal or even informal in constitution, and vary in size from those with half a dozen members or less, to national organisations like the National Trust (which claims a membership of over two and a quarter million). The study of voluntary-sector leisure organisations by Hoggett and Bishop (1986) reported in Chapter 2 was limited since it identified only a proportion of organisations which met leisure needs, excluding those which did not constitute mutual aid organisations and restricting itself to a relatively small area. One of the few attempts at a detailed and wide-ranging inventory of voluntary organisations, including those for leisure, is Newton's (1976) study of voluntary-sector political activity in Birmingham. Two points are worth emphasising from Newton's study. One is the sheer number of voluntary organisations in a major city such as Birmingham (some three thousand); the second is the large proportion (more than half) which had a primary or subsidiary leisure function.

The structure of the voluntary sector involves more than hobby, arts or sports organisations through which individuals cater for their own leisure interests. It incorporates a range of organisations which have primary goals other than those relating to leisure (e.g. Scouts and Guides) or which exist to provide leisure for people other than members. If we are to comment on the nature of the sector it will be important to identify the range of organisations which constitute it. Such organisations might be characterised by one of the following five categories:

- **recreation and sports organisations;** these are perhaps regarded as archetypal leisure organisations; interest groups which have grown up around a common interest among their memberships for a central activity. They represent what Hoggett and Bishop (1986) term 'mutual aid' organisations since they operate for members to meet leisure needs, rather than for any other social purpose.
- **community service groups;** where the group is 'client-centred and its membership is providing a service. PHAB clubs, which bring physically disabled and able-bodied people together, illustrate the nature of such groups (though perhaps strictly speaking this could be seen as a 'mutual-aid' group with two different categories of member). A further example is that of the Women's Volunteer Service, which concerns itself with leisure (and other) needs of the housebound.
- **community development groups;** where the theme of 'self help' is central: such organisations differ from community service groups in that though they may start as client or service-centred groups, their aim is self-reliance, to empower 'clients' to meet their own needs. Such a pattern is not unusual in community arts where groups may be established initially by community artists in a proactive manner but which then become self-governing.
- **community action groups;** such organisations focus activities on a particular 'cause', acting as a pressure group, often in relation to the

activities (or inactivity) of a public body. Groups may be issue-specific in their focus (e.g. a pressure group conducting a campaign for the establishment of children's play facilities) or may be rather more generic (e.g. a local sports council).

● **'social' groups;** those with 'socio-emotional' goals, but for which recreation forms an important element in activities. Groups may initiate community recreation projects (Working Men's Clubs not only promote leisure opportunities within their own premises but also sports teams, hobby and interest groups, competitions, trips to events, etc.). Organisations may well have potential for meeting leisure needs of groups which public sector provision finds difficult.

Voluntary organisations existed prior to the period of urbanisation and industrialisation in the form of political coffee clubs of the early eighteenth century, or more simply as informal groups such as church choirs. Indeed, voluntary groups have a considerable history in earlier societies such as ancient Greece. The emergence and burgeoning of formal leisure organisations in our society is, however, a function of the erosion of traditional ties of kinship and community. Voluntary organisations provide the medium for development and pursuit of common interests which might previously have been met by the extended family or the local community. Thus voluntary sector organisations became increasingly important when, rural, agrarian society gave way to urban, industrial society in the first half of the nineteenth century, or when working class urban communities in the second half of the twentieth century were shattered by housing redevelopment schemes, or out-migration to new towns.

In the period since 1976 'voluntarism' has become important. The concern of the 'New Right' is to 'roll back the state', to reduce state spending and state social provision. Increasing emphasis has been placed on voluntary organisations providing benefits for their members which the state can no longer afford to provide. However, the argument is not simply that the economy can no longer support the level of public sector provision envisaged in the early 1970s, rather that voluntary sector provision is *superior* to public sector provision in two important ways. Firstly it is argued that people will be much more committed to a facility or service built from their own efforts and, therefore, the service will be used more regularly. Physical facilities will be less subject to vandalism since they will be valued (and protected) by those who provide them. Secondly, voluntary organisations are more likely to be flexible in approach, responsive and innovative, since they are not bound by bureaucratic procedures which stifle the work of public bodies. Thus voluntary sector provision is likely to generate a wider variety of forms of provision than the public sector, which will tend to 'play safe' since it has to be accountable for the way public funds are spent. Support for a flourishing voluntary sector is also evident in some socialist commentators. Gary Whannel (1983) argues that the public-sector provision is predominantly controlled by professionals who, as middle class bureaucrats, are likely to be insulated from working class needs and preferences. The replacement of public sector paternalism with voluntarism is, Whannel argues, to be welcomed.

Unfortunately, voluntary-sector provision is likely to be uneven, and dependent on available local enthusiasm and expertise. As noted in Chapter 2, Bishop and Hoggett's (1986) review of voluntary sector provision in two contrasting locations, one suburban Bristol, the other, inner-city Leicester, demonstrated this. Their review was limited to the activities of mutual-aid organisations, but nevertheless, highlighted that inner-city Leicester had far fewer voluntary organisations, and these tended to have shorter histories, be less well resourced, and were likely to have been supported in some way through public funding. Nevertheless, these authors regard the range and diversity of the voluntary sector as its major strength, and argue that to maintain such diversity, or 'fragile pluralism', public sector support should be avoided, where possible. Government aid, particularly through the Urban Programme has aimed to foster voluntary effort in the inner-city. In 1986, £94.7 million was spent on inner-city social schemes, of which £31.3 million represented expenditure on sport, leisure, and children's play; more than the amount spent on social services in the urban programme and almost three times the amount spent on education. Government has ensured that much of this expenditure finances voluntary organisations. Redevelopment of city housing, the break-up of traditional working class communities and the influx of ethnic-minority groups within many inner cities has amplified the need for development of a voluntary sector structure in these areas, given the problems of poverty, unemployment, poor housing and low levels of amenity which such communities face.

Membership of voluntary-sector organisations has expanded since the mid 1970s, although as Gratton and Taylor (1987) point out, the picture is far from uniform. Growth exists, as one might expect, in organisations representing the elderly, with membership of three organisations, Pensioners' Voice, Royal British Legion and Age Concern having a 1984 membership of over 2 million, a 50% increase on 1971. At the other end of the age spectrum, youth organisations have recorded relatively small increases or significant decreases in membership. 'Traditional' youth bodies such as the Scout and Guide organisation, Girls' and Boys' Brigades and Cadet Forces fall into this category. However, youth club membership may have increased over the same period (a 110% increase in membership was recorded for the National Association of Youth Clubs, though this may simply represent wider levels of affiliation than previously). Among traditional organisations for women there was a falling-away of membership. Over the 1971–84 period, Women's Institute membership fell by 20%, Mothers' Union membership by 36%, and Townswomen's Guild by 33%. However, membership of sports organisations generally expanded. One notable exception was angling where membership of clubs declined by approximately 118 000 over 1971–85. Thus, despite the growth of privatised, home-based leisure forms, voluntary organisation membership continues to sustain an important role in the pattern of provision (including self-provision) in contemporary Britain.

QUESTIONS AND EXERCISES

1 Why do people become involved in voluntary sector leisure organisations? Make a list of reasons which you think might reasonably explain the willingness of some people to make efforts on behalf of such organisations. Are people from different backgrounds (or of different sexes) likely to provide similar explanations?

2 Select a local voluntary leisure organisation and undertake a survey of its membership seeking information on age, gender, occupation, ethnic identity and other data of significance. Present your findings and explain the significance of the patterns of membership identified.

3 The public sector

The role of the state in provision for leisure is complex and fragmented. As Travis (1979) points out, organisation of leisure responsibilities in central government involves four major departments (the Departments of Environment, Education and Science, Employment, and the Ministry of Agriculture, Fisheries and Foods). Critics bemoan the lack of an organisational framework to allow development of a coherent comprehensive set of leisure policies. Dennis Howell, the former Labour Minister for Sport, has consistently argued for a single Ministry of Leisure, suggesting that if government is serious about tackling inequalities in access to leisure then it will require policy machinery capable of achieving significant policy change. Other commentators, such as Ken Roberts (1978), argue that fragmentation is actually desirable because it militates against a 'Big Brother' approach to leisure policy in which government interferes with free choice by the imposition of centrally devised policies.

Notwithstanding these arguments, the fragmentary framework for state policies makes description and analysis of the public sector detailed and lengthy. For this text, commentary is restricted to consideration of major vehicles of policy in sport, the arts and countryside recreation, from the leisure quangos (the Sports and Arts Councils and the Countryside Commission) and local government. Commentary will focus on the post-1976 period, identifying changing rationales for state involvement in each policy area, changes and continuities in policies, and changing relationships of quangos and local government with central government.

(a) The Sports Council and Sports Policy

Establishment of a Sports Council was resisted by the Macmillan Conservative Government, apparently because of fears of government intervention in an 'apolitical' activity. However, when the Labour Government established a Sports Council with advisory status, the incoming Heath Administration provided a Royal Charter, which gave effective control over its budget in pursuance of policies laid down in that charter. This granting of executive status rendered the Sports Council a quasi-autonomous non-governmental organisation, in an attempt to insulate sport from party politics by appointing experts to a Council which would make decisions on resource allocations not on politically partisan criteria, but with reference to the 'needs of sport'. This quasi-autonomous status still exists in theory, but in practice, insulation from governmental influence has been eroded.

As we have seen, the Wolfenden Report which led to the establishment of a Sports Council was primarily influenced by two principal concerns; with sporting performance and with the problem of youth. Statements by both major parties also indicated recognition of leisure as an area in which government provision was desirable, simply as a means of enhancing quality of life. These extrinsic rationales (supporting provision because of its side effects) and intrinsic rationale (supporting provision as worthwhile in its own right) were echoed in both the House of Lords Select Committee Report *Sport and Leisure* and the subsequent White Paper *Sport and Recreation*. Indeed, the latter document argues that leisure provision is a need and, therefore, constitutes a necessary welfare service. However, addition of leisure to the portfolio of welfare services funded under the welfare state, came at a time when the ability of the economy to sustain public expenditure at levels established in the early 1970s was being questioned within the UK and by the International Monetary Fund. The 1975 White Paper is something of a watershed. After that the intrinsic rationale received less and less emphasis in policy documents. Expenditure on sport and recreation through grant-aid to the Sports Council was sustained and although local-government capital projects for leisure were curtailed by the end of the 1970s, local government revenue expenditure on sport and recreation was relatively stable.

Sports provision might seem to represent the 'luxury' end of welfare and therefore to be most likely to suffer cuts when central government is looking to reduce public expenditure. However, grant-aid to the Sports Council since it gained executive status, has not diminished in real terms, though it has decreased marginally in the late 1980s. Large-scale cuts in spending have, therefore, not been effected. Reasons for continued support for public-sector sports provision are related to claims made for sports provision in the inner city. The 1977 White Paper *A Policy for the Inner Cities*, and the Department of Environment report *Recreation and Urban Deprivation*, underline the claim that boredom and frustration of the young in urban settings can be alleviated by provision for recreation and thus the costs of policing inner cities and repair of vandalised property are likely to be greatly reduced by investment in recreation opportunities, particularly for young, unemployed people.

This claim has been made regularly in political statements and professional literature and yet there is no empirical evidence to support it. The rationale for leisure service, and sport in particular, has shifted from one which emphasised the state's role in reducing social inequalities by providing access for all groups ('Sport for All'), to one of economic benefit. Leisure and recreation, together with sport and play have emerged as major areas of government funding through the Urban Programme since publication of the inner-cities White Paper in 1977. It also resulted in reoriented Sports Council spending since the mid-1970s, with the emergence of funding for 'Areas of Special Need', 'Football in the Community', 'Urban Deprivation Grants', 'Pound for Pound Schemes', and most recently 'Action Sport'. One possible effect of this emphasis on reducing the costs of policing and repair is that groups who are recreationally disadvantaged but who are less likely to cause costly damage or problems of social order (such as women, the elderly, or the disabled) are more likely to be neglected in resource allocation.

Policy change since the early 1970s shows a number of trends. In addition to funding national governing bodies of sport and the management of national sports centres, the major policy aim of the Sports Council in the early 1970s was promotion, through grant-aid to local authorities, of facilities of 'larger than local significance'. Where a local authority had to provide facilities with a catchment beyond its boundaries, it was appropriate that local ratepayers should not bear the burden of all capital costs. Subsequent research, however, demonstrated that large-scale sports facilities did not always have an appreciably bigger catchment area than smaller-scale provision. By the mid-1970s, therefore, a complete reversal of policy had come into force with the Council only willing to grant aid to small-scale, local provision (except in special cases) which were seen as rather more cost effective than more grandiose forms of provision.

Throughout the 1970s user surveys of sports facilities demonstrated the dominance in usage of sports centres and similar public-sector facilities by certain groups, such as those with cars, middle class users, the young, and/or white males. This evidence together with encouragement from government to cater for disadvantaged groups in inner cities, persuaded the Council that provision of facilities was not enough, and that investment in personnel to act as animateurs, stimulating awareness and participation among target groups, would be more productive. The dominant emphasis on grant-aid for facility construction has given way to emphasis on investment in leisure workers, and small-scale grants to voluntary bodies operating in inner areas.

Concomitant with shifts in rationale for state intervention in sports and recreation and changes in policy over the decade, are changes in the Sports Council's relationships with central government. While establishment of executive status for the Council was an attempt to insulate it from direct government involvement in the Council's policies, subsequent events have undermined that independence. The principle of arms-length funding assumes that the government will allocate a global sum as grant-in-aid but will not attempt to influence the way it is spent. However, when the Callaghan Labour Government provided £802 500 in 1978, in mid-financial year for the Sports Council, it stipulated that the money should be used for alleviating urban deprivation and provided further monies (£1.7 million) specifically for schemes to provide links between football clubs and their communities (in part a response to football hooliganism). The Council, in accepting these funds and agreeing to implement policies decided by the government, assisted the breaching of their own independent status. Since the election of the Conservative Government of Margaret Thatcher in 1979, this erosion of independence has continued. The Department of Environment's representative on the Sports Council has been redesignated from 'observer' to that of 'assessor'. The assessor has the opportunity to represent the views of the Minister to the Council at its meetings, and now may no longer be excluded from meetings of certain Council committees. As Coalter *et al.* (1987) point out, the Chairman of the Sports Council acknowledged its dependent state in the 1981/82 Annual Report, remarking:

The Council's Royal Charter refers to the setting up of an 'independent Sports Council'. But in this modern world, which of us is independent? Not the Sports Council which is dependent on the government. . . .

In the same report with reference to the 'Pound for Pound' schemes launched by the Sports Council in response to the urban disorders of

1981, the Minister described the Council as 'acting for me on this initiative'. In subsequent public expenditure White Papers the Government has intermittently indicated its continued support for the Sports Council, while referring to policy programmes it wished emphasised.

The status of the Sports Council and its future role and policies are the subject of continuing debate. In an open letter to the Chairman of the Sports Council, Colin Moynihan, the Conservative Minister for Sport, argued for an even closer link between Council and government on social policy matters, with funding of governing bodies achieved through commercial sponsorship. Moynihan sought the Sports Council's response to a series of questions:

Should the Council concentrate its grant-aid more towards community provision and especially to areas and groups of special need like the inner cities, the unemployed and other target groups? . . . Should the Council develop more effective guidelines, advice and programmes for helping sports governing bodies to look more effectively to the private sector for funding, thus freeing more resources for the Council's own community programmes? . . . Should the Council disengage itself from provision of support for elite competitors and leave this to governing bodies, the British Olympic Association and the Sports Aid Foundation?

(Open letter from Colin Moynihan to John Smith, 19.11.87)

Whether or not reorientation of policy will be attempted or can be achieved is open to question, but the Minister's concerns are a reflection of just how far thinking on policy, rationale for provision and relationships with government, have changed since the granting of executive status in 1972.

(b) The Arts Council and arts policy
Although the Arts Council and Sports Council are both leisure quangos there are fundamental differences in their policy traditions. Whereas the Sports Council promotes both excellence and participation in sports, and funds are aimed at benefiting amateurs, the Arts Council is concerned solely with funding professional artists and fostering excellence. While the Sports Council's activities are supported by a social welfare and social order rationale, the Arts Council's activities are justified largely on grounds that they are culturally improving and generate invisible earnings through tourism. Apart from grant-aid to governing bodies of sport, the Sports Council's budget is largely one-off grants, or revenue grants with a limited time-span. The Arts Council, however, has traditionally provided revenue funding on an annual basis. Finally, the Sports Council is involved in some direct provision of sporting opportunities through its management of national sports centres, while the Arts Council has worked almost exclusively through its grant-aid

recipients to promote cultural opportunities. Despite these contrasts, since the mid-1970s the Arts Council, like its sporting counterpart, has been subject to changing emphasis in the justification for state support of the arts, in arts policies, and in its relationship with central government.

Despite the 'liberalisation' of arts policy in the Government White Paper of 1965 which emphasised promoting wider access to the arts, broadening the art forms promoted by the Arts Council, and decentralising provision from London, the Council faced a challenge to its legitimacy in the 1970s from the community arts movement. Community arts constitute a reaction to the promotion of 'high' or 'established' arts by the Arts Council, arguing that such art forms have no meaning or significance in the lives of working class people. Rather than pursuing a policy of making traditional high arts available to all (a policy of 'democratisation of culture') the community arts movement argues that arts policy should seek to offer all groups the opportunity to develop their own cultural expressions (a policy of 'cultural democracy'). Community arts tend to incorporate such activities as mural painting, community festivals, video, community photography and newspapers, drama and so on, but the phenomenon of community arts is not to be defined by reference to the activities it encompasses but by the way such activities are employed. For example a Greater London Arts Association Policy Paper describes it in the following terms:

Community arts proposes the use of art to effect social change and affect social policies, and encompasses the expression of political action, effecting environmental change and developing the understanding of and use of established systems of communication and change.

(Quoted in Kelly, 1984)

By this definition the value of community art is to be judged on the emancipatory criterion of its ability to effect positive social change rather than on any aesthetic criteria. The traditional 'high arts' are viewed negatively from this perspective since not only do they *not* challenge social inequalities, they may even serve to reinforce them by providing social status for those who have the 'cultural competence' to understand and appreciate 'high art' forms such as opera and ballet.

The way the Arts Council responded to this challenge was to set up a working party to monitor expenditure on this area of work in 1975–7. Debate about the merits of community arts raged, with some commentators asserting that such forms were only of artistic value if they weaned people on to more serious art forms. The legitimacy of the community arts protagonists' claim to promote more socially relevant art forms was also undermined by the fact that, like the traditional art forms which they rejected, community arts also represented minority interests for many of the groups at which they were targeted. The findings of the working party were unlikely to result in major change of Arts Council policy, since those who ultimately sat in judgement on the community arts critique, were the very group (the cultural elite) whose expertise and aesthetic judgement they sought to challenge. It is hardly surprising, therefore, that the funding of community arts continued to be a marginal activity for the Arts Council and that in 1979 the Council decided to delegate responsibility for support of community arts to the Regional Arts Association, arguing that they were of predominantly local significance and would, therefore, be better dealt with at local level.

The sting in the community arts critique was drawn not simply by the marginalisation of the issue, but also by the emerging public expenditure crisis of the late 1970s and early 1980s. This crisis presented another challenge to the dominance of the policy goal of 'democratisation of culture'. In the late 1970s it became apparent that a number of Conservative Party arts commentators associated with New Right thinking were advocating a reduction of state involvement in the arts. Although the formal policy statement by the Conservative Party in opposition, *The Arts: the Way Forward* (Conservative Party, 1978), promote a broadly traditional line of support for the 'high arts', policy statements by commentators such as the Selsdon Group (which published *A Policy for the Arts: Just Cut Taxes* in 1978), and Kingsley Amis (1979) challenge state subsidy. The argument was that public money tends to be wasted in purchasing and promoting experimental art forms, since arts administrators strive to demonstrate their commitment to the 'avant garde' by making purchases at inflated prices of items which would fetch little in the unsubsidised, private market place. Thus, it is argued, private patronage should be fostered which would allow goods to be realistically valued (in monetary and aesthetic terms), and such private patronage might take the form either of individuals purchasing works of art or supporting an artist, or of business sponsorship of worthwhile artistic events.

The Arts Council was sufficiently concerned about policy ideas promoted by the New Right for the Chairman to write to Margaret Thatcher, while she was in opposition, to ask for assurances that the arts would not be subject to cuts if the Conservatives were to win the 1979 election. In a well-publicised reply Mrs Thatcher wrote:

I do not believe in the present economic situation it would make sense for any government to look for candle end economies which yield a very small saving, whilst causing upset out of all proportion to the economies achieved. Public expenditure savings directed at the arts would come into this category . . . I can assure you that we will continue to support the arts . . .

(Quoted in Baldry, 1981)

Following the election, however, the Conservative Administration reduced financial allocation to the Arts Council for the then current financial year by £1.1 million. Subsequent squeezes on expenditure have led to a radical review of Council policy. The product of this review was expressed in the policy statement, *The Glory of the Garden*, which devolves responsibility or funding to the regions and increases their support, but does not introduce radically different funding priorities.

Devolution of decision-making about grant-aid might cynically be seen as a means of sloughing off a particularly unpleasant responsibility, and one made all the more difficult in times of reduced funding. In 1981 the Arts Council caused uproar in the arts world by cutting aid to 40 client organisations. This furore was in part responsible for the policy review which *Glory of the Garden* represents. Nevertheless, the review was also a way of responding to criticisms that the Arts Council is an undemocratically constituted body made up of vested interests in the arts world which were invariably served by the Council's spending. When an Arts Council member is to be replaced, a new member is appointed by the Minister for the Arts, usually from the 'arts world' and often with advice about potential candidates from existing Arts Council members. Robert Hutchison (1982) neatly illustrates the kind of incestuous relationship between the Arts Council and its clients which can result, when he points out that among those who had served on the board of the Council's major beneficiary, the Royal Opera House, were four of the seven Arts Council chairmen, and of 47 board members, 19 had direct Arts Council experience.

Regional Arts Associations, in contrast, incorporate councillors from local authorities in each region and therefore have an electoral link with the taxpayer who foots the bill for public-sector arts spending. In recent policy statements the Labour, Liberal and Social Democratic Parties have all indicated a wish to see membership of the Arts Council opened up to interests other than the 'high arts' lobby.

As in the case of the Sports Council, the 1980s have seen increased involvement by central government. Appointments have been widely seen as political, made on the basis of willingness and ability to carry out policies which are consonant with the government's wish to reduce reliance on public subsidy.

There has also been a shift in state involvement in the arts which is similar to that for sport. The notion that the arts are of intrinsic value and that government has a role to play in preserving and promoting them was implicit in the White Paper of 1965, and the support of successive governments up to 1979 for increased spending. This has given way to emphasis on the economic rationale for arts provision, based on the notion that investment in arts provision provides a return in the spending of tourists attracted to Britain. It is the extrinsic benefits of both sport and

198 _____ _Understanding Leisure_

the arts which have attracted limited approval of a government concerned to reduce state expenditure.

(d) The Countryside Commission

The rationale for state involvement in countryside recreation has also
undergone subtle change in emphasis over the last two decades. Establishment of the Countryside Commission under the Countryside Act 1968
to widen the remit of its predecessor, the National Parks Commission,
reflected the Wilson Government's concern that the National Parks were
providing for a relatively small proportion of the population (those with
access to one or more of the parks) and that such groups tended to be
those with private transport. Furthermore there was recognition that the
parks as environmentally sensitive areas were subject to increasing pressures from car-borne users. In order to improve access to countryside
recreation opportunities, and to protect the National Parks, the Countryside Commission was given the remit of fostering development of
country parks and other urban-fringe provision. The emphasis was on
conservation and access for recreation. However, by the time the Countryside and Wildlife Act came into force in 1981, the emphasis was on
protecting the interests of agriculture, rather than those of recreation and
conservation.

The Countryside Commission did not become a quango until 1982.
Prior to its change in status it was part of the Department of
Environment. The Sports and Arts Councils were primarily concerned
with consumption issues and therefore peripheral to the national
economy (except in the link between culture and tourism) and
government had been willing to forgo control of these. Policies for the
countryside, however, involve production (particularly agricultural and
extractive industries) and, therefore, are of greater economic significance.
This may explain the difference in status between the other leisure
quangos and the Countryside Commission before 1982. However, in
conservation and recreation policy goals the Countryside Commission
was always likely to conflict with other arms of government such as the
Ministry of Agriculture, Fisheries and Food, and it therefore sat
unhappily in the portfolio of responsibilities of the Department of
Environment. This clash of interests with government departments led to
a system of competing grants. Where the Countryside Commission (or
the Nature Conservancy Council) might seek to preserve a particular
environment such as a wetland habitat, the Ministry of Agriculture,
Fisheries and Foods might offer a grant for the reclamation of that land
for agricultural production (for other examples see Blunden and Curry,
1985). This conflict of interests across governmental departments was a
tension which surfaced when there was direct conflict between the
concerns of production and those of conservation. An important example

was cited in Coalter *et al.* (1986) when the Countryside Commission opposed the Department of Transport's scheme to route the M25 through an Area of Outstanding Natural Beauty. The proposal was subject to an inquiry of 1979 at which the Countryside Commission (a Department of Environment sponsored organisation) engaged legal representation to oppose the Department of Transport's case for the planned motorway route. Counsel for the Department of Transport attempted unsuccessfully to argue that the Countryside Commission had no right to present a case relating to an area outside National Park boundaries. This move failed, and subsequently a letter was sent by the Department of Environment to the Chairman of the Countryside Commission complaining of the waste involved in the Countryside Commission's use of public funds to engage a barrister to oppose the plans of another government Ministry. This kind of friction was a major factor in the decision of government to accede to the Countryside Commission's request that it be granted quango status.

Passage of the Wildlife and Countryside Act in 1981 and the circumstances surrounding this piece of legislation, provide further insights into the relationship of the Countryside Commission with government and the strength of conservation and amenity interests related to agricultural and landowning interests. In the early 1970s concern about loss of open moorland in National Parks was growing. In Exmoor, in particular, 25% of all moorland recorded in 1954 had been ploughed by 1972. The CPRE and the Countryside Commission placed pressure on the Labour Government to investigate and an inquiry was set up under Lord Porchester. The recommendations of Porchester led to the drafting of a Countryside Bill in 1978. The Bill incorporated powers to control ploughing of open moorland and other sites of conservation and amenity interest. However, there was considerable opposition to these proposals from the agricultural lobby, most notably the National Farmers' Union and Country Landowners' Association, and the Conservative Opposition delayed passage through Parliament sufficiently for the Bill to be dropped in favour of more urgent legislation. Within weeks of the Conservative election victory of 1979 the Country Landowners' Association and National Farmers' Union sought a meeting with ministers to discuss prospective legislation, and on 20 June 1979 the Countryside and Wildlife Bill was announced. This Bill differed from that defeated under Labour in that it promised voluntary agreements rather than government powers to control ploughing of moorland, and furthermore, in later amended form, it required conservation and amenity interests to compensate farmers for loss of earnings when a successful appeal was made against plans for agricultural development on conservation and amenity grounds. The Countryside Commission and the Nature Conservancy Council were placed in a position in which they could not afford to object successfully to plans since they would be unable to meet the cost of compensation for a large number of successful appeals. In their account of the passage of this legislation Blunden and Curry (1985) note that the Government prepared six consultation papers while drafting the legislation but did not consult the Countryside Commission until after the public consult:.tion period, while the National Farmers' Union and Country Landowners' Association were instrumental in development of the Bill. This represents clear evidence of the marginality of conservation and recreation interests and the 'incorporation' of agricultural interests in development of government policy.

Change of government in 1979 during a period of economic recession has resulted in a policy shift from earlier emphasis on improving access to the countryside and on conserving assets for future generations, to one of ensuring that agricultural interests are not unduly hampered by restrictions imposed because of recreation and conservation. Membership of the National Park Committees incorporates a high proportion of those with agricultural and industrial interests (McEwan and McEwan, 1982), and recent appointments to the Countryside Commission and the Nature Conservancy Council of individuals from the agricultural lobby, have confirmed this tendency. Thus, the very organisations which are charged with establishing a balance between competing interests in the countryside are finding it increasingly difficult to represent conservation and amenity interests in the face of powerful industrial lobby. Despite the fact that quango status should in theory have allowed the Countryside Commission greater freedom of action to pursue its own policy goals, the financial climate and the power of large-scale agriculture have combined to erode its effectiveness. This is compounded by the fact that where Countryside Commission grant-aid was intended to foster action by local government, the financial situation of local authorities is such that stimulation of spending has become increasingly problematic.

(e) Local Government
Although each of the leisure quangos is important in policy terms, none makes as substantial an investment in public-sector leisure provision as local government, which spent £1882 million in 1985/6 under the revenue budget headings of recreation and leisure. Local government is also experiencing significant change in its relationship with central government, though this change is more radical than that experienced by the leisure quangos. Progressively more stringent legislation has been introduced by the Conservative Government since 1979, with first spending limits and then penalties for overspending, and subsequently rate-capping imposed on local government. The object of these measures had

been the curtailing of public spending, but a consequence of the legislation has also been that local government power and freedom have been seriously eroded. Because the maximum local rate which can be set is effectively (though rarely directly) stipulated by central government, room for manoeuvre on the part of local government, in developing new service provision, is greatly restricted.

Legislation to take effect in the late 1980s will further accentuate this trend. The 1987 Local Government Bill seeks to place a requirement on local authorities to open up management of a range of services, or 'defined activities', to competitive tendering so that commercial-sector operators can operate public-sector services where they are able to do so at a greater profit or smaller loss than local-government managers. The Minister of State for the Environment has indicated that the government wish to add sport and leisure management to the list of 'defined activities'. Thus local government is experiencing reduced autonomy, is operating with reduced resources, and may well play a declining role in direct provision.

In addition to political and financial pressures originating from central government, there are a range of other pressures which local government has been facing since the mid-1970s. Increasing social pressure, particularly in the major conurbations, with unemployment, poverty and social order problems, has resulted in greater demands on local-government service provision. Economic pressures in areas of industrial decline have meant that for many local authorities, economic development has become a major concern. In many older industrial cities much of the Victorian infrastructure of roads, buildings and sewers, is reaching the end of its useful life, and environmental pressures may therefore require a local government response.

This increasingly hostile climate has fostered changing practices and these are reflected in changing approaches to leisure policy. The initial response to reduced economic resources in local-government leisure services has been to take one or both the following options. The first is to reduce costs and levels of service provision in order to achieve target savings. The second has been to maximise income by adopting a more entrepreneurial style of management. However, these are not the only policy trends in leisure. Failure of traditional approaches to facility management in the 1970s to attract a clientele representative of local populations has resulted in the growth of community recreation approaches to public-sector leisure management (Haywood and Henry, 1986). Community recreation implies giving local people a greater say in running local leisure services, a focus on disadvantaged groups, and a range of non-standard forms of provision, such as outreach work.

A further area within which local government leisure policy has begun to make a contribution is that of economic development. This is particularly evident in areas where the traditional industrial base has been eroded. Tourism is one sector which has attracted interest as a means of stimulating local economies. Bradford, for example, has actively sought to attract the second-holiday, short-stay market for week-end packages in the city, while Portsmouth has developed a marketing strategy based on its association with Britain's naval history. Tourism may not be able to replace jobs or finance, lost recently, but is seen as an area of potential growth by many local authorities. Leisure developments also play an important role in some environmental improvement schemes carried out in industrial cities. Redevelopment of docklands in Liverpool, Salford and London incorporates water sports and cultural facilities in an attempt to stimulate use of once-derelict areas.

These new policy developments represent a shift in rationale for local-government leisure services. Whereas in the early 1970s when local government experienced major growth the expansion of leisure services was seen as equalising access to leisure opportunities, particularly those whose interests were not served by the commercial sector; in the 1980s this 'social democratic' rationale has been undermined. Certainly community recreation represents an extension of concern with inequalities in access (though only perhaps for certain groups), but financial pressures have been such that services are often either reduced in scope or operated in a manner more akin to the commercial sector. Economic development, though it seeks to serve social needs by stimulating local employment, has a predominantly economic rationale. Thus the economic imperative has shaped leisure services in ways which represent a distinct break with earlier local government leisure policy traditions.

Conclusion

This chapter provides a framework for understanding developments in leisure provision in the commercial, voluntary and public sectors. These developments are in part a function of wider social, political, economic, and technological environments. In the following chapter how these environments might change in the future is explored.

QUESTIONS AND EXERCISES ───────────────────────

I Review the annual reports of the Sports Council, Arts Council or Countryside Commission for the last ten to fifteen years. What evidence is provided from these sources of significant changes in policy?

2 Through sources such as the Humanities Index, find references in the national press about the role and activities of the Sports Council, Arts Council and Countryside Commission. What are the issues raised and why are they important?

3 Through sources such as the local press, records of Council minutes, and interviews with local council officials, identify the range of leisure activities supported by your own local authority, and the nature of local debates about council investment in leisure services.

Further Reading

(a) Leisure histories
There are a number of books which focus on leisure in industrialising Britain, including Malcolmson (1972), Cunningham (1980), Bailey (1986) and Yeo and Yeo (1981). Those which review twentieth century leisure history are, however, relatively rare. Jones (1986) and Howkins and Lowerson (1979) cover the inter-war period, while Walvin (1978) spans the period 1830–1950.

(b) The leisure sectors
Material on the voluntary and commercial sectors is also relatively sparse. Tomlinson (1979) reviews the voluntary sector in leisure, while Hutson (1979) evaluates voluntary sector activity in a small section, Hoggett and Bishop's (1986) research is of central importance, representing the only major review of voluntary sector leisure activity.

In terms of the commercial sector Gratton and Taylor's (1987) book provides useful background data, while Roberts' (1979) analysis remains one of the few attempts to describe systematically the role of the commercial sector.

In contrast to the other sectors there are several texts on the public sector. Some are devoted to specific areas of the public sector – one of the leisure quangos or local government while others range across the whole sector. Sources which deal predominantly with the activities of the Arts Council include Hutchison (1982) and Baldry (1981), of the Sports Council, McIntosh and Charlton (1985) and Whannel (1983), and the Countryside Commission, McEwan and McEwan (1982) and Blunden and Curry (1987). Local government leisure services are the primary focus of Bennington and White (1986). Items by Travis (1979) and Coalter *et al.* (1986) range across the public sector as a whole.

See also Haywood (1994) which looks at community leisure and recreation.

LEISURE FUTURES

Introduction

For many writers the future is seen as 'the leisure society' while for others, this comes as a shock. Indeed, an important book by Jenkins and Sherman carries the title *The Leisure Shock*. In it they argue that people are not prepared for the impending future of leisure. The social networks they belong to, the political and educational institutions they have created, the belief in work and the work ethic, will make little or no sense in the future pattern of employment awaiting the next two generations. It is time to face the future and it is one where leisure and social change figure strongly.

The last three decades have been a period of crisis both for the world economy and world politics but particularly for the UK and the industrialised nation states of Western Europe. For the optimists, the state of crisis is temporary as the old industrial economies shift into a new phase of development, aptly described by the term 'post-industrialism'. The age of industrialism is over, as the textile factories and coal mines become museums and tourist locations for a wide variety of visitors. Post-industrialism means the disappearance of old patterns of employment, the growth in education and leisure and not least in information industries founded on computing and microprocessing. This shift into a 'service' or 'leisure' economy may be uncomfortable but such new technologies offer choices only dreamed about by previous generations. For the pessimists, the crisis is permanent and destructive.

While industrial society was progressive in the nineteenth century, by the late twentieth century it has literally run out of energy (particularly in the form of fossil fuels), as the costs of industrialism outweigh its benefits. Whether seen as a hiccough in the path of progress or as a major breakdown, social change has political, economic, cultural and ecological dimensions. These may lead to new work-leisure relationships, shifts in patterns and periods of unemployment, and to a growth in the informal sector or 'invisible economy'. Such changes will reverberate through the world economy.

It is not just the industrialism of the USA, Japan and Western Europe that has been thrown into disarray. So too has the second major sector of the world economy, the state socialist societies of Eastern and Central Europe. The Soviet block faces rapid economic liberalisation, problems with democratic political systems, especially bureaucratic planning structures and growing cultural changes which will fuel ethnocentrism, liberalise the arts and witness the growing infiltration of Western popular culture and consumerism. Such radical changes have been signified throughout the fragmenting and defunct USSR. China too has opened itself up to the influence of Western capitalism. During the 1960s the cultural revolution of the Maoists attempted to rid communist China of Western imperialism, whereas now it is possible to buy a MacDonald's hamburger in close proximity to the Square of Heavenly Peace. The 'third-world' of the newly industrialising nation-states have a central role to pay in the trajectory of the world economy. Although consigned to the periphery of power in the world economic system, certain parts of the third world are the locations for substantial foreign investment in primary industries such as steel, shipbuilding and manufacturing. It also provides the cheap labour-power to assemble consumer durables, linked to micro-technology which dominate Western leisure markets. Perhaps, more importantly, the third world is tied into the world economy not only by tourism and by a balance of trade which favours the industrial West, but also by a world banking system which is presently in chaos.

The nature of the relationship between the 'core' and the 'periphery' of the world economic system will provide a crucial dimension to any future developments. To take one example – multinational companies in leisure markets, such as Nike, depend upon third world labour-power and markets for raw materials for its production of leisure goods. Cheap 'trainers', leisure wear and music systems in the UK are possible because of the world economy and the third world's dependent position in it. Although many of their jobs have been exported overseas, the unemployed in Britain may still be able to afford 'trainers' and other leisure items made overseas. One of the many ironies is that unemployed youths may be wearing them as they participate in sports initiatives funded by the Sports Council or in employment schemes to help the unemployed in inner-city areas in the UK.

Given the long chains of interdependency in leisure markets and the resulting relationships that are generated, it is important for those studying and working within leisure industries, to comprehend the nature and the direction of the substantial changes taking place.

This chapter reviews three principal approaches to understanding leisure futures:

1 The first draws upon 'futuristic' analyses of the future, including literary accounts of how future societies might be organised.
2 The second studies the predictions and forecasts made by social scientists who substantiate their projections by analysing social science data drawn from a range of sources.
3 Finally, an overview of major theories of social change will be provided and their implications for leisure will be examined.

Visions of the future

Looking forward in a rear view mirror?

The title of this section appears paradoxical yet the bulk of 'futuristic' novels were written in the distant past and mirrored, or at least reflected upon, the societies in which the authors lived. It is also important to realise that many visions of a future ideal society often draw their inspiration from pre-industrial society. Somehow the clock must be turned back before industrialism.

In the area of choice that selects quietness over noise, smallness over largeness, slowness over speed, local over metropolitan, public over private means of transportation, individualised over standardised products, skilled craft work over mechanised mass production, rural over urban pursuits, home based over mass forms of entertainment, clean air and water over polluted skies and seas – in these areas it is clear that the range of choice has been diminishing very sharply.

(Kumar, 1978)

'Futuristic' visions percolate through all three sections, although critics would claim that some writers included here have been blinded by their visions. Supporters of futurism stress the need for such thinking and prefer to see utopianism as spectacles which sharpen and clarify the nature of leisure experiences in present society. In a sense, futuristic visions see further than conventional studies of leisure and of society. Such thinking serves three major functions:

1 To explore future alternatives.
2 To place the present in perspective.
3 To examine the necessary and pre-conditions for change to occur.

Utopian thinking (about an ideal future-state) serves to fire the imagination and is radical in the sense that it breaks with present institutions and arrangements for leisure by suggesting possible 'blueprints' for new arrangements. From this perspective, the traditional institutions of work, family and leisure do not *have* to be as they are presently arranged and therefore one crucial task is to rearrange these three major building blocks of society into another more human structure. Needless to say, the project of rebuilding society, institutions and people is not welcomed by all. The vast majority dismiss utopias as unrealistic and unworkable. Many writers, usually, though not exclusively of a conservative disposition, fear that utopian visions of new institutional arrangements often carry with them totalitarian schemes of political intervention and planning. Not least for utopian thinkers is the problem of moving out of the 'old' society into the 'new'. For anti-utopians, the cure for the ills of the old social order seems more unpleasant than the disease itself.

In sharp contrast with present industrialism, social order prevails within utopias; the economy yields goods in abundance (often secured by new technologies); the political system is not coercive and provides natural justice and the individual is free and strives to develop his or her skills, abilities and interests while belonging to part of a wider community – of both shared material and cultural resources. Utopian writers struggle to come to terms with three values, liberty, equality and fraternity, that were central to the French Revolution, so as to produce a harmonious balanced society. Two themes inside utopian literature are the perfectability of human nature and pleasure. Given the right economic, political and cultural conditions, individuals are free to develop themselves, and significantly, utopias are pleasant places to be – as a child, an adult or in old age. It is no coincidence that play and pleasure meet with freedom and self-development to produce the essential qualities of leisure, as defined by many philosophers of leisure (e.g. De Grazia, Huizinga and Dumazedier).

It is important to examine futuristic literature to assess its possible contribution to a deeper understanding of leisure and social changes. Each novel tells us something, if only by its silence, about the organisation of:

1 Work – paid employment, new technologies and class relationships.
2 Family – the social division of labour, gender relations and education.
3 Leisure – freedom and 'the licensing' of leisure forms; high and low culture.

Many of the key utopian novels offer Christian (Penty), or socialist values of different sorts (Bellamy and Morris), whereas others draw on a mixture of values (Huxley, Wells, Vonnegut). Recent feminism and feminist publishers have rediscovered utopian-feminist writers (Perkins-Gilman). It is an important task to examine the leisure and cultural forms envisaged by each book and read them as reflections of the social organisation of future society.

Not all visions of future society are optimistic about the development of industrialism. Some visions idealise the pre-industrial past and romanticise country life and recreations into natural, healthy, 'rural retrospective regret'. Other writers fear for the future and offer totalitarian visions of control and surveillance, usually aided by new technologies. Such pessimistic visions are commonly described as 'dystopias', in which work, family and leisure are permeated by state control and monitoring and the plot usually revolves around the struggle of one/two 'deviant' individuals fighting to gain some personal space and pleasure from the grey world of bureaucratic state controls. Huxley's _Brave New World_ and Orwell's _1984_ are good examples of such tradition and both books offer interesting insights into leisure and the licensing of leisure.

Some futures have been worked out on paper. Others have been tried in practice. There have been social experiments during the past two centuries, and their physical expressions remain today. Some were visions of industrial capitalists to provide a planned industrial urban community such as Saltaire, Bourneville or New Lanark. There have been feminist experiments to reorganise domestic labour into communally based kitchens, laundries and nurseries so as to release women's time for leisure activities (Hayden, 1981). Others have attempted to provide an integration of work, family and leisure as Ebenezer Howard's planned garden cities. More recently in the 1960s there have been small-scale attempts to provide alternative communities, or communes, that offer a solution to many of the personal, social and political problems facing modern industrial society. Many of the experiments were anti-urban, anti-capitalist and anti-patriarchy and many failed. What is important is not these 'successes' and reasons for 'failure' but rather how different experiments or alternatives constructed the social organisation of work, family and leisure. Certainly, many of the social experiments in the 1960s were directly inspired by the cultural messages of expressive revolution in the 1960s in popular culture, or what some have described as 'counter-culture'. New movements in cultural criticism, attitudes to sexuality, popular music and drug use (or abuse) found their expression in alternative communities. Critics of alternative communities may with hindsight point-up fatal flaws or contradictions in the rationales and organisation of such groups. What is important is how such experiments approached leisure and pleasure and constructed new leisure forms or practices – whether of a legal or illegal nature.

Although kaleidoscopes of leisure and pleasure are to be found in utopias and dystopias, either on paper or in practice, an important source of visions on future leisure is to be found embedded in mass or popular culture – particularly films. The cinema has played a crucial role in formulating and also reflecting leisure forms and lifestyles. There are obvious examples of films which directly address future visions of leisure – for dated examples: 'Rollerball', 'Clockwork Orange', 'War Games' and so on. More recent films such as 'Blade Runner' and 'Jurassic Park' spring to mind and the reader is invited to think of current films, videos and TV series that carry messages about leisure lifestyles. Perhaps much more important were films constructed around a particular lifestyle like 'Pretty Woman' and 'Three Men and a Baby'. Science-fiction films and literature also provide visions and fears of future developments. Indeed, science-fiction writing in the twentieth century has generated a wealth of accurate predictions about new technologies, health care and space travel. These provide many of the images and cultural artefacts for children's toys which reproduce and reinforce stereotypes of gender and consumerism. Yet, while fads and fashions change (who plays Space Invaders now?), science fiction provides an important source for leisure potential and repertoires.

Forecasting change

Having journeyed through some leisure fictions, this section examines the alternative leisure futures propounded by social science. The two approaches work within very different traditions. The utopian novel is pure fiction and usually draws inspiration from the past, utopian social science looks forward and is grounded in theories, models and complicated data profiles and analysis.

Even the most routine science-fiction writer has more imagination and understanding than was revealed in the technocratic, jargon-ridden, commission reports, think-tank projections, and social forecasts. . . . If we were indeed facing 'future shock', the most shocking thing about the future seemed to be its prose, and its ponderousness.

(Kumar, 1978)

As the above quote suggests one cannot automatically assume that social science will be more accurate or insightful about leisure futures than literature. How do social scientists go about planning, predicting and forecasting the future? What assumptions do they have and do these affect their views of the future and incipient developments in leisure? What questions do they ask about leisure, the changing nature of society and the future?

It is worth pointing out from the start that some writers feel that speculating about the future and future leisure trends are not activities that should bother social scientists. But if we put such objections temporarily to one side, the question remains why should we want to predict the future? The answer differs for different sections of leisure provision as outlined in Chapter 5.

1 *The commercial sector* requires market intelligence on which to base investment decisions. Knowledge of future developments in demographic profiles, household ownership, levels of disposable income, and lifestyles help the private commercial sector to invest wisely, develop the best recruitment policies and to locate plant/resources in the most economically viable region or nation-state. Marketing principles encourage organisations to think about product, price, place and promotion and therefore it is essential to have accurate knowledge about market structure and segmentation to facilitate marketing, service delivery and to encourage diversification into new markets.

2 *The public sector* requires data on future trends as a necessary feature of social and leisure policy and planning. Central and local government need such information to fulfil their statutory duties to provide education, health, social and leisure services as well as a democratic mandate to provide the legal, physical and economic infrastructure for the electors. As in the private sector, medium and long-term provision of such services require some grasp of the likely future developments in patterns of employment, the likely age structure of the population and the allocation of spatial and financial resources to conserve and develop the leisure potential of facilities in the public sector – whether it be in education, sport, recreation, tourism or planning the urban infrastructure of metropolitan areas.

3 *The voluntary sector* may be under less pressure to plan for the future, although future decisions by the state and the commercial sector can create massive obstacles or opportunities for voluntarism. Consequently, faced with the need for long-term financial security and to meet future needs of its members, the voluntary sector too must make investment decisions to meet future needs for resources – both spatial and financial.

Consequently, all three sectors are drawn for different reasons to think about the future and make provision for it, although the rationales underpinning their assessment of future leisure are different. Nevertheless, 'contingency' theories point out that organisations (in whatever sector) must gather some information about the environment they are working within and have some sense of impending change. The commercial, public and voluntary sectors must make assessments of likely future scenarios. Dominant groups inside organisations have some say in deciding what leisure markets to operate in, what leisure services to provide and how to meet members' and consumers' demands.

The rationale of planning or leisure, the form it takes and how policies are implemented varies from one state to another. The balance between the commercial, public and voluntary sector is the product of national culture, historic tradition, position in the world economy and not least political alliances and allegiances. Political ideologies spell out the strengths and weaknesses of certain planning practices and offer recipes for leisure policies, and define roles for the three sectors. The three major political ideologies of conservatism, liberalism and socialism have been outlined elsewhere (Henry, 1993) and some have attempted to deduce leisure plans directly from the key values of each ideology. A major task for all political parties is to design policies which clearly implement their own political preferences and those of the electorate. All three political ideologies mentioned have been challenged by feminist theories for focusing on the public world of politics and economics and ignoring the private sphere of the household and the family (and the dependent position of women in that sphere). Students of leisure should start to think about these four ideologies (conservatism, liberalism, socialism, feminism), and their many variants, and try to work out some guidelines for directing leisure policy and future practices. Clearly in Britain much planning and forecasting is carried out by providers such as the Arts Council/Countryside Commission/Sports Council and they are imperfect vehicles for transmitting 'pure' political ideals. The result is often that their policies and future plans are curious, uneven mixtures of ideologies and therefore they often reflect a 'social democratic' compromise. Such compromises become even clearer on closer reading of crucial policy documents, although shifting political alliances are clearly discernible too.

It is easy to point out the pitfalls of making predictions in the social sciences. It seems that natural science can explain facts because it can isolate the key factors that cause changes to take place. By being able to isolate and identify causes, scientists can provide explanations of what has happened and therefore can predict accurately what will happen in future circumstances.

The crucial difference with social science is the latter's failure to provide precise explanations of events. Because social theorists cannot explain the causes of social events (e.g. revolutions, wars, leisure styles) they are unable to predict when these events will occur and how they will subsequently develop. Another related problem is that the 'facts' at issue are social facts already 'interpreted' by people living in society so that social scientific predictions may be rendered null and void if people are aware of them and accordingly change their actions. Social scientists point to this paradoxical feature of social life as a 'self-fulfilling prophecy'; to paraphrase G. H. Mead – if men define circumstances as real, then they will have real consequences. It is no accident that multinational media organisations spend millions to promote 'new bands' and 'new releases' so as to ensure their subsequent success.

Leisure researchers have access to reliable knowledge about existing forms and levels of participation in leisure and these can be correlated with other socio-economic factors (e.g. occupation, gender, age, race, etc. – see Chapter 3). Forecasting means 'making intelligent assumptions and extrapolations about how the parameters of the future world of leisure will change' Elson (1982). It is essential to separate reliable data (e.g. demographic profiles) from variable data (e.g. changing economic, political, personal factors) which must be added to 'forecasting' to make a 'prediction'. For example, can one assume that those buying a car in the next ten years will have the same leisure profile as present car owners? Will the growing proportion of elderly in society generate different and more varied lifestyles than the present elderly, who may function as a vanguard in generating new leisure lifestyles, opportunities and resources? It is also important to remember that hard, reliable data (e.g. household size) are a function of social changes and choices. Members of the present generation of 18–30 year olds may choose to marry and remain childless because they are keen to pursue a lifestyle in which leisure plays a central part, which will be jeopardised by childcare.

Futurologists argue that 'modernity' (i.e. present industrial society) is under pressure from a variety of sources. Such pressure can be subdivided into six major areas:
(a) *demographic changes*: diversity in household structure; childless marriage and small families; dual-career families and leisure lifestyles; single parent families; an ageing population, particularly those in retirement.
(b) *economic changes*: 'stagflation'/inflation in the world economy; changing relationships between the core and periphery of world consumption and production; divisions of incomes within nation-states – growing real incomes for some, poverty for others; inequalities in work, employment and the informal sector.
(c) *political changes*: change in world politics and defence alignments (change in the relationship between central/local government in terms of funding/responsibilities, etc.). Change in relationships between the state, the market and citizen welfare; in nation-states divisions between the public and private spheres.
(d) *cultural changes*: secularisation – the marginalisation of religious beliefs and the growth of individualism, consumerism. Changing attitudes to work, domestic labour and gender divisions, changing attitudes to health/diet/sexuality.

(e) *ecological changes*: the social limits to growth – problems of pollution/conservation/access; the growth of cities, urban processes and transport systems; cost of energy production and nuclear power.
(f) *technological changes*: innovation and growth in new technologies – information technology, cable communications and satellite systems; problems of surveillance and control.

This section introduces the data bases used by futurologists to construct various leisure scenarios, depending upon the assumptions they introduce into their models, and the way in which the key elements or factors are integrated. Previous attempts to predict future leisure patterns have floundered because of faulty extrapolations. When leisure forecasting took off in the 1960s, built into the models were assumptions of even population growth, car ownership and patterns of participation in existing leisure forms at current rates, yet predicting rates of participation in leisure and, hence, demand is a notoriously difficult exercise.

Veal (1987) stresses five major measures of leisure (a) participation rate, (b) number of participants, (c) volume of activity, (d) time, (e) expenditure. He then proceeds to outline nine techniques of forecasting:

(a) speculation – personal insights;
(b) trend extrapolation – current rates of participation;
(c) respondent assessment – preferred future choices of interviews;
(d) the Delphi technique – panels of experts ranking likely future events;
(e) scenario writing – building assumptions into simple models;
(f) comparative method – analysis of one society against another developed one;
(g) spatial models – cost benefit and gravity models of access;
(h) cross-sectional analysis – analysis of leisure participation amongst members of society;
(i) composite methods – usually based on analyses of trends in leisure expenditure.

Students can turn to Veal's book for very brief summaries of the limited amount of literature which has developed in the 1960s and 1970s in the field of leisure forecasting. Perhaps the bulk of speculation has been about recreation, particularly in rural areas and has developed for the USA and Australia to a lesser extent. The results of such forecasting have been poor and even when predicting trends in the right direction, have hardly been earthshattering with their level of insight into leisure and leisure participation. Nevertheless, certain general conclusions may be drawn from the various attempts tried to forecast futures:

(a) successful forecasting requires a mixture of quantitative data on demographic profiles, class, disposable income, car ownership, but that

must be matched to cross-sectional qualitative data about leisure lifestyles and subcultural styles in leisure.
(b) long-term forecasting seems particularly hazardous and at best must
be linked to a variety of alternative future scenarios based upon
different assumptions about economic growth, political control and
leisure time and expenditure.
(c) forecasting models that pay little attention to the supply of leisure
facilities, which naturally can crucially stimulate levels of demand,
appear doomed to failure.
(d) increased research is essential in the economics of leisure, especially
into the influence of prices of leisure commodities and services. Such
data need to be related to cross-sectional surveys so as to gain
insights into how increases and decreases in disposable income affect
leisure choices, consumption and participation.
(e) it is important to embark on long-term re-studies of such forecasting,
so as to examine systematically the fit between predictions and reality
of leisure experiences. Retrospective analysis may encourage forecast-
ers to develop more complicated models for predicting leisure and
thereby avoid previous errors and glaring omissions. Of course, as
Keynes noted, in the long run we are all dead, yet medium-term
decisions must be made by those working in the leisure industries. It
seems reasonable to multinational companies to build theme parks,
develop particular tourist locations, encourage 'leisure' fashions, to
invest in satellite TV systems, develop multi-million pound,
multifunctional shopping centres and so on. Are these best understood as demand-led or supply-led leisure provision? Will they be
spectacular successes as was the case with packaged foreign holidays
or will they be failures such as skateboarding? What sorts of leisure
forms and activities will thrive in the future and what sorts will
stagnate or fail? To whom will the activities appeal and how will they
be developed?

Rojek (1985) discerns four major tendencies in modern leisure –
privatisation, individuation, commercialisation and pacification. Privatisation stresses that the home is the major site of leisure experience.
Individuation refers to the processes that demarcate the individual as a
specific person from others. Commercialisation means that leisure is increasingly run on business lines for profit and not need. Finally,
pacification is the product of a complex division of labour within which
individuals are expected to exercise self-control over passionate emotions
and physical violence. (This view of leisure stresses passivity and is
symbolised by the personal stereo.) Leisure and leisure consumption legitimate capitalism (because it *can* supply leisure goods and free time)
but capitalism equally denies human freedom from want and promotes

scarcity as it divides material and cultural resources, along the structures of class, gender and race. Not all social theorists are as gloomy about the constraints that mass society exercises; there is always some space for human choice. People, with personal audio systems, can listen to the radio on it, or to their favourite tapes (or other people's) or learn a foreign language or listen to background music as they travel on the train/bus/cycle, roller boots or on foot. One can always not buy the stereo or not use it. Rojek's pessimistic analyses of the tendencies in leisure seem a long way from the technical pursuit of forecasting and predicting trends from existing rates of participation. It is therefore time to look briefly at the theoretical assumptions that are built into and therefore colour social scientists' views on leisure and the future 'leisure society'.

4 Theorising change

This section provides the briefest outline of important theories of society and of social change. Most books tend to set out two major theories of social change. First, an optimistic 'post-industrial' view of progress and innovation and this is subject to a pessimistic critique which points out the problems and divisions in advanced industrial societies. The approach favoured here is to outline three major theories of society and social change. This is to highlight the complexity of arguments offered by different writers, which are sometimes lost in the debate between post-industrialists and their critics. Nevertheless, each of the three traditions outlined here carry many variations and overlaps. Some writers are more interested in leisure than in social change and vice versa, yet all can contribute to an exploration of social changes and their direct and indirect consequences for leisure and leisure provision.

The three traditions can broadly be labelled 'post-industrialism', 'mass society' and 'radical alternatives' (Marxism/feminism). The background assumptions and key arguments behind each tradition are to be found in Ken Roberts' seminal work, *Contemporary Society and The Growth of Leisure* (1978). This book is somewhat silent on feminist perspectives and Rosemary Deem (1985) *All Work and No Play?*, and Eileen Green et al. (1990) *Women's Leisure: What Leisure?* provide a fuller discussion of leisure and how it is differentially experienced by women in present society. Clarke and Critcher (1985) *The Devil Makes Work*, attempt a synthesis of Marxist and feminist perspectives on leisure and culture in Britain.

Social theory has attempted to understand the changing relationships between work, family and leisure and to capture the long-term shifts in the nature and structure of society. Perhaps predictably, writers develop different terms to refer to society such as industrial (e.g. Durkheim), urban (e.g. Wirth) or capitalist (e.g. Marx). Others are happier with compound terms such as urban-industrial, industrial-capitalist and so on to do justice to the profound changes that have unfolded. Feminist theory has exposed these gendered perspectives on the world of industry and politics and argues that society is best described and understood as 'patriarchal', i.e. the rule of men over women, of which, 'industrialism' or 'capitalism' is but one phase.

The reason for digging at the roots of social science, is that one of its central purposes has been to understand the long-term changes or transformations taking place and their implications for people's lives, and not least, their leisure. Throughout earlier chapters there have been numerous examples of how leisure has been changed by these wider processes in society. There is also substantial literature on the changing forms in the nineteenth century, e.g. Malcolmson (1973); Cunningham (1980); Bailey (1978); Walvin (1985) and the ways in which leisure forms reflect wider changes in society. Current and future leisure forms and activities will be as much an expression of wider changes in society as has been the case in the past. Consequently, one way of understanding these three traditions in thinking about leisure futures is to realise that they grow out of social theory's concern with understanding social change.

There is only sufficient space here to present the three views of leisure futures in tabular form. The particular arguments about developments in leisure are available from the writers listed in Table 6.1.

These three perspectives offer different predictions about future society and the changing nature of leisure. There are many ways of evaluating these general theories:

- What do the theories choose as the key trends or tendencies in leisure and in society?
- What are the precise mechanisms of change? Are they to be found inside society or are they somehow neutral or external to society?
- Will the changes envisaged be evolutionary or revolutionary?
- Which groups will support/resist which changes?.
- How do the theories relate to political ideologies and the likely distribution of power and resources in the future?
- Do the theories omit key features that may play a significant role in future developments?
- What evidence is there that these theories can be realised in practice?
- Which tradition do you find most acceptable? Most realistic? Most unacceptable?
- Can the theories explain and predict all leisure forms or do they only make sense of particular leisure activities?

Conclusion

This chapter has explored different visions of leisure futures. One has been gleaned from futuristic novels. A second vision comes from social science forecasting and predictions in the field of leisure. A third is derived from mainstream sociological theories which focus on social change. Many of these visions are contradictory and make different predictions about future developments both in leisure and in society. Whether one treats these leisure futures as optimistic, realistic or pessimistic depends on a variety of factors including one's personal biography and not least one's understanding of leisure and the nature of society.

QUESTIONS FOR DISCUSSION AND RESEARCH ————

1 Examine the assumptions built into the long-term strategies of such leisure quangos as the Sports Council; Countryside Commission; Arts Council; Tourist Boards, as illustrated by in-house publications.

2 Imagine yourself as an expert consultant in leisure futures; what key factors would you build into your advice about future developments (say during the next 20 years) in leisure activities? Would your advice differ if the organisation was drawn from
   (a) commercial sector?
   (b) public sector?
   (c) voluntary sector?

3 What skills do leisure professionals need to develop in the next ten years?

4 Which major writer do you find most convincing in analysing leisure futures?

5 Conduct interviews with a variety of organisations (private/public/voluntary sector) to discover their medium/long-term plans, and how these plans are to be put into practice?

6 Are there any convincing arguments to support a convergence of leisure futures with the second and third world developing along the same lines as American Society?

Further reading

Tony Veal (1987) *Leisure and the Future*, offers a comprehensive summary and reference point for major writers on future society and techniques of

Table 6.1 Perspectives on leisure futures

	Post industrialism	Mass society	Radical alternatives (Marxism/Feminism)
Key writers	Bell, Toffler, Stonier	Leavis, Tourraine Early Frankfurt School	Gorz
Economy	Growth in Market privatisation; abundance	Growth in State Intervention and surveillance	Redistribution of wealth income – changing patterns of work, employment, and domestic labour
Politics	Pluralism – increased individualism and diversity	State Control authoritarianism, planning	Socialist/Feminist Egalitarianism
Work	20 hour working week, service economy	State sponsored 'work'/and leisure schemes; cuts in welfare	Work and domestic labour recast
Driving mechanism of change	New technologies biotechnology; automation; IT	Mass culture – Americanisation of popular culture: false needs and consumption	Class/gender struggle
Leisure	Leisure society – diversity of life-styles, experience, innovation	Mass society – privatised mass passive leisure	Socialist/feminist society work and income are separated

forecasting; the key writers dealt with in Table 6.1 are to be found in the general bibliography.

Leisure consultants such as MINTEL and the Henley Centre for Forecasting are interested in predicting new market opportunities for leisure industries. The PSI Report (1991) *Britain in 2010* represents the most interesting overview of the future on a local, national and global level for the UK. It examines the changing world economy, political and environmental pressures, as well as demographic and social policy issues facing the UK.

LEISURE AND SOCIAL THEORY

This chapter reviews various contributions made by social theory to an understanding of leisure and leisure forms. As in the world of the theatre, reviews scarcely ever please everyone. Reviewers are accused of bias and favouritism, of omission and misunderstanding, of intellectualism and undue criticism. It is, therefore, no easy task to pick out the key writers or debates which have significantly informed an understanding of leisure. The previous chapters and their contents contribute towards a leisure theory. But such a task is daunting since textbooks on leisure draw upon a wide variety of disciplines to come to grips with the diversity of leisure forms and experiences. All the main social sciences are out in force – psychology, sociology, geography, economics and history, as well as more recent fields of study such as social policy, political economy and urban studies. Each discipline or field of study can muster its own influential writers and internal debates.

It is not the claim of this chapter, nor of the book as a whole, that one single discipline can understand or explain leisure. Each discipline has and will make important contributions to the broader task of developing social theory and research. The primary focus of this present book has been on understanding the *social* dimensions of leisure. The questions posed by each chapter – what is leisure? Who participates in leisure? Where are leisure spaces? Who provides leisure? What of the future – are all broadly conceived of as *social* questions. Such questions demand an understanding of people and of the context within which social relations of leisure take place. One of the central problems of social theory has been to link people with the society in which they live and many of the writers mentioned in this book have worked within that tradition. Raising questions about the social dimension of leisure may mean a break with traditional research into some leisure forms (e.g. sport) which have been conceived primarily as physical rather than social interaction. Research into sport has focused on performance not participation, with physical science perspectives (e.g. biomechanics) dominating the social sciences.

The aim of this chapter is to find out what social theory can tell us about leisure and to evaluate the arguments of those writers who claim to have developed a 'leisure theory'. There is need for some caution – finding one's way about leisure theory mirrors neatly some of the forms of outdoor recreation. For some, getting to grips with social theory is a 'wilderness experience' as one disappears into an alien, hostile environment, lost in a landscape of books written predominantly by 'dead Germans'. For others, social theory becomes a whistle-stop tour of important sites of knowledge where slivers of key text are consumed, then one is marched back on to the bus to travel to the next destination. Another response is to trust in one guide or single textbook and depend upon that authoritative source to make sense of what is happening, just as one might depend upon Wainwright's books for walks in the Lake District. Finally, for the few, social theory becomes an aesthetic landscape where one appreciates the form, scope and the powerful insight of theories, research methods and findings. All these responses to social theory are equally valid and yet some are more rewarding than others.

What follows is not a comprehensive survey of each particular contour but key writers have been chosen to provide some orienteering skills to assist in finding one's way around the intellectual terrain of social theory (if we dare prolong the analogy with outdoor recreation). The chapter divides into two parts. The introductory section maps out the major contours in social theory; the second half examines strategies for coming to terms with the main features and offers some innovative techniques for getting round the course.

Before starting out, it is important to realise that there is no clearly defined tradition of 'leisure theory'. What counts as 'leisure studies' and 'leisure theory' varies from one nation-state to another. For example, in the UK 'leisure' and 'theory' have remained quite distinct, with one or two major exceptions. Why should leisure be undertheorised in this way? This lack of theory finds its obvious expression in the four separate definitions of 'leisure' introduced in chapter one. Each definition is embedded in a broad theory which brings together people's experience and the context of leisure in a particular way. Each definition of leisure implicitly offers clear understanding of the social i.e. the relationship of people and society.

One explanation for the absence of leisure theory is that leisure is a late arrival to a field of studies dominated by other traditions of research. Writers have been much more concerned to understand other major institutions in society – those of work, organisation, politics and family. For example, the nature of work and its distribution has long been the focus of major social scientists and leisure is traditionally studied *in relation to* work and occupation. Consequently, leisure is left-over and peripheral to mainstream theories which have been developed while viewing the 'richer' and more 'important' themes of work, politics and family. Key writers such as Marx, Durkheim, Weber and Freud provide little direct guidance to later theorists applying their perspectives upon people and society to make better sense of leisure.

It may be that the well-worn theories developed on other topics need substantial rethinking when applied to an understanding of leisure. Indeed, some writers look to leisure theory to generate theories, concepts and research which will make substantial contributions in mainstream social science.

A second reason why leisure is left over and left out of social theory stems from its own history. Leisure is very much a product of nineteenth-century capitalism and conceived in terms of 'free-time', (as outlined in Chapter 1). E. P. Thompson has traced the shift in history from thinking of 'time-as-past' to thinking of 'time-as-spent'. Leisure becomes associated with free-time and more recently, with the production and consumption of mass markets around the home, through the mass media and the culture industries. Leisure lacks a distinct history of its own. There are some detailed histories of leisure forms but few which relate leisure to change in social structures and processes. Despite one or two notable exceptions, leisure, like gender, is hidden from history and hidden in it.

A third and final reason why leisure is undertheorised lies in the complexity of understanding 'leisure' and 'leisure forms'. This book has begun to explain this complexity and has introduced a classificatory scheme in Chapter 2. Many have attempted to define leisure and then have proceeded to study it. Others have contented themselves with equating leisure with a commonsense understanding of free-time and then studied the patterns of participation in free-time activities. Consequently, there is a strong tradition of taking leisure and leisure forms for granted, and for studying the policy and practical concerns generated by leisure participation, usually in the public sector.

It may be of little comfort to know that leisure is both 'problematic' and is undertheorised. It is however, an essential starting point as these two features help to explain the debate within 'leisure theory'. In Chapter 1 it was suggested that the Latin root of leisure, 'licere' implies two major dimensions of leisure – the freedom to choose (licentiousness) and permission to choose (licence). These positive and negative elements in the definition give a useful clue to dividing social theorists into two major traditions or perspectives. The first tradition theorises leisure as freedom while the second treats leisure as control. In order to clarify the differences between the two major perspectives they are presented here as direct opposites. They will be presented as two different, mutually contradictory, ways of thinking about people and society and their relationship to leisure. Indeed, in an influential article written in 1970, Alan Dawe defined them as two sociologies – one of action and one of structure. These terms are flawed but are useful for introductory analysis of these two competing major traditions of thought. They provide the major physical contours which must be recognised and negotiated, if there is to be any hope of getting round the course.

Action: leisure as freedom

In this tradition leisure is seen to be distinct from all other aspects of life. It is non-serious, non-productive and emancipatory. It is defined as relaxation from work and as human self-expression. Leisure then is an end in itself; it is intrinsically satisfying and demanding.

This approach suggests that any attempt to attach functional labels on leisure activities must be frowned upon, as this subverts the nature, the internal logic of leisure – whether it be active (games, sport, recreation) or more passive forms of consumption (music, theatre, mass media). Leisure is seen as a sacred realm that must be preserved and there are clearly defined rules that preserve the reality or more properly the 'unreality' of leisure. Writers in this tradition fear that the amateuristic accumulation of pleasure is under attack by corrosive processes of commercialism, competition, bureaucracy, nationalist ideology and so on. It considers that the gratuitous challenge and the experience of free-time activities underpin the meaning and attraction of leisure forms. Consequently, writers celebrate the form rather than the function of leisure.

An important assumption of this perspective is its focus on the individual and his or her freedom to choose particular leisure forms and activities. Whereas children play, leisure is the quest by adults to take 'time-out' from serious concerns of work, politics and culture. Leisure becomes synonymous with pleasure and society is made up of a variety of 'taste publics', actively pursuing their chosen leisure form. In this view individual leisure choices produce spatial and cultural consequences (both intended and unintended) but there are no shared criteria for valuing the diversity of leisure pursuits. There are no grounds for suggesting that high culture (ballet versus bingo), or active recreation, is better than passive (playing is better than spectating).

Individuals are free to choose which clubs they wish to be members of, and which leisure services and commodities they wish to consume.

To conclude, this perspective treats leisure as freedom. Its central focus is upon human agents, i.e. on individuals who actively choose and give meaning to leisure forms and express themselves within these diverse forms. People control their own leisure. This stress on individuals, particularly in the consumption of leisure, finds the fullest expression in a collection of writers whose work can best be captured by the category 'leisure studies'. Although perhaps resisting the label themselves there are many American, Australian and British writers who exemplify this approach.

Structure: leisure as control

If the 'leisure studies' tradition celebrates form over function, a structuralist perspective emphasises function over form. Structuralism starts from the power of society over individuals. Control lies not with the individual and his or her leisure choices but rather with the existing institutional structures which constrain choice and direct leisure into legitimate forms. Structuralism usually draws upon society as a system in which each part maintains and supports the whole. Consequently, leisure functions to preserve the existing social order. Society is often presented as an external coercive and collective fact which controls the individual's instincts and desires. The individual is integrated into existing structural arrangements and is seen as a 'cultural dope' who matches the present social order. Such a structuralist perspective offers two versions and these reflect differences in attitude towards the present social arrangements of industrial capitalism:

1 A conservative view may be exemplified in the work of Talcott Parsons. Although starting out to develop a theory of action, Parsons provides a structuralist account of society. Leisure is seen as a part of a wider social system, with institutional frameworks that permit adults expressive emotional self-development.

   The privatised nuclear family is seen as best suited to the functional requirements of modern industrial capitalism as it serves to provide a private sphere for legitimate adult, sexuality, child rearing and leisure. The family is seen as a haven within which adults can relax and recuperate from the pressures of the public spheres of work, politics and culture. Consequently, the family and leisure function to provide individual security and collective solidarity. This 'structural functionalist'

approach has found its strongest support in American studies of sport.
2 For Marxists too, the starting point is not so much leisure and leisure
activities but the wider economic and political structure of capitalism.
Whereas structural/functionalists regard inequality and present cultural arrangements as both inevitable and desirable, Marxists see capitalism as flawed by the power of capital and markets to override the
interests of labour and human needs. Present leisure and leisure forms
are mirrors of capitalist society. They are inegalitarian, competitive,
privatised, individualistic and commodified. Access to leisure depends
on class relationships, particularly the control over capital (land,
wealth, income), although the state may intervene but only to protect
the long-term interests of market and capital.

Many writers stress that leisure forms in industrial capitalism mirror
the hierachical relationships of capitalist work with its stress on individualism, performance, efficiency and, not least, nationalism. There
are several examples of structural Marxism viewing leisure forms as
direct reproductions of capitalist forms (e.g. Brohm 1978).

For critical theorists from the Frankfurt school, freedom in leisure is
illusory, as people live in a demoralised capitalist society. Individuals
have little or no control over the serious matters of work or politics.
Leisure becomes packaged, promoted and processed for mass markets,
like any other commodity. From this perspective, the freedom of individual choice offered through the leisure markets is no choice at all.
Individuals are trapped within the ideology of consumerism and capitalism. Human instincts and creativity are repressed into false needs
and desires. Writers such as Marcuse, Adorno and Horkheimer criti-
cise the 'culture industry' of capitalism (i.e. mass media, and popular
culture) and the state for denying leisure and freedom and debasing
culture. Critical theorists can take no pleasure from capitalism.

Although subscribing to differing conservative and radical political
ideologies, both these structural approaches are similar in that they are
underpinned by a functional analysis of society. Both perspectives offer
a strong version of social order – one for industrial society, the other
for capitalism. Much writing about changing leisure forms is guilty of
a naive functionalism, as clearly pointed out in Gareth Steadman
Jones' seminal article – 'class expression versus social control?' This has
done much to make Marxist historians and social theorists recast this
structuralist account into a weaker, and hence more defensible form.

To conclude, this second perspective treats leisure as control. Its
central focus is social structure, i.e. on institutions which dominate
individuals and channel them into acceptable leisure forms which sustain social order. Ideological and material controls on leisure find fullest expression in the structuralism of Parsons and Althusser. The most

influential tradition has been that of Marxist critical theorists and at times more recently, feminism.

This section has presented two views of social theory in extreme form because they often seem to be set against each other. Action theorists are critical of structure theorists for not paying attention to individual experience whereas the latter are critical of the former for ignoring the social and cultural context in which leisure takes place. Both perspectives are partial and both action and structure views on leisure have promising strengths and telling weaknesses. Both perspectives are guilty of 'talking past each other' in that what are the strengths of one perspective are also seen as major weaknesses by the other.

Action:

1 focuses on individuals' meaning/experience of leisure.
2 highlights diversity of leisure forms and pleasure as a qualitative experience.

Structure:

1 focuses on the function/outcomes of leisure for society and in history.
2 stresses communality of leisure activities – self development/relaxation, etc.
3 highlights institutional contexts/constraints on leisure forms.

Leisure as freedom and control

Having outlined the two distinct traditions in the study of leisure, it is important to emphasise that these have been presented as competing views of action and structure. The two perspectives represent leisure as both freedom and as control, with the constituent features of leisure *experience* emphasising actions; while the social *context* emphasises structure. Dawe presented the two sociologies of action and structure in 1970, but by 1979 he attempted to integrate the two as different 'dialogues' within the central problems of social theory. The aim of this section is to review four contemporary perspectives which in their own distinct ways attempt to avoid the pitfalls of action and structure. These seek to overcome the partial explanations outlined above by being aware of the limitations and going beyond them.

It will become clear in the following sections that some key writers seek to integrate action and structure whereas others recast the action/structure problem and ask different sorts of questions about people's experience and the social context in which it occurs. Different concepts reflect distinct perspectives on the social relations of leisure. The following sections attempt to spell out the distinctive approach of figurational sociology, cultural studies and feminist analysis using relevant examples. Each theory offers a more or less clearly defined strategy for thinking about leisure, social relations, people and society. Each captures a different tension between social action and structure. To stay with the analogy of orienteering, the previous section on action and structure delineated the key physical contours of the field of social theory, these three contemporary perspectives reorientate the compass bearing for circumnavigating the course.

Before setting off, it is worth reminding oneself of one or two points made earlier about the lack of leisure theory in the UK. All four perspectives may be seen as substantive social theories, i.e. they offer distinct perspectives on the historical development and nature of society. All four offer explanations about the 'serious' worlds of work, politics and religion. They also claim to provide distinct and potentially rewarding theories for understanding leisure, as well as conducting specific research into leisure forms and activities. Figurational sociology, cultural studies, feminist analysis and postmodernism can claim to be both social theory and leisure theory. There are major writers such as Elias and Bourdieu who have made significant contributions both to social theory in general and leisure theory in particular. It is worth remembering that figurational sociology, cultural studies, feminist analysis and postmodernism are very broad labels and that each tradition is neither equally nor fully developed. There are also other major social theories, such as Gidden's theory of structuration, that offer considerable potential for understanding leisure. However, the following is confined to just four approaches because each informs current leisure publications and has established theories and research traditions in the field of leisure. There are two final points to bear in mind. First, these perspectives are not always clearly defined but they are useful labels to distinguish differing perspectives on leisure. Secondly, some critics may feel that one or all of these perspectives are not breaking new ground at all but are following the well trodden paths of earlier writers about leisure.

Contemporary perspectives on leisure and society

1 Figurational sociology

Norbert Elias has developed his 'figurational' approach to sociology and social theory over a period of 40 years. He worked at Leicester University and his associates, notably Eric Dunning, extended and applied Elias's theorising to studies of sport, although the insights from figurational sociology have yet to be fully realised in studies of leisure generally.

Elias argues that ideas of figurations form a more adequate analytical tool for understanding the complexity of social life than debates about action and structure, or freedom and control reviewed earlier. In the first section the key elements of Elias's social theorising about 'figurations' are outlined together with illustrations of this approach.

Elias has applied his theory through an extensive analysis of what he calls 'the civilising process'. In two massive volumes, originally written in Dutch in the 1930s, he argues that over the centuries, emotions have gradually been 'flattened out', and instinctual desires and pleasures have been increasingly sublimated and channelled into 'civilised' forms of cultural activity. So, for example, the levels of bodily violence tolerated in physical activity forms like games and sports have progressively diminished. Combat sports like boxing and wrestling, and animal sports like hunting are increasingly subject to controls over what is considered acceptable or 'civilised'.

Figurations

Elias argues that many social theory problems are caused by the tendency to reduce the study of people to one or other of a series of partly overlapping divisions such as agency or structure, individual or society, freedom or constraint, actor or activity. He argues that such dualistic terminology, does not capture the complex and changing inter-relationships between individuals in societies. The basis of analysis for Elias is not individual or social action rather it is the 'network of interdependencies' which bind people together. He calls these networks 'figurations' – structures of mutually oriented and dependent people. Everyone, in all aspects of their lives, is interwoven into a network of people. Their personal identities are closely connected through relationships with other people and their position within groups of interdependent individuals. So the actions of any individual (e.g. their leisure activities) can only be understood by studying the 'web' of interdependencies in which such action or activity is situated.

Think for example of some leisure activities such as gambling, eating out at a restaurant, shopping and playing football. In each case, an individual's actions are dependent upon, inter-linked with, and only make sense with reference to other's actions. Consider also a facility such as a leisure centre in which groups of individuals have particular responsibilities for technical services, administration, cleaning, catering and coaching. The centre is a figuration in which any particular individual is part of an interdependent whole. The centre is, of course, part of a larger figuration of leisure services in a local authority, a figuration which includes other centres, alternative leisure attractions, policy makers in the local authority and funding agencies. All these parties are involved in leisure provision. Elias therefore talks of increasingly complex 'chains of interdependence'. The more complex the 'chain' the less likely it is that the properties of any one link can be explained or understood as if it were an independent entity. For example, the meanings of any one individual's work within a leisure centre are related to the social context of that work.

But in this wider figuration of public sector leisure services in a local authority, each of the groups (e.g. policy makers, centre managers, catering staff, coaching staff, maintenance staff) have particular interests which are related to their position in the figuration. Moreover, each group also has power and resources relative to other groups. For Elias, power is a fundamental property of any figuration. Even in a simple figuration such as a conversation between two or three people, individuals have particular resources which affect the processes and the outcomes of that conversation. Similarly in complex figurations there are more or less unequal balances of power and resources which affect the 'interweaving' of social life and crucially the outcome of those processes. Elias uses a series of 'game' models as devices to illustrate the possible permutations of power distribution within figurations. His key argument is that in a figuration where one individual or group possesses most of the power and resources, then they are more likely to be able to have control over the outcome of the figuration. In an analogy with a game of chess, consider a situation where a good player is playing ten separate games against ten other players simultaneously. Here the power-balance shifts, since the good player has to distribute his resources more widely. The balance will be altered yet again if the ten players decide to pool their resources to play one game.

The figuration would be even more complex if each of the eleven players start to play games against the other ten. At this complex level, as in the case with public sector leisure services, the greater the balance of power between the links in the chain, the less likely it is that any one of these links can dictate or determine the outcome.

This is a central plank in Elias's explanation of how the social dynamics of figurations operate. Out of the interweaving of individual interests and intentions, something eventually emerges that, as it turns out, has not been planned or intended, or necessarily anticipated by any single individual. Yet this outcome has been brought about by the actions and intentions of all the relevant individuals.

To return to the example of the leisure centre peopled by individuals who have particular interests in the organisation and administration of the centre, each individual, and more generally each group of administrative, maintenance, catering and coaching personnel, has relative amounts of power and resources. This power stems from their work during those times when the centre is operational, their particular skills which are bought and sold for wages, their links with professional or trade associations such as the Institute of Leisure and Amenity Management, their representation upon policy-making bodies in the local authority, and upon committees which decide upon staffing levels, plant maintenance and capitation requirements. It is easy to understand that any one individual might feel powerless within a complex figuration.

This shows why individuals group together in associations in order to provide collectively a mechanism through which their common interests can be brought to the notice of other groups. Even users of leisure centres possess power in terms of their patronage of a particular facility. Ultimately, policy is orientated towards encouraging use and discouraging the withdrawal of patronage – there are plenty of examples of users of leisure facilities organising themselves into associations in order to increase their power and resources (like the nationwide Consumer Association, or the Rambler's Association).

Elias's enduring contribution to understanding leisure activities is therefore to suggest that explanations of individual *actions*, whether as providers or consumers, can only be explained by reference to the chains of interdependency within which such action takes place. Moreover, social *structures* are to be understood not as an abstract entity, but as networks of actors. Hence, the idea of figurations is an explanation both of individual action and of social structure.

Elias's theory yields insights and explanations of individual actions and activities which are crucially different from other more standard explanations. To illustrate this, consider the much publicised occasion of a game of rugby played between England and Wales in 1987. The game excited much critical comment in the media because of 'non-sporting' violations, not just of the game rules, but of the law of the land. Outside the game the actions of some players would be labelled as inflicting 'grievous bodily harm'. The outcome was the sacking of the England captain and the suspension of two other England players. The game was a travesty of Rugby Union Football because of the failure of the players to follow the rules. The response by the games administrators and by journalists was to place the blame firmly on the shoulders of particular *individuals*, responsible for their own *actions*.

However, what explanation might be offered using Elias's idea of figurations? Firstly, it can safely be assumed that neither the players nor the coach intended the game to develop as it did, especially as the outcome (the dismissal of players and subsequent suspensions) disadvantaged their interests. The outcome must therefore be explained with reference to the figurations within which the actions took place. The primary configuration is the 30 players, but this game did not take place in a vacuum. Players and coaches devised tactics and strategies with respect to knowledge of their own strengths and weaknesses, i.e. an interpretation of the power and resources possessed by the 30 individuals.

These understandings need to be set against knowledge that the visiting team (England) had not won in Cardiff since 1963. Another factor is that the players around which the controversy took place are part of the figuration of English and Welsh club sides and frequently play with and against the players in the opposing team – such prior knowledge influencing the ways in which they interact with one another. To this add the knowledge that both teams lost their opening matches of the International Series and that previous games between the two countries had been characterised by 'foul play'. Employing Elias's account of action within figurations of interdependent individuals, it is credible to offer an account of this particular game which offers insights ignored by conventional condemnations of individual players' actions. Such an account moves away from the individual in order to consider the interweaving of individuals in association, not to condone such action (since in this case it resulted in the spoilation of the game), but rather to offer an explanation which is not couched solely in terms of individual biography, personality or motivation.

Therefore figurational sociology attempts to explain individual action with reference to figurations of interdependent people. The reader is invited to consider other leisure activities, and to situate individual expressions of leisure choice and individual strategies of leisure professionals, within larger configurations.

The civilising process
Much leisure activity provides the opportunity for 'letting one's hair down'; for relaxing conventions which normally apply in domestic and work lives, and for having 'a good time'. Leisure for relaxation, recuperation and recreation is taken for granted. It provides opportunities, from pop-concerts to sports spectatorship, for the emotional or 'affective' domain of one's being to override the rational or 'cognitive' self. Elias argues, however, that emotions are intrinsically bound by the particular historical circumstances in which one lives. More specifically, the characteristics of leisure behaviour (what is condoned and is acceptable rather than what is condemned and inadmissible) are historically relative and change over time.

There are current debates about various aspects of leisure behaviour. There are censors who preside over what is admissible material for the television and cinema. There are groups who campaign against fox-hunting, bull-fighting and game-shooting as well as battery-hen farming practices. There are others who want to make boxing illegal, and much publicised debates about violence in sports. Increasingly the legal system is becoming involved in cases of 'grievous bodily harm' on the rugby and football pitches in this country. Note, also that football hooliganism is deemed to be a problem of such proportions that the Government is driven to intervene for its suppression.

In the 1880s, and perhaps only 50 years ago, issues such as these might not have arisen. Elias's argument is that people's perception about what is socially acceptable behaviour has changed over time. The thresholds of shame, guilt, repugnance and embarrassment have risen. This is one key element of Elias's account of the civilising process explored in the first of two volumes subtitled 'A History of Manners'. This history, embellished with the most detailed account of etiquette through the ages, traces a social process whereby individuals have gradually learned to exert self-control over their bodily functions, instincts and passions. Emotions have become 'flattened out' instinctual desires have been sublimated, and passions channelled into socially acceptable and 'harmless' pursuits. From toilet functions to love-making, from physical recreations to eating habits – all are affected by this process. The epitome of good manners in dining in the Middle Ages (as described in Erasmus's *Book of Manners*) would nowadays be regarded as animalistic in the relaxed stylised setting of a restaurant in modern Europe.

Elias's analysis, however, is more far-reaching than a mere description of the 'civilisation' of leisure behaviour. Such behaviour, including expressions of taste and distaste, of tolerance and intolerance, does not arise or develop of its own accord. Elias suggests that the characteristics of personalities (of which our leisure behaviour is but one expression) is intimately connected with the type of state system in which they are formed. Over the centuries, the gradual formation of large nation-states from a host of smaller warring fiefdoms has resulted in increasing control by the state over the legitimate use of violence. Such power is now centralised in national armies and police forces. Through this process, the lives of individuals have gradually become more secure, more pacified, and more predictable. Also as the state has become larger and more encompassing, so the chains of interdependencies have become longer, the social figurations more complex. The outcome of these 'lengthening dependencies' together with 'internal pacification', is that both the opportunity and the necessity for violent and impulsive expressions of emotion have decreased.

Consider for example, the experience of travel in different historical epochs. Travel today is both ordered and relatively secure. Cars are subject to stringent safety checks, the wearing of safety belts is compulsory, rules for the proper use of roads are adequately policed, insurance policies are available to offset misfortunes from windscreen breakages and towing charges to breakdown services and loss of luggage. Similar protective procedures apply to rail and air travel. Compare this with the experience of travel in the Middle Ages which must have been much more adventurous, and full of risk. One ventured into unpoliced spaces from relatively safe city walls (designed to keep intruders out). The experience was unpredictable not solely because of the low level of travel technology but also because of the real possibility of attack by 'vagabonds'. The only insurance policy against attack was to travel with one's own do-it-yourself police force which, in relative terms, was much more expensive than modern insurance packages, and therefore only available to the few. Travel, as with other aspects of life, was less secure, more unpredictable, and less peaceful. The modern connotation of 'fending for oneself' takes on a different meaning in situations where violence was the only preservative measure available, and different personal attributes and qualities were required to cope with travel conditions. In modern Britain, if an individual, involved in an accident, were to leap out and bodily assault the other party, then the action would almost certainly override any judgement of blame in terms of the original clash of motor vehicles.

Dunning has undertaken an extensive analysis of games-playing from about 1300 AD to the present, and applied Elias's insights about the civilising process. Folk games such as early forms of 'football', Cornish 'hurling' and Welsh 'knappen' were wild and uproarious affairs. There were no limits on the numbers of players, no elaborate written rules and no boundaries in playing space or time. Even if rules had been introduced there was no way to ensure that they would be adhered to. In short, these games were close to real fighting characterised by a high level of tolerance for physical violence and injury. An extract from Carew's account of hurling in Cornwall in 1602, provided by Dunning, gives evidence of the uncivilised nature of these proceedings:

The ball in this play may be compared to an infernal spirit: for whosoever catcheth it, fareth straight awayes like a madde man, struggling and fighting with those that goe about to holde him: and no sooner is the ball gone from him, but hee resigneth this fury to the next receyver, and himselfe becommeth peaceable as before. I cannot well resolve, whether I should more commend this game, for the manhood and exercise, or condemne it for the boysterousness and harmes which it begetteth: for as on the one side it makes their bodies strong, hard and nimble, and puts courage into their hearts, to meete an enemie in the face: so on the other part, it is accompanied by many dangers, some of which do ever fall to the players share. For proofe whereof, when the hurlings ended, you will see them retyring home, as from a pitched battaile, with bloody pates, bones broken, and out of joynt, and such bruises as serve to shorten their dais; yet al is good play, and never Attourney nor Crowner troubled for the matter.

Dunning's point is that these mock fights (and other 'recreations' such as cock-fighting, bull or bear-baiting, dog-tossing, burning cats alive in baskets, watching public executions) are a reflection of the level of violence and violence control in society at large. These 'entertainments' are typical of people in a society at an early stage in a civilising process in comparison with the relatively stable, relatively impersonal central control of the means of violence which characterises contemporary nation-states. The fact that such activities appear barbarous and repugnant to us is evidence of this civilising process.

Table 7.1 is an edited version of Dunning's summary of the historic development from folk-games to the stylised, organised and highly controlled sports of the present where action is monitored both by codified rules and in some cases by the tacitly understood ideas of 'fair-play and 'sportsmanship'. Players are allocated particular roles, and specific individual skills and group strategies and tactics are developed within specific space and time boundaries.

Table 7.1 Characteristics of folk-games and modern sporting games (After Dunning)

Folk games	Modern sporting games
High toleration of physical violence; open and spontaneous 'battle-excitement'	Low toleration of physical violence; controlled and sublimated 'battle-excitement'
Simple unwritten rules transmitted orally	Formal, codified rules transmitted through bureaucratic channels
Regional variations in rules, equipment.	International standardisation of rules, equipment
No precise space and time boundaries or numbers of participants	Precise space and time boundaries, or numbers of participants
Emphasis on force as opposed to skill	Emphasis on skill as opposed to force
Little division of labour (role differentiation) amongst players	High division of labour (role differentiation) amongst players
Playing and spectating roles loosely distinguished	Playing and spectating roles strictly separate

QUESTIONS FOR DISCUSSION ————————————————

1 As noted in the earlier sections on countryside recreation, most of the issues about leisure in the National Parks give rise to conflicts of interest. Applying Elias's insights, map out the figuration of interdependent interest groups and consider the different resources and power which particular groups have in influencing the outcome of conflicts.

2 In the figuration of your study group, how are power and resources used to influence the processes and outcomes of discussions? How different are the processes or characteristics when the leader is not present?

3 How do commercial, voluntary and public sectors of leisure provision function as a figuration of interdependency?

4 How would the figuration of leisure provision be restructured if public leisure services were privatised?

5 Consider a situation where you are promoting and organising a particular event at an Art Centre or a Sports Centre. How is this promotion and organisation dependent upon a network, web, or figuration of other individuals in association?

6 According to Dunning, football hooliganism is not a new phenomenon. He indicates many examples of 'crowd disturbance' in matches earlier this century. Does 'football hooliganism' in the 1980s contradict Elias's theories about the civilising process?

7 The increasing violence in sport is frequently highlighted by the media. This seems to contradict Elias's thesis about the civilising process. How does 'figurational' sociology explain this phenomenon?

8 What conventions surround toilet functions in contemporary Western society?
   As an aid to the sluggish imagination:
   (a) think of the different euphemisms used to denote 'the toilet' (e.g. the 'little room', the John (USA), the lav)
   (b) what euphemisms are used to denote urination? (e.g. passing water)
   (c) how does modern decor/tastes in bathroom design and toilet 'requisites' mask the primary function

9 What conventions surround:
   (a) eating?

(b) drinking?
(c) meeting and parting?
(d) shopping?
(e) money transactions?
(f) committee deliberations?
(g) playing squash?

10 Recently, an incidence of dog-fighting (between two Staffordshire Bull Terriers) excited much media comment and condemnation. Such events would not have been news a century ago. What leads us to condemn such practices today?

Further reading

S. Mennell (1980) *Sociological Theory: Uses and Unities*, Nelson. In Chapter 2, entitled Interaction and Interdependencies, Mennell provides an excellent review of both figurations and the civilising process.

N. Elias (1978) *What is Sociology?*, Hutchinson. In Chapters 1–3 Elias mounts his criticism of conventional sociological debates about agency and structure, and then proceeds to outline his figuration theory. Chapter 3 is devoted to a consideration of game models to map out changes in balances of power and resources. The foreword to this book, by R. Bendix, is worth reading.

E. Dunning (1979), 'The Figurational Dynamics of Modern Sport' in *Sportswissenschaft*, 9.4. This application to sport of figurational sociology suggests that the growing seriousness and competitiveness of top level sport, and the consequent demise of amateurism is the unintended outcome of the interweaving of the actions of several interdependent groups over several generations.

See also E. Dunning (ed.) (1971) *The Sociology of Sport*, Frank Cass, which contains a contribution by Elias and E. Dunning and K. Sheard (1979) *Barbarians, Gentlemen and Players* Martin Robinson. See particularly chapters on the Civilising Processes and The Formation of the RFU.

2 Cultural studies

'Cultural studies' includes a large number of writers who have been interested in a variety of cultural forms and their development during the nineteenth and twentieth centuries. Unlike figurational sociology, which can be identified with Norbert Elias, cultural studies cannot easily be located in one single writer or with one single research tradition. Many would point to Frankfurt in the inter-war years, as the home of critical theory and later cultural studies. But cultural studies have also been heavily influenced by versions of French structuralism, Italian studies in ideology and an English tradition of literary criticism. This brief introduction will map out the key ideas behind Critical Theory as they have been developed by the Centre of Contemporary Cultural Studies (CCCS) at Birmingham. Tomlinson (1989, 1990) suggests that leisure studies and cultural studies constitute alternative paradigms to explain leisure, consumption and culture.

In the final section, particular attention will be paid to the prolific work of Pierre Bourdieu and his analysis of cultural styles, cultural reproduction and cultural competence. Although the approach and analysis of individual writers are substantially different, certain themes are common to the cultural studies tradition:

1 A concern with the economic processes of capitalism and their relationships with cultural forms; certain forms are seen to be relatively autonomous or independent from capitalism, whereas others are seen to be direct expressions of capital's ability to make objects into commodities and sell them to mass markets.
2 An interest in 'high' and 'popular' cultural forms; particularly the impact of mass media technologies on art, music, drama and literature.
3 A focus on the role of the State within capitalist society and its building of a 'national' ideology based on popular forms, obscuring divisions, inequalities and constraints in society while providing opportunities for individual freedom to consume.
4 A commitment to social class and its relationship to cultural forms. Each class generates its own culture which is both a product of its own 'lived' experience (at work, in the family and in leisure) and also of its relationship to other classes (ones of dominance and dependence). The concept of hegemony is central to understanding how ruling classes win the active consent of subordinate classes yet such processes are negotiated and historically constructed (*see* Clarke and Critcher, 1985).

Although more recently cultural studies have become more interested in gender relations, their central focus is one of class, community and employment rather than domestic labour and women, hence they remain distant from feminist theory and analysis.

The Frankfurt School – Critical Theory

Writers in the Frankfurt School set out to make sense of their own experience of Germany in the 1920s and 1930s. Many were Jews caught up with the rise of Fascism in the 1930s and many were Marxists attempting to make sense of the fascism that was unfolding before them. Why had there been no socialist revolutions as Marx's theories of capitalist economics and class struggle had predicted? Why were they witnessing a growth of the capitalist state, the collapse of socialist resistance and menacing authoritarian mass-culture fuelled by state propaganda? Why were working class movements mobilised by ethnocentrism and depleted by unemployment?

Such questions encouraged key writers such as Marcuse, Adorno and Horkheimer to revise Marxist analysis (so drastically that many critics claimed that they were no longer Marxists). They began to review the nature of the relationship between the individual and capitalist society, and began a complex integration of Freudian views of the personality with Marxist views of capitalism. The clearest and most accessible statement of just such a synthesis is to be found in Herbert Macuse's (1964) *One Dimensional Man*. This is a rich and complex work full of solutions and problems. One important theme for understanding leisure is the argument that resistance to the inequalities of capitalism is absorbed and diverted by the prevailing ideas of the ruling class, by the processes of hegemonic control. By managing the state and 'the culture industry' (a term used by Adorno and Horkheimer), the ruling class binds the individual into consuming. As with other goods, leisure becomes a commodity to be consumed. Instead of consumers buying commodities, it is more accurate to suggest that 'commodities buy consumers'. The culture industry provides mass entertainment in 'people palaces'. The market offers household durables and leisure styles of immense diversity; these become false needs, fuelled by advertising and on display in 'consumption palaces'. Such views of demoralised leisure have been rehearsed in previous chapters (viz. on consuming and on mass-society leisure futures).

CCCS Birmingham – Cultural Marxism

A more optimistic view from cultural studies is to be found in the work of the Centre of Contemporary Cultural Studies, at Birmingham University. Rather than seeing mass audiences and popular culture as demoralised leisure, they view them as a site for cultural struggle and resistance against capitalism by ordinary working people. Rather than being used by the culture industry, the thrust of the work by the CCCS is to emphasise the popular expression of ordinary working people through their own cultural forms. Harris (1992) has suggested that CCCS research has been nostalgic in romanticising working-class communities. Football, working-men's clubs, allotments, pigeon-racing and so on are seen as collective working-class cultural forms which have won some space from the reality of capitalist work-relationships. While critical theorists have been thought of as 'elitist' with their focus on the 'high' arts, the CCCS have looked towards popular culture as an arena or site for the development of leisure, both in terms of pleasure and freedom. Early research from the CCCS focused upon the resistance through rituals of working-class youth, but later contributors examined racism, ethnic minorities and women.

Bourdieu on taste in leisure

The work of Pierre Bourdieu and his associates at the centre of European sociology in Paris has only recently begun to have an impact upon studies of leisure in this country. Over a period of 20 years, he has carried out extensive research into leisure activity and lifestyles to demonstrate how the prevailing system of class-based inequalities is sustained.

Much of his research focuses upon tastes and preferences in art but has a more general application to all forms of cultural activity and consumption such as sports, holidays, outdoor recreations, media, home decor, cars, clothes, drinks and other leisure-time activities.

Earlier in this text, reference has been made to various writers who have argued that social class divisions have only limited power in explaining leisure activity. Many leisure activities are not starkly arranged along class lines. Moreover, in different ways, post-industrial theorists such as Daniel Bell and the 'mass culture' theorists such as Adorno argue that contemporary developments in patterns of employment and in mass communication systems have had a profound social impact. In both cases, the idea of separate and conflicting social-class groupings (with their own distinctive cultures and leisure lifestyles) is seen to be anachronistic in modern Western society.

Nevertheless, Bourdieu considers that an individual's upbringing within a particular family and class has a powerful influence upon leisure choice. This choice is not solely confined to activities, but extends to the 'styles' and 'dispositions' adopted in their pursuit. Therefore, although surveys of most leisure activities might suggest that participants and/or consumers are not drawn from any particular social strata, Bourdieu invites us to go beyond such descriptive data to analyse styles, tastes, preferences and the meanings of particular activities for different people.

As noted in Chapter 3, individuals are restricted in their choice of leisure activities through a range of factors related to cost, demands of employment, the cost of the activity, age, and gender. But, given these constraining and enabling factors, which limit what Bourdieu calls, 'the field of possibility', how are tastes and preferences acquired for different leisure activities, and on what basis choice made? To answer this key question, Bourdieu suggests that only a partial explanation can be offered, by interviewing individuals about why they choose particular activities. He suggests that tastes, preferences, perceptions and dispositions for leisure activities are learned and developed in early childhood within the family and its social surroundings. Bourdieu's 'Theory of Practice', is that childhood practices and experiences give rise to a 'habitus'. This habitus is a 'system of transposable dispositions' which function as a collection of perceptions, tastes, preferences, appreciations and actions; forming a way of perceiving the world and distinguishing between appropriate and inappropriate activities. By transposable, Bourdieu means that an individual's tastes and preferences in any one leisure activity are inter-related with or interdependent on the taste and preferences manifested in all other leisure activities.

The habitus operates according to a coherent 'logic of practice' and because it is internalised in early childhood, it operates unconsciously, and cannot be wholly supplanted.

To summarise these points: 'conditions of existence' are the family and class situations into which an individual is born (*see also* Chapter 3); which gives rise to a set of 'conditioning' (the habitus) which translates into a 'system of dispositions' (the logic of practice). This, according to Bourdieu, is the basis upon which leisure lifestyles are generated. The same system of dispositions, the same logic of practice operates unconsciously in all tastes and preferences for leisure activity from sports and arts, through membership of clubs and associations, to holiday-making and informal activities such as media consumption and home-based leisure. Bourdieu acknowledges the obvious point that tastes and activities might change through later experiences but he argues that such choice is invariably made *according* to the structural logic of the existing habitus.

A more detailed account of Bourdieu's idea of the 'habitus' as the principle upon which leisure activity is based is provided in Garnham and Williams' (1980) extensive review of Bourdieu's work.

This explanation of the origin of dispositions in leisure activity is the foundation of Bourdieu's subsequent analysis of leisure. The habitus is the basis upon which all choices of leisure are made, and through the formation of the habitus, individuals acquire a range of 'cultural competences' or 'cultural capital' which makes particular leisure activities more or less accessible or possible for them.

On the basis of this Theory of Practice, Bourdieu develops an account of how choices in leisure operate. He suggests that leisure activities should be conceived as a 'field of stylistic possibles'. In this field are different types of leisure activity, different spaces where they may be pursued (e.g. public facilities and private clubs) and different styles or approaches which an individual might adopt. All of this offers the individual choice, depending upon his/her own particular material circumstances. Bourdieu then argues that the 'significance' of particular activities, spaces and styles is related to their social 'distribution'. This means that individuals make choices with respect to their knowledge of other individuals' choices. Some activities, styles and spaces are common, easily accessible and 'vulgar', others have rarity value, are distinctive and are relatively inaccessible. Their inaccessibility relates not just to material factors such as their high cost, but also to the particular and distinctive cultural competences which they demand.

So, for example, opera and other 'high' culture forms are distinctive not necessarily because they involve large material outlays. Indeed the cost of a night at the theatre is not significantly different from costs incurred in attending a Football League match or a night's gambling on the greyhounds. Rather its distinctiveness arises from the cultural competences required for its appreciation; competences not possessed by the majority. Therefore theatre patronage is symbolic of a distinction from the common, mundane and ordinary.

Tastes and preferences are therefore to be explained in terms of their 'distributional significance'. Tastes are social breaks. Tastes are, in effect, *distastes* of others, marks of distinction, and it is this pursuit of distinction, which for Bourdieu, provides the motor for leisure activity and styles.

The significance of tastes is that they are always relative to other tastes. This is apparent in the development of holiday locales. In former times, Brighton (through Royal patronage) was a distinctive holiday resort but its increasing accessibility and popularity rapidly made it 'distasteful' to original patrons who consequently sought new, untainted and therefore distinctive spaces. Biarritz was once distinctive as was Corfu and the French Riviera, now it is Goa or the Bahamas. A similar dynamic operates in ski-resorts and indeed in all leisure activities. The example of holiday resorts is a crude representation of taste. Bourdieu indicates the complexity and subtlety of tastes operating in all forms of consumerism from food and drink to clothes and house decor and this extends to postures, gestures, mannerisms, speech modes, forms of address and various techniques of sociability. All of these provide the small number of distinctive features which, functioning as a system of differences, differential deviations, allows the most fundamental social differences to be expressed . . . and offers well-nigh inexhaustible possibilities for the pursuit of distinction.

Summary
Bourdieu's analysis is a significant advance upon conventional leisure research which merely describes but does not explain the distribution of leisure activity amongst the population. It also develops beyond explanations couched solely in terms of either structural constraints or in terms of individual freedom. Moreover, his Theory of Practice and account of

the dynamics of leisure choices is an attempt to explain the impulse behind *all* leisure activity. The key elements of Bourdieu's thesis reviewed above are as follows:

(a) through early experiences, individuals acquire particular and different dispositions which translate into perceptions, tastes and preferences.
(b) dispositions are transposable, i.e. operate in all forms of leisure activity and consumerism.
(c) individuals vary in their perception of leisure activities, and the meanings with which such activities are invested.
(d) different activities and styles require different types of cultural competences.
(e) the significance of particular leisure activities, spaces and styles arises from their distribution amongst social groups.
(f) leisure choice arises from this distributional significance. Tastes and preferences are social breaks.
(g) leisure choices are an endless, on-going game in which tastes are significant in terms of their relationship and distinction from other tastes.

QUESTIONS FOR DISCUSSION

1 Consider the range of alcoholic drinks available. How does choice operate? Think of mixes such as whisky and . . . , gin and . . . Think also of terminology (e.g. half-pint/small beer: martini/vermouth).

2 What techniques of sociability and cultural competence are required in a private golf club? How do these differ from a public course? How do the 'rules' of social intercourse differ?

3 How do the dynamics of taste operate in a game like squash?

4 Not all 'high' culture offers the same possibilities for the pursuit of distinction. For example, one can now buy any number of reproductions of Constable's painting 'The Haywain' or of Beethoven's 5th Symphony in a local hypermarket. What are the dimensions of taste within so-called elitist high culture?

5 Which leisure activities retain images of social exclusivity beyond any consideration of their accessibility in purely material terms?

6 The Sports Council promotes a 'Sport for All' policy. But which sports? For whom? What effects would this have (if successful)?

7 Why is there no 'Art for All' policy by the Arts Council?

8 In Chapter 6, it was noted that leisure is provided through the public, voluntary and commercial sectors. Using Bourdieu's analysis, examine how these sectors inter-relate with one another.

Further reading

Bourdieu's own writings are difficult to understand. His major work is entitled *Distinction: a social critique of the judgement of taste*, Routledge and Kegan Paul (1985). It is now available in paperback. Section 4 on 'The Dynamics of the Fields' can be read in isolation. Also recommended is an article in *Media Culture and Society*, **2**, 2, 1980 entitled 'The Production of Belief' and an article in *Social Science Information* entitled 'Sport and Social Class'.

N. Garnham and R. Williams (1980) in *Media Culture and Society*, **2**, 2. This provides an excellent review of some of the main elements in Bourdieu's work, particularly his Theory of Practice. The article also suggests how Bourdieu's work is an advance on other perspectives within Cultural Studies. Some criticisms which might be levelled at Bourdieu are also offered, including the lack of any consideration of gender divisions.

Recent discussions of cultural studies and leisure include: A. Tomlinson (1989), 'Whose side are they on? Leisure Studies and Cultural Studies in Britain', *Leisure Studies*, **8**, pp. 97–106; C. Rojek (1993), 'After Popular Culture: Hyperreality and leisure', *Leisure Studies*, **12**, pp. 277–89; D. Harris (1992) *From Class Struggle to the Politics of Pleasure*, Routledge and Kegan Paul.

3 Feminist studies

A number of feminists working in the leisure field have argued convincingly that leisure has different meanings for men and women. Most research into leisure reflects men's experience of leisure forms and activities. Definitions which equate leisure with free-time from paid employment fail to consider the everyday experience of most women. Policy-makers may see women as a 'problem' and introduce policies to increase women's participation. The fusion of free-time, leisure activities and pleasure is differently experienced by men and women. Stated bluntly, women have less leisure than men. Leisure as conventionally defined, makes little sense of women's experience, yet they form 50% of the workforce, receive 25% of total wages and do 100% of domestic work within the majority of households. Such inequality is felt by some writers to override other factors such as class, race, education, income and car-ownership.

Within feminist studies, leisure is seen as a site of patriarchy, which may be broadly defined, for present purposes, as the control of women by men. The institutional structures and strategies whereby men control women in general and their leisure in particular, are diverse, complex and resilient. Such control is achieved by men collectively; individual men who claim not to be male chauvinists, can passively acquiesce to wider structural arrangements which secure male dominance over women's lives.

Throughout this book, most social theorists have focused upon the inter-relationship between three major institutions.

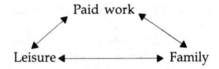

Figure 7.1   Work, leisure and family inter-relationships

Yet feminist analysis argues that such a commonsense model is one dimensional and ignores the dimension of gender in social relations. People are 'gendered' individuals and the fundamental sexual division between males and females permeates life and living. Hence, human sexuality is a crucial factor in social relations and in many studies, is *the* determinant of opportunities and constraints in leisure. The previous model needs recasting:

It is truism that men and women occupy different spheres in social relations. Women are more likely to be in the 'private' sphere of the household/family, providing emotional care and domestic work, where-

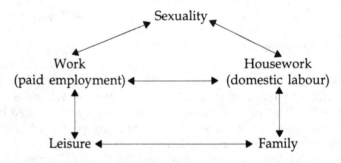

Figure 7.2   Sexuality and leisure

as men occupy the 'public' sphere of work, politics and leisure, and are supported by the 'private' sphere, serviced by women. Women who work face 'the dual burden' of paid employment and domestic work. Such sexual divisions within social relations have recently been challenged and explored by leisure research. It is as if leisure researchers, predominantly male, have never asked the question why they always go to the male changing rooms when going swimming.

Anti-feminists argue that the sexual division of labour is natural and inevitable. Biological differences between the sexes ensure that the reproduction of the species demands that women are childbearers. But such a view assumes that biology determines social and cultural behaviour; that instinct drives women 'naturally' towards motherhood, housework and childcare. Human beings may be seen as sticks of lettered rock, which are imprinted throughout with the message male or female. Yet the feminist position is more complex as it argues that the biological message of sex gradually changes through childhood and adulthood and develops into one of 'gender'. That means the biological division between male and female finds its expression in social differences in maleness and femaleness or more usually masculinity and femininity. There are immense difficulties in understanding 'natural' and 'social' divisions and they need not detain us, as the relationship between people and their physical being is one of the undertheorised problems confronting any social theory. Sex becomes *gender* as people express their physical being in social relations. Cultural definitions of gender change over time both within and between different societies. Men and women define themselves in different ways as each generation comes to terms with the sexual division of labour. In the negotiation of gender roles, there are constraints and opportunities and feminist work has highlighted the constraints experienced by women which have been ignored or taken for granted by previous research.

It is difficult to grasp the breadth and diversity within feminist studies, especially for men. What follows is a very simplified outline of three important perspectives in feminism. In stark contrast to figurational sociology and cultural studies, feminism is not an academic discipline, but a political practice, and one that is constantly developing. It is important to realise that most feminism integrates and inter-relates these three perspectives both in academic work and political practice. Nevertheless, textbooks still find it is useful to differentiate *Liberal feminism*, *Radical feminism* and *Marxist feminism*, as these often reflect different political strategies in dealing with women's oppression. One way of thinking about the three strands is to see radical feminism focusing on women's oppression, Marxist feminism on the exploitation of women's labour and liberal feminism on discrimination.

Liberal feminism
Liberal feminists take the position that capitalism or industrial society is capable of addressing itself to meeting women's needs, provided there is change. Liberal feminists working within the Women's Liberation Movement in the 1960s organised campaigns to secure equal rights and opportunities for women. Campaigns struggled to guarantee equal legal rights for women in work and education. As liberals, many demanded anti-discriminatory legislation and radical changes in social policy. Crucial sites for change within capitalism are ideas and attitudes about women and femininity. Society socialises women into not only reproducing children, but also the corrosive ideas of femininity, domesticity and the family. Such ideas stand in the way of those women who wish to be treated as people – who want to pursue careers, engage in leisure and succeed in the 'public' sphere.

It is therefore essential to change ideas about leisure. Women themselves are often bearers of patriarchal ideology by accepting that men do 'real work' and therefore should be entitled to leisure. In fact, research suggests that many women experience guilt when they find themselves with free-time and engaged in leisure activities. Consequently, listening to the radio, or watching television, must be supplemented by additional domestic tasks such as ironing, washing-up or knitting. The subordination of women is achieved through ideas about domesticity and caring relationships.

Women who complain about servicing the needs of others are defined as 'unnatural', 'uncaring', or 'deviant' if they challenge these traditional cultural expectations and choose to live their lives as independent women.

The sources of cultural expectations about appropriate feminine and domestic behaviour are to be found everywhere, but primarily within early childrearing and schooling. Liberal feminists, therefore, amongst others, stress the need to change patterns of socialisation and schooling which are sexist. Girls must not be discriminated against both within school and within wider institutions of leisure such as voluntary organisations, youth clubs, and recreation provision. (The barriers to access and participation have been explored fully in Chapter 3.)

Another important source of ideas about femininity and domesticity is the mass media, particularly images of advertising and consuming. Gender differences are highlighted in selling products – particularly leisure commodities, and the subordination of women is celebrated within popular culture. Much insightful work has been developed in the ideology of romantic love and its expression within gender relations, particularly the family. Romantic love is the life-blood of literature, films, magazines and popular music. Women are the majority of consumers of popular romantic novels and feminists are starting to address the question of why women enjoy soap operas and romantic literature and whether they strengthen ideas about the subordinate position of women in society. It is inadequate to say that women are their own worst enemies by subscribing to patriarchal ideas. Women acknowledge that they experience a 'gender problem' in the political, economic or cultural spheres. It is the 'feminist' label and analysis that is resisted.

Radical feminism

There has been a long history of radical feminism and one aspect of the feminists' task is to rediscover women's place in and contribution to human history. Nevertheless, the 1960s represent a significant watershed for radical feminism as the women's movement began to develop a comprehensive critique of both social theory and society. Since then radical feminism and Marxist feminism have enriched each other and it is difficult to separate the strands. 'The Women Question' defines men as oppressors and explores the ways in which men exercise power and control over women and their bodies. Radical feminism sees patriarchy as an important constituent of social relations; power and politics are important not only in the public sphere of government and policy making but also in the private sphere within sexual relationships, especially within the family. Radical feminists raise the question of 'social politics' with slogans such as 'the personal is political' and the 'anti-social family'. They catalogue how patriarchal power is exercised and taken for granted in social relationships, particularly as men attempt to exercise control over women's biological reproductive capacity and the sexuality of their bodies. 'Private' personal matters become public issues – domestic violence by men against wives and children, rape and the public safety of women, abortion and contraception, childcare and child-minding all become policy issues. Sexual relations and the family are seen as the natural site of patriarchy, an arena of struggle. In the final analysis, the oppression of women is secured by male violence and coercion, but it rarely comes to that. Women experience mental and emotional oppression, and social policies under capitalism fail to address women's issues adequately. Given such an analysis of patriarchy highlighted in physical violence, a growing demand from radical feminists was one of 'separation', i.e. that women should avoid men altogether, or deal with them at a distance and rely on other women to withstand male oppression. To quote one slogan, 'A woman needs a man like a fish needs a bicycle'.

Marxist feminism

Whereas radical feminism focuses on issues of sexual politics and oppression, Marxist feminism highlights the economic exploitation of men and women under capitalism. The sexual division of labour under capitalism means that not only do women biologically reproduce people, they also reproduce the labour power of workers. It is within households that such work is done and Marxist feminism has engaged in 'the domestic labour' debate about how domestic work serves the interests of capital. Leisure for men in the home makes work for women. Men are free to participate in leisure within or outside the home because women take the major responsibility for domestic labour such as housework, shopping, cooking and childcare. Imagine a world full of children without women – how would the present organisation of work and leisure persist? Research by Green *et al.* (1987) stresses that women fatalistically accept, with some complaints, that their leisure interests will be restricted by marriage and family but such restrictions do not apply to men in the same way or for the same length of time.

The dominance of this primary role of wife and mother means that women do not see domestic responsibilities as work, even though research suggests that women with no paid work spend an average 77 hours a week doing housework, which is unskilled, monotonous, routine and invisible in that one only appreciates it when dinners aren't cooked clothes aren't clean and no one will look after the children. As one of the slogans of the feminist movement suggests 'You fall into his arms and your arms fall into the sink'. The position of women within the home is much closer to slavery than to normal contracted work in industrialised society.

The housewife is much more 'task-orientated', as was the case with the natural rhythms of work in pre-industrial society, rather than 'time-orientated' as is the case with male paid employment. A constant theme in feminist studies is that women simply have too much to do and the day is one of 'ceaseless activity' with rounds of housework, meals and caring for children. Consequently, 'coffee breaks', listening to the radio and 'gossiping' are not so much leisure but 'rests' from the daily routine of domestic labour. Paradoxically, there is some evidence that women set themselves increasingly high standards of childcare, domestic cleanliness and culinary skills, thereby ensuring that labour saving devices within the household do not necessarily reduce the amount of time women spend involved in domestic labour. Fiscally, financially and socially, women are dependent upon institutional structures within marriage, the household and the family, which define women as domestic labourers and carers in the private sphere of the home and men as workers in the public sphere of paid employment or work. Both groups are dependent on capitalism as consumers. The state reinforces women's dependence on men through tax allowances, pension schemes and social welfare policies, particularly those with a community care dimension. Consequently, women have the primary function of servicing men's sexual and domestic needs, and their domestic labour provides time, space and resources for men, and husbands in particular, to enjoy leisure.

Women, work and leisure

The experience of women under capitalism has changed and is changing. Constraints and opportunities for leisure find their expression in each individual's own biography. All biographies are mediated by inequalities of both class and race but because of women's domestic labour there are also strong common experiences, particularly within families. The mother of small children with too much to do and 'available' 24 hours a day, gradually finds herself with little to do once childcare skills are redundant as children leave home. Like the unemployed, older women can find themselves with too much free-time, which can hardly be described as leisure or pleasure. Most feminist studies also acknowledge that marriage, housework, and childcare provide opportunities for leisure and pleasure for women. Despite being induced by 'male medicine' and hospital technology, babies and young children provide opportunities for play and leisure which are hard to find for childless couples. Children bring parents into sports, music, and leisure because of their involvement with clubs, voluntary organisations and schools. Although mums may have to provide the transport, spectate, and wash the kit, there are also opportunities to participate and increasing leisure opportunities are geared towards the whole family rather than the individual. Indeed, working class male spectator sports such as soccer, are finding it hard to recast the game as a family sport and entertainment, despite the efforts of certain 'family clubs' and well-known television commentators. Within this book there have been many examples of the family as the site for leisure both in the section on countryside recreation and on consuming. Indeed, 'shopping as leisure' provides an important exemplar for understanding changing patterns of leisure and of gender relationships. Researchers argue that window shopping and shopping itself provide ideal activities for women to experience leisure. They provide opportunities to be outside the home, in safe public places and engaged in leisurely consumption within a traditional and culturally legitimate role. Husbands and children have been drawn, sometimes reluctantly, into these 'consumption palaces', so that the whole family may embark on the weekly hypermarket shop. Needless to say, late-night or weekend shopping depends upon access to car transport, family work-schedules and the usually tight timetables for children's out of school leisure activities. However, it is usually the mother/housewife who organises the shopping trips while children and husbands console themselves by filling shopping trolleys with numerous bottles of non-alcoholic and alcoholic drinks.

If women do participate in the public sphere, they do so on gendered terms. Because domestic and family responsibilities are defined as non-work, women usually enter paid employment as part-time workers. The concept of the 'dual-labour market' highlights gender divisions in paid employment. Men are to be found in the primary labour market which offers full-time contracts, pensions, job security and promotion, whereas women are in the secondary labour market which usually offers inferior conditions in every aspect. These divisions often reinforce those of racial divisions so that black women find themselves as objects of extreme exploitation at work, reinforced by a traditional sexual division of labour within domestic responsibilities. If women compete in the same job market as men they may be a 'reserve army of labour' to be recruited during periods of economic expansion and to be dismissed during periods of recession. Women's position of exploitation both at home and at work carry clear restrictions on women's leisure as they often lack time, transport and income to engage in leisure. Many women carry the double burden of paid employment and domestic work. Research by the Rapoports has documented how dual-career families manage family life, leisure and work careers. Such management often depends upon employing other women to work as domestics. Ironically, research on unemployment by Pahl (1984) suggests that male unemployment in the household may result in further domestic labour for the wife. In addition to coping with the pains of her husband's unemployment, welfare payments may result in the wife stopping her job and having to work harder in the domestic sphere (budgeting, cooking, etc.) to manage much reduced household income more efficiently. For many working women 'leisure' is the time during which domestic and caring work is done. Indeed, so many women are trained to care and have their 'double burden' that their fantasy of leisure may be to wish for more time to do yet more domestic labour.

During the 1980s and 1990s there have been considerable shifts in patterns of employment as the UK economy has witnessed a growth in service sector employment. These developments and their social consequences are theorised in the final section on postmodernity. However, it is clear that economic restructuring has had a differential impact on labour markets which has resulted in male unemployment and growth in female employment, particularly in sectors with flexible, often part-time, working conditions. Some writers suggest that this constitutes a feminisation of labour, or paid employment, with capital eager to employ a flexible female work force. Previous research into male occupational communities highlighted the central importance of work in men's lives and also on their families. The feminisation of work will clearly have both short-term and long-term impacts on gender roles, expectations, free time and consumption patterns. In short, the economic and social policy foundation of 'the family wage', with men as sole breadwinners as in the postwar period, sits uncomfortably alongside the more diverse household arrangements of flexible work practices associated with the 1990s.

Women, sexuality and control

Oppression is not achieved solely by physical coercion. Language is an important medium form exercising control over others. 'Calling people names' seeks to discredit and devalue their stance and perhaps it should come as no surprise that feminists have been labelled as 'extremists' 'unnatural lesbians' and 'failed women'. The power of language to control people can broadly be seen as 'discourse' theory and is perceptively illustrated by Sue Lees' work on female sexuality and the way in which it is controlled by the terms 'slag' and 'drag'. Lees set out to show how the discourse of sexuality controls young women:

> Patriarchal power and the control of women's sexuality and labour are frequently cited in the feminist literature but little attempt has been made to describe how power is exercised in the social domain and to examine the mechanisms both material and ideological – that underline this dominance.
>
> (Sue Lees, 1986)

In *Losing Out* Lees argues that all women must maintain their sexual reputation. In the public sphere of leisure – for example, in pubs or at parties, women are judged in sexual terms in ways that men are not. Independent women who are, or who are thought to be, sexually active may be labelled as 'slags' and pressured into steady relationships which may result in marriage. Having a steady boyfriend, resolves the 'slag–drag' reputational dilemma and secures access to the public sphere without the anxieties of worrying about sexual harassment from other males. The young women interviewed by Lees rely upon networks of closeknit friends to resolve their sexual identities, as friends can be relied upon to counter accusations of sexual promiscuity made by outsiders. As has been suggested in Chapter 3, women leaving school not only have to get and keep a job, but they also have to get and keep a man. For some, pregnancy may be seen as a 'solution' to long-term unemployment, just as for others prostitution may be defined as a well-rewarded career, compared with other women's work. Prostitution and pornography are clear examples of how women's sexuality is sold through the market, often illegally to the willing male consumer. Women's bodies and women's time are used to service male visions of female sexuality, not to mention undercurrents of violence, conjured up by masochism and rape. Although prostitution and pornography may be seen as extreme examples of male oppression, women have to resist male control over their bodies and masculine notions of femininity. Sheila Scraton's analysis of teaching physical education explores the ways in which sport and physical activities at school can be regarded by some girls as 'unfeminine' and therefore may be resisted. Schools do little to encourage young women to participate and develop skills in sports and recreation. Research suggests that women 'sports personalities' often defer marriage to pursue their 'careers' while television commentators persist in quizzing successful women athletes as to when they will embrace the 'natural' role of wife and mother. To challenge such assumptions about hetereosexuality, as did Martina Navratilova in tennis, is to fuel moral panics about lesbianism and independent women or to encourage (short-sighted?) sports officials to demand compulsory sex-tests for female athletes as they approach male standards in performance.

Feminist work documenting the dependence of women and their relationship to leisure can be observed in a range of material and cultural contexts. As Chapter 5 has argued, institutional networks carry clear policy implications and consequences, both intended and unintended. For women to be free to enjoy leisure, they need some of the conditions which characterise men's lives. They need time, freedom from domestic chores, and paid employment, an absence of maternal responsibilities, sexual freedom, confidence and cultural competence to engage in existing and new leisure forms. There are obvious divisions in terms of age, class and race in women's experience which must be built into any telling analysis For example, young women define pre-marriage as freedom yet Griffin's work suggest that young working class women are actively involved in the work of 'getting a man' – a stable relationship to cope with the vicissitudes of being working class in a patriarchal society. Race too may also impose severe restrictions on the leisure lives of young women growing up in Asian and in Afro-Caribbean communities. Black women, such as Alice Walker and Bell Hooks, have highlighted the oppression experienced by women under the further burden of racism. Class, income, and education can also reduce some of the restrictions that patriarchy imposes on women's opportunities for leisure.

Just as structuralism offers different versions of functionalist analysis, feminist writers provide different views of patriarchy. Feminism documents how women are constrained by the physical, economic, and ideological power of men. Leisure and the family are reduced to the oppression and control of women. Leisure forms revolve around sexuality and women's sexuality is defined by men and, at worst, is treated as a commodity to be consumed by men or used in advertising to sell other leisure commodities. On the other hand, other versions of feminism acknowledge that marriage and the family are not vehicles solely for constraint, but provide opportunities and leisure choices. Childcare provides rewards that are denied by paid work and provides control over time in ways that paid work cannot.

What is obvious is that women's access to leisure depends in part upon the construction of commercial and public-sector leisure policy. This means more than local authorities providing 'women-only' swimming days for Asian women (although such a policy is to be welcomed). Women's leisure and pleasure are grounded in a whole range of public sector provision of collective goods. Women's time is a function of health-care services, ancilliary support, location of recreation/sports facilities, provision of school dinners, supervision, cost and reliability of public/private transport in a way that men's time is not. This is because men can depend upon women to organise private domestic resources (both material and temporal) to meet the shortfall in public provision.

Another crucial dimension in feminist studies of leisure is the exploration of ways in which the commercial, public and voluntary sectors challenge or reinforce cultural stereotypes of women and women's leisure. Feminist analysis has perceptive things to say about each sector and their potential for increasing women's leisure. It has been suggested that the different currents in feminist analysis have converged in a broader socialist feminist position. Some critics suggest that the feminist movement has gone too far (anti-feminist perspective) or is no longer relevant because of the gains made by the women's movement (non-feminist perspectives). There have also been debates with postmodern arguments about the difference and diversity within women's experience and resistance to the claims of post-feminist positions (Scraton, 1994).

EXERCISES AND DISCUSSION ———————————————

1 What policy decisions would you take to make your local sports centre more open to women?

2 Why do bingo/adult education/the romantic novel/aerobics attract high rates of participation amongst women?

3 Can one talk of a leisure policy for women? Examine the ways in which the needs of women can change with marriage, or with class, age and race.

4 Why have women not developed their own distinctive women's leisure forms either in sports, recreation or tourism? Which area of leisure activity is most amenable to be developed?

5 How would you set about encouraging young women to participate in physical education both in a school or a youth club setting?

6 What are the arguments for and against mixed sporting events, e.g. mixed team games such as hockey/football; racket games such as badminton; athletics/swimming, etc.?

7 Set up three separate interviews with women to find out their attitudes towards feminism and women's leisure; if possible try and get a group of women together to discuss feminism and leisure. Beforehand, do you expect the results of individual and group discussions/interviews to be different or the same?

Further reading

Rosemary Deem (1986) *All Work No Play?*, Open University Press and E. Green, S. Hebron and D. Woodward (1990) *Women's Leisure: What Leisure?* Macmillan, provide definitive overviews of the field and the substantial contribution that feminist analysis can make to leisure studies. Recent theoretical developments in the feminist work are lucidly summarised in Sheila Scraton's chapter on 'Leisure' in M. Haralambos (1992) *Developments in Sociology*, Ormskirk, and more recently in 'The Changing World of Women and Leisure?', *Leisure Studies* **13**, July 1994.

4 Postmodernism

Some social theorists claim that in the late twentieth century we are entering a qualitatively different era or social epoch which can be described as 'postmodernity'. Others, including those writing in cultural studies and feminist traditions, dispute the term postmodernity and dismiss postmodernists as nihilistic intellectuals who have misrepresented art as life. Such critics argue that the term 'high modernity' or 'late capitalism' more closely expresses the condition of the 'New Times' (Hebdige, 1988). However, most intellectual domains recognise the 'postmodern' and acknowledge the radical nature of contemporary changes taking place in all spheres of life. While these changes are often contradictory and strong continuities with the past remain, there are, it is argued, features of a 'postmodern' society which are significantly different from a previously 'modern' era.

Postmodern changes
The issues raised by postmodern thinking and the birth of postmodernity are multi-dimensional and complex. Change permeates several spheres of life: the economic, the political, the social and the cultural. One key feature of the postmodern is difference and *dedifferentiation* – traditional hierarchies, divisions and boundaries collapse. Certainty implodes as 'all that is solid melts into air'. Divisions between high and low culture are deemed to be no longer relevant. Postmodern analysis posits 'the death

of the author'. There can be no one uncontested interpretation of a book, painting or film, and intellectuals therefore have no authority to speak for 'others', or to present their analysis as the privileged account.

Dedifferentiation occurs within ordinary people's everyday life. For example, the organisation of both time and space becomes more flexible and fragmented as individuals deconstruct traditional patterns and reconstruct their own individual pathways and life course. Whether one looks at patterns of work, ethnicity, leisure tastes, sexuality, meal times and tastes, media consumption, lifestyles, holidays and so on, traditional and collective patterns have become more diverse and individualised. To take just one example, the video recorder weakens the constraints of time and space. Individuals can record programmes while viewing another channel, still catch up with favourite serials when somewhere else, and can watch over and over again favourite films, sporting events and so on, not to mention watching commercial videos and creating personal camcorder records.

Whether one examines the economic, social, political or cultural spheres, significant shifts in experiences of leisure, life styles and social circumstances have been encountered in recent decades. Although the term 'postmodernity' derives largely from cultural experiences and in particular the language of architecture, it has been adopted as an inclusive term to incorporate major economic and social changes.

Different perspectives emphasise the dominance of particular processes of change. Neo-Marxism retains its emphasis on the mode of production of commodities, their circulation and consumption. Many would acknowledge the prime significance of economic shifts dating from the mid-1970s onwards within developed economies as industry adopted what has been termed a post-Fordist regime of flexible accumulation. This is contrasted with historic Fordist structures of industrial capitalism centred on Henry Ford's development of the assembly-line method of working and the economies of scale associated with routine mass production.

Dynamic economic change experienced in advanced economies since the 1970s has involved a shift from manufacturing industry to service

Table 7.2 Categorisation of change

Historic		Contemporary
Fordism	(Economic)	Post-Fordism
Welfarism	(Political)	Post-welfarism
Industrial	(Social)	Post-industrial
Modernity	(Cultural)	Post-modernity

'production', with finance capital replacing manufacturing capital in economic significance. Occupational restructuring has also taken place and still continues, with a growing division between a 'core' workforce enjoying benefits of continuous well-paid employment and a 'peripheral' workforce consisting of lower paid, part-time and often de-skilled and insecure employees. There is also a discernible long-term process of the feminisation of paid employment with increasing proportions of women in work and sections of the male population facing long-term unemployment.

Such economic changes have wider repercussions in the changing nature of class, gender and status patterns and the growing emphasis on individualised consumption in all areas of social life. Recently, Marxists such as Stuart Hall and Dick Hebdige have acknowledged that market processes have opened new choices in patterns of consumption for all sectors of the public which traditional Marxist politics have denied.

For theorists like Jameson (1984) these postmodern forms reflect a culture which in late capitalism is increasingly commodified and consumed. In this context, images, styles and representations become products, as does information itself, as culture is integrated into commodity production as part of the logic of late capitalism. David Harvey (1989) in particular has attempted to make sense of these socio-cultural changes in terms of the physical reality of urban spaces. Like all other areas of life and existence, urban places reflect change, so the postmodern city emphasises quality of life experiences and the importance of city image. There is competitive civic investment in malls, plazas and marinas and the holding of spectacular mega-events both sporting and cultural. Heritage features are developed in an effort to produce an attractive environment for tourism and commerce. In a variety of ways, through the gentrification of certain residential areas, the improvement of historic quarters, or the transformation of waterfronts, the city comes to reflect the image, aspirations and expectations of a postmodern public.

Political theorists have linked these socio-economic changes to the growth of liberal individualist anti-collectivist ideologies in western democracies. There has been a shift from postwar welfare states to more flexible post-welfarism. There is a collapse of the social as collective provision and policy becomes deregulated, fragmented and privatised, whether in health, pensions, housing, transport or education. New patterns of capital accumulation require complex systems of regulation, negotiated and legitimated by new ideologies and policies. The role of the state, politics and public policy changes along with the shift from Fordism to post-Fordism, as powerful groups inside nation states seek to move towards more flexible systems of regulation which are symbiotic with the needs of transnational capital and global corporate investment strategies. Chapter 5 has traced such shifts in policy. Leisure and leisure policies, like all aspects of life, have been affected by the growth of private provision in housing, transport, health, education, and welfare. Increasingly, private market competition and contracting of services have come to replace mass municipal or collective state provision. Leisure services exhibit a growing economic rationale and a market-based discourse rather than one of social welfare.

For postmodern theorists the links between new life-styles and consumption are significant for leisure and in the formation of personal identities. Featherstone (1990) has argued that consumer culture celebrates the aestheticisation of everyday life – fashions become significant and one must live with style(s). The media endorse not products but lifestyles. Consumption from this perspective is not so much about commodities but is of signs and status signifiers. These represent a substantial investment and embodiment of cultural capital and competence for the growing educated service class of late capitalism.

Baudrillard (1983) suggests iconoclastically that 'history is over' and we now inhabit a two minute 'depthless culture'. He has emphasised the impact of mass media, particularly television, in the full emergence of a consumer society, characterised by 'hyperreality' in the playful substitution and simulation of 'fake' and the 'real'. Language and texts have been displaced by figural forms. For many, authenticity and real life nostalgically belong in the past but these can be represented and reconstructed in theme parks and heritage centres for tourists, not only to gaze upon but also to experience, interact and engage with. Leisure, as part of the patterns and styles of life and consumption, plays a significant role in defining people's identities, experience and consciousness.

These approaches have been adopted by Hebdige in analysing developments in Britain in the 1980s, particularly in relation to popular culture and 'consumer identities'. One's life course becomes a reflexive project during which one *must* make choices and develop and discover one's self and identity (Giddens, 1991). Free time and leisure practices provide an ideal and legitimate site for just such a quest.

Social theory about the postmodern tends to elevate the everyday realities of work and leisure into esoteric debate and obscure terminology. Whatever their theoretical position, whether acknowledging a distinctive break with past existence or not, all recognise significant recent change and attempt to understand it. Leisure also conforms to these cumulative changes. Increasingly commodified, individualised, diverse and flexible, it is represented by the television and video, Sega and Nintendo games, the personal stereo, virtual reality games, and the interactive CD player. It is much more about high technology and individualism than collective participation and communal enjoyment. Participants are restless, sensation seekers and demand direct involvement and high quality, and only those leisure forms which can respond succeed in such a context.

The accumulation of such changes in economy, society, politics and culture has led some to designate a qualitatively new era of postmodernity. Part of the debate has also involved a questioning of the nature of social theory itself. Postmodernists argue that the 'crisis of modernity' is not merely a matter of economic, political, social and cultural dynamics but is an intellectual crisis in understanding the social world. Intellectuals are no longer authoritative legislators but interpreters. The Enlightenment 'project' and its key ideas on the nature of scientific objectivity, progress and emancipation are being questioned, as just one language game. 'Open questioning' and deconstruction of knowledge are central to Lyotard's thesis, as is the rejection of the notion of objectivity in the form of grand theories or meta-narratives which he associates with 'myriad stories and fables' (Lyotard, 1984). Social theories thus need to be reflexive and to explore both new times and old paradigms.

Whether or not the more extreme claims of postmodernists are accepted, these approaches to social theory highlight significant recent economic, social and political changes and attempt, paradoxically given the scepticism about meta-narratives, to make sense of them comprehensively. The focus on individual consumption and its emphasis on current lifestyles and cultural forms ensures its importance in attempting to understand leisure in the 1990s. For the postmodernists, leisure is no longer a fixed entity, characterised by freedom or control but is fragmented, dedifferentiated and de-centred.

Further reading

A general overview of the state of leisure theory can be found in C. Rojek (1991) 'Leisure and Recreation Theory' in E. Jackson and T. Burton *Understanding Leisure and Recreation*, Ventura Publishing. Chris Rojek has done much to disseminate postmodern debates in various recent *Leisure Studies* articles and in *Ways of Escape*, Macmillan (1993). David Harvey (1989) *The Condition of Postmodernity*, Basil Blackwell, provides a comprehensive overview of theory applied to urban change. Mike Featherstone's book on *Consumer Culture and Postmodernity*, Sage (1990) provides a comprehensive and sophisticated introduction to consumer culture. Zygmunt Bauman in *Intimations of Postmodernity*, Routledge (1992) examines postmodern thinking as an intellectual crisis.

Conclusion

The aim of this chapter and of the book as a whole has been to develop some understanding of leisure. To quote A. E. Housman, 'perfect understanding will sometimes almost extinguish pleasure' and some readers may feel these many pages have had the unintended consequence of both extinguishing pleasure and heightening mental fatigue. Nevertheless, all the writers reviewed in this last chapter are determined both to understand and to explain leisure. They seek to develop a theoretical understanding of leisure and its distinctive contribution to social relations.

Throughout many of the previous chapters there has been a tension, sometimes hidden, sometimes manifest, between writers who see leisure as freedom and choice for individuals, and others who stress the control and constraints exercised by structural processes over leisure. The relations of class, race, gender and the State intervene to distort leisure and to use it to legitimate broader rationales of social order and inequality. The tension between individual freedom and control appears (and is rarely resolved) by competing definitions of leisure. It also provides an important perspective upon the typology of leisure forms introduced in Chapter 2. Leisure forms range across an active-passive continuum, with the state seeking to encourage certain types of leisure and license others.

In Chapter 3, the choices individuals make about their leisure were highlighted, yet such choices are severely constrained by other factors such as class, gender and race. Chapter 4 explored the spatial expression of land values and uses, providing both opportunities and constraints on leisure, either in the home or elsewhere. Access to leisure facilities and locations have represented an important and well-developed tradition in recreational analysis. The next chapter examines the opportunities and constraints generated by providers in the commercial, public and voluntary sectors and, not least, how these opportunities and constraints have developed historically. Chapter 6 took a step further by outlining different futuristic visions of both leisure and of society.

This final chapter has provided the briefest of summaries of four important perspectives that can contribute to our understanding of both leisure and society – (namely, figurational sociology, cultural studies, feminist analysis and postmodernism. All four have important strengths:

- they transcend sterile dualisms which set individual against society or action against structure;
- they acknowledge that individuals live within physical bodies or selves and think of them as important resources or agents for realising pleasure and leisure;
- they stress that these dimensions have been ignored or taken for granted by other leisure theories;

- they are aware of the importance of power, particularly of the State, which may facilitate or constrain leisure;
- they broaden the concept of leisure and locate it in a more open-ended developmental view of human history.

What more could one ask? Needless to say each perspective provides different theories and evidence in answer to the above issues. The important point is not so much the answer but getting to the right sort of questions. Apparently Gertrude Stein on her death-bed asked 'What then is the answer?', only to murmur to her bedside companion 'Ah, but what is the question?'

BIBLIOGRAPHY

Alonso, W. (1982) in Blowers A., Brook C., Dunleavy P. and McDowell L. (eds), *Urban Change and Conflict*, Harper and Row, London.

Amis, K. (1979) *A Policy for the Arts?* Centre for Policy Studies, London.

Arts Council (1984) *The Glory of the Garden: Strategy for a Decade*, Williams Lea, London.

Bailey, P. (1986) *Music Hall: The Business of Pleasure*, Open University Press, Milton Keynes.

Baldry, H. (1981) *The Case for the Arts*, Secker and Warburg, London.

Barker, D. and Allen, S. (1976) *Sexual Divisions and Society: Process and Change*, Tavistock, London.

Barnes, C. (1991) *Disabled People in Britain and Discrimination: A Case for Anti-Discrimination Legislation*, Hurst and Co., London.

Barrett, M. (1980) *Women's Oppression Today*, Verso, London.

Bateman, M. (1982), 'City Development in a Hinterland' D202, Unit 5, *Urban Change and Conflict*, Open University Press, Milton Keynes.

Baudrillard, J. (1983) *The Precession of Simulacra*, Semiotexte, New York.

Bauman, Z. (1992) *Intimations of Postmodernity*, Routledge, London.

Bell, D. (1976) *The Coming of Post-Industrial Society: a Venture in Social Forecasting*, Penguin Books, Harmondsworth.

Bennington, J. and White, J. (1986) *The Future Role and Organisation of Local Government: Functional Study No 4: Leisure*, Institute of Local Government Studies, University of Birmingham.

Bishop, K. (ed.) (1992) *Off the Beaten Track: Access to Open Land in the UK*, Countryside Recreation Network.

Blunden, J. and Curry, N. (eds) (1985) *The Changing Countryside*, Open University, Milton Keynes.

Bourdieu, P. (1978), 'Sport and Social Class' in *Social Science Information*, 17, **6**, 819–40.

Bourdieu, P. (1980), 'The production of belief' in *Media, Culture and Society*, 2, **2**, 261–93.

Bourdieu, P. (1985) *Distinction: a social critique of the judgement of taste*, Routledge and Kegan Paul, London.

Brake, M. (1980) *A Sociology of Youth Culture and Youth Subcultures*, Routledge and Kegan Paul, London.

Bramham, P. *et al.* (1984) *New Directions in Leisure Studies*, Applied and Community Studies Occasional Paper 1: Bradford and Ilkley Community College.

Brohm, J-M. (1978) *Sport: a prison of measured time*, Ink Links, London.

Brown, A. (1987) *Active Games for Children with Movement Problems*, Harper and Row.

Burkhart, A.J. and Medlik, S. (2nd ed) (1982) *Tourism Past, Present and Future*, Heinemann, London.

Byrne, D. (ed.) (1986) *Waiting for Change? Working in hotel and catering*, Low Pay Unit/Hotel and Catering Workers' Union, GMBA TU, London/Esher, Surrey.

Caillois, R. (1961) *Man, Play and Games*, The Free Press, New York.
Carrington, B., Chivers, T. and Williams, T. (1987), 'Gender, Leisure and Sport: A case study of young people of South Asian descent,' in *Leisure Studies*, 6, 3, 265–79.
Cashmore, E. (1990) *Making Sense of Sport*, Routledge, London.
Cashmore, E. and Troyna, B. (eds) (1982) *Black Youth in Crisis*, George Allen and Unwin, London.
Central Statistical Office (1987) *Social Trends*, HMSO, London.
Centre for Leisure Research (1986) *Access to the Countryside for Recreation and Sport*, Sports Council, London.
Chadwick, R.A. (1981), 'Some Notes on the Geography of Tourism: a Comment,' *Canadian Geographer*, 25, 191–7.
Chambers, D.A. (1986), 'The Constraints of Work and Domestic Schedules on Women's Leisure', *Leisure Studies*, 5, 3, 309–25.
Clarke, J. and Critcher, C. (1985) *Devil Makes Work*, Macmillan.
Clawson, M. and Knetsch, J. (1986) *Economics of Outdoor Recreation*, Johns Hopkins, Baltimore.
Cloke, P. (1987) *Rural Planning: Policy into Action*, Harper and Row, London.
Coakley, J.J. (1986) *Sport in Society: Issues and Controversies*, C.V. Mosby.
Coalter, F., Duffield, B. and Long, J. (1986) *The Rationale for Public Sector Leisure Services*, Sports Council/Economic and Social Research Council, London.
Cohen, E. (1972), 'Towards a Sociology of International Tourism,' *Social Research*, 39, 164–82.
Cohen, E. (1979), 'Phenomenology of Tourist Experiences,' *Sociology*, 13, 179–202.
Cohen, P. (1984), 'Subcultural Conflict and Working-Class Community,' in Butterworth, E. and Weir, D. (eds), *A New Sociology of Modern Britain*, Fontana, London.
Collins, V. (1984) *Recreation and the Law*, E. and F.N. Spon, London.
Conservative Party (1978) *The Arts, The Way Forward*, Conservative Political Centre, London.
Cornish, D.B. (1978) *Gambling: a Review of the Literature*, Home Office Research Study, No. 42, HMSO, London.
Countryside Commission (1977) *Tarn Hows: An Approach to the Management of a Popular Beauty Spot* (CCP 106), Countryside Commission, London.
Countryside Commission/Sports Council (1986) *Access to the Countryside for Recreation and Sport:* Report to the Countryside Commission and the Sports Council by the Centre for Leisure Research (CCP 217), Countryside Commission/Sports Council, London.
Countryside Commission (1987) *New opportunities for the Countryside*, (CCP 224), Countryside Commission, London.
Countryside Commission (1992) *Countryside Stewardship: An Outline* (CCP 346), Countryside Commission, London.
Countryside Commission (1994) *Informal Countryside Recreation for Disabled People – a practical guide for countryside managers* (CCP 439) Countryside Commission, London.
Cowling, D., Fitzjohn, M. and Tunatt, M. (1983) *Identifying the Market: Catchment*

Areas of Sports Centres and Swimming Pools, Study No. 24, Sports Council, London.

Critcher, C., Bramham, P. and Tomlinson, A. (1995) *Sociology of Leisure: A Reader*, E. and F. N. Spon.

Csikzentmihalyi, M. (1975) *Beyond Boredom and Anxiety*, Jossey-Bass, San Francisco/London.

Cumming, E. and Henry, W.E. (1961) *Growing Old: The Process of Disengagement*, Ayer Publishing Co.

Cunningham, H. (1980) *Leisure in the Industrial Revolution c. 1780-1880*, Croom Helm, London.

Davidson, R. (1992) *Tourism in Europe*, Pitman, London.

Davidson, R. (1993) *Tourism*, Pitman, London.

Davies, B. (1986) *Threatening Youth*, Open University, Milton Keynes.

Dearden, P. (1983) 'Tourism and the Resource Base,' in Murphy P.E. (ed.), *Tourism in Canada: Selected Issues and Options*, University of Victoria, West Geographical Series **21**, 75–93.

Dearlove, J. (1973) *The Politics of Policy in Local Government*, Cambridge University Press, Cambridge.

Deem, R. (1982), 'Women, Leisure & Inequality,' *Leisure Studies*, 1, **1**, 29–46.

Deem, R. (1986) *All Work and No Play?*, Open University Press, Milton Keynes.

De Grazia, S. (1964) *Of Time, Work and Leisure*, Anchor Books, Doubleday and Co. Inc., New York.

Delphy, C. (1984) *Close to Home*, Hutchinson, London.

Dennis, N. *et al.* (1968) *Coal is Our Life*, Tavistock, London.

Devereux, E.C. (1949) *Gambling and Social Structure*. Unpublished PhD. Thesis, Harvard University.

Dixie, R. and Talbot, M. (1982) *Women, Leisure and Bingo*, Trinity and All Saints College, Leeds.

Downes, D.M. *et al.* (1976) *Gambling, Work and Leisure*, Routledge and Kegan Paul, London.

Dunning, E. (1979), 'The Figurational Dynamics of Modern Sport,' *Sportswissenschaft*, 9.4.

Dunning, E. (ed.) (1971) *The Sociology of Sport*, Frank Cass, London.

Dunning, E., and Sheard, K. (1979) *Barbarians, Gentlemen and Players*, Martin Robinson, London.

Elias, N. (1978) *The Civilising Process* (translated from the German by E. Jephcott), *Vol. 1: The History of Manners*, Blackwell, Oxford.

Elias, N. (1978) *What is Sociology?* Hutchinson, London.

Elias, N. (1982) *The Civilising Process, Vol. 2: State Formation and Civilisation*, Blackwell, Oxford.

Elias, N. and Dunning, E. (1986) *The Quest for Excitement: Sport and Leisure in the Civilising Process*, Blackwell, Oxford.

Eliot, T.S. (1948) *Notes towards the definitions of culture*, Faber, London.

Eliot, T.S. (1953) *Selected Essays*, Faber, London.

Ellis, M. (1973) *Why People Play*, Prentice Hall, New York.

Elson, M. (1982) 'The Poverty of Leisure Forecasting' in Collins, M. (ed.) *Leisure Research*, SSRC/SC/LSA, London.

Elson, M.J. (1986) *Green Belts*, Heinemann, London.

Elson, M. (1987), 'The Urban Fringe – Will Less Farming Mean More Leisure? A Critical Review of Recent Events,' *The Planner*, October, 19–22.

ETB/RDC/CC *The Green Light: A Guide to Sustainable Tourism,* English Tourist Board/Rural Development Commission/Countryside Commission.

Featherstone, M. (1987), 'Lifestyle and Consumer Culture,' *Theory, Culture and Society,* 4, 1, February, 55–70.

Featherstone, M. (1990) *Consumer Culture and Postmodernity,* Sage, London.

Frankenberg, R. (1976) *Sexual Divisions and Society: Process and Change,* Tavistock, London.

Fraser, D. (1984) *The Evolution of the British Welfare State,* Macmillan, London.

Garnham, N. and Williams, R. (1980) 'Pierre Bourdieu and the Society of Culture' in *Media Culture and Society,* 2, 2.

Getz, D. (1982) *The Impact of Tourism in Badenoch and Strathspey,* Highlands and Islands Development Board, Edinburgh.

Giddens, A. (1991) *Modernity and Self Identity,* Polity Press, Cambridge.

Gilg, A. (1978) *Countryside Planning,* David and Charles, Newton Abbot.

Glyptis, S. (ed.) (1987) *Leisure and the Home,* Newsletter Supplement, Leisure Studies Association, London.

Glyptis, S. (1991) *Countryside Recreation,* Longman, London.

Goffman, E. (1972) *Interaction Ritual,* Penguin, Harmondsworth.

Goffman, E. (1974) *Frame Analysis,* Penguin, Harmondworth.

Goldthorpe, J. *et al.* (1964) *The Affluent Car Worker,* Cambridge University Press, Cambridge.

Gratton, C. and Taylor, P. (1987) *Leisure in Britain,* Leisure Publications, Hitchin.

Greater London Enterprise Board (1985) *London Industrial Strategy: the Culture Industries,* Greater London Enterprise Board/Greater London Council, London.

Green, E., Hebron, S. and Woodward, D. (1988) *Women's Leisure: Constraints and Opportunities,* Leisure Studies Association, Newsletter Supplement, London.

Green, E., Hebron, S. and Woodward, D. (1990) *Women's Leisure: What Leisure?,* Macmillan, London.

Gregory, S. (1982) 'Women among others – Another View' *Leisure Studies,* 1, 1, 47–52.

Griffin, C. (1985) *Typical Girls?,* Routledge and Kegan Paul, London.

Groombridge, B. (1964) *The Londoner and His Library,* Research Institute for Consumer Affairs, London.

Grossin, W. (1986), 'The Relationship between Work Time and Free Time and the Meaning of Retirement', *Leisure Studies,* 5, 91–101.

Gruneau, R. (1983) *Class, Sports and Social Development,* Amherst University Press.

Hackman, C. (1978) 'Influential Factors in the Development of Sport for women' *Physical Education Review,* 1, 1.

Hargreaves, J. (ed.) (1982) *Sport, Culture and Ideology,* Routledge and Kegan Paul, London.

Harris, D. (1992) *From Class Struggle to the Politics of Pleasure,* Routledge and Kegan Paul, London.

Harris, M. (1987), 'Lush Fruits of Nudge and Gamble,' *Daily Telegraph,* 20.1.87.

Harrison, C. (1991) *Countryside Recreation in a Changing Society,* The TMS Partnership Ltd.

Harvey, D. (1973) *Social Justice and the City,* Edward Arnold, London.

Harvey, D. (1989) *The Condition of Postmodernity*, Basil Blackwell, Oxford.

Hayden, D. (1981) *The Grand Domestic Revolution*, MIT Press, Cambridge, Mass.

Hayes, J. and Nutman, P. (1981) *Understanding the Unemployed, the psychological effects of unemployment*, Tavistock, London.

Haywood, L. (ed.) (1994) *Community Leisure and Recreation*, Butterworth-Heinemann, Oxford.

Haywood, L. and Henry, I. (1985) *Leisure and Youth*, Leisure Studies Association, Annual Conference Proceedings.

Haywood, L. and Henry, I. (1986) 'Policy Developments in Community Leisure and Recreation' in *Leisure Management*, **6**, 7; and **6**, 8.

Haywood, L. and Kew, F. (1988), 'Community Recreation: New Wine in Old Bottles' in Bramham, P., Henry, I., Mommas, H. and Van der Poel H. (eds) *Leisure and the Urban Process*, Methuen, London.

Hebdige, D. (1979) *Subculture: The Meaning of Style*, Methuen, London.

Hebdige, D. (1988) *Hiding in the Light: on images and things*, Routledge/Chapman & Hall, London.

Henry, I. (ed.) (1986) *Leisure Policy and Recreation Disadvantage*, Newsletter Supplement, Leisure Studies Association, London.

Henwood, M. (1987) *Inside the Family: changing roles of men and women*, Family Policy Studies Unit.

Hill, H. (1980) *Freedom to Roam*, Moorland Publishing, London.

Hobson, D. (1981), 'Young Women at Home and Leisure,' in Tomlinson, A., *Leisure and Social Control*, Brighton Polytechnic, Brighton.

Hoggett, P. and Bishop, J. (1986) *Organising Around Enthusiasms*, Comedia, London.

Hoggett, P. and Bishop, J. (1986) *The Social Organisation of Leisure: A Study of Groups in Their Voluntary Context*, Sports Council/Economic and Social Research Council, London.

Howkins and Lowerson (1979) *Trends in Leisure 1919–1939*, Social Science Research Council, London.

Huizinga, J. (1980) *Homo Ludens. A study of the Play-Elements in Culture*, Routledge and Kegan Paul, London.

Husband, C. (ed.) (1982) *Race in Britain*, Hutchinson, London.

Hutchison, R. (1982) *The Politics of the Arts Council*, Sinclair Brown, London.

Hutson, S. (1979) '*A Review of the Role of Clubs and Voluntary associations based on a study of two areas in Swansea*', Sports Council/SSRC.

Huxley, A. (1932) *Brave New World*, Granada, (1977 edn.) London.

Jafan, J. (1982), 'Understanding the Structure of Tourism in Interrelation between Benefits and Costs of Tourism Resources,' *AEIST*, **23**, St Gallen, Switzerland.

Jahoda, M. (1979), 'The psychological meaning of unemployment', *New Society*, 6 September, 492–5.

Jameson, F. (1984) 'Postmodernism, or the cultural logic of late capitalism', *New Left Review*, 146, 53–94.

Jarvie, G. (1991) *Sport, Racism and Ethnicity*, Falmer Press.

Jenkins, C. and Sherman, B. *The Leisure Shock*, Eyre Methuen, London (out of print).

Johnson, R.J. (1984) *City and Society*, Hutchinson, London.

Jones, S.G. (1986) *Workers at Play: A Social and Economic History of Leisure 1918–1939*, Routledge and Kegan Paul, London.

Kaplan, M. (1975) *Leisure: Theory and Policy*, John Wiley and Sons Inc., New York.

Kelly, J. (1982) *Leisure Identities and Interactions*, George Allen and Unwin, London.

Kelly, J.R. (1982) *Leisure*, Prentice Hall, Englewood Cliffs, New Jersey.

Kelly, O. (1984) *Community, Art and the State: Storming the Citadels*, Comedia, London.

Kendell, P. and McVey, M. (1986), 'Tourism and Politics,' *Leisure Management*, August, 17–20.

Kerr, H., Ashton, H. and Carless, R. (1959) *The Challenge of Leisure*, Conservative Political Centre, London.

Kew, F. (1987) 'Sporting Challenge', *Youth and Society*, May, 16–18.

Kew, F. (1994) *Sport and Structural Inequality*, National Coaching Foundation, Leeds.

Knox, P. (1987) *Urban Social Geography*, Longman, Harlow.

Koch, E. (1973) *The Leisure Riots*, Tundra Books, Montreal.

Labour Party (1959) *Leisure for Living*, Labour Party Publications, London.

Lake District Special Planning Board (1985) *Lake District National Parks Plan Review* (draft copy for consultation), Lake District Special Planning Board, Kendal.

Leaman, O. and Carrington, B. (1985), 'Athleticism and the Reproduction of Gender and Ethnic Marginality,' *Leisure Studies*, 4, 2, 205–17.

Lees, S. (1980) *Losing Out*, Hutchinson, London.

Limb, M. (1986) 'Community Involvement in Leisure Provision,' in Coalter, F. (ed.) *The Politics of Leisure*, The Leisure Studies Association, Chelsea School, Brighton Polytechnic, Brighton.

Long, J. (1987) 'Continuity as a Basis for Change: Leisure and Male Retirement,' *Leisure Studies*, 6, 1, 55–70.

Loy, J. and Kenyon, G.S. (eds) (1971) *Sport, Culture and Society*, Macmillan, London.

Lyotard, J.F. (1984) *The Postmodern Condition*, Manchester University Press, Manchester.

McCabe, T. (1981), 'Girls and Leisure,' in Tomlinson, A. (ed.) *Leisure and Social Control*, Brighton Polytechnic, Brighton.

MacEwan, A. and MacEwan, M. (1982) *National Parks: Conservation or Cosmetics*, George Allen and Unwin, London.

MacEwan, A. and MacEwan, M. (1987) *Greenprints for the future?*, George Allen and Unwin, London.

McIntosh, P. (1984) *Sport in Society*, Macmillan, London.

McIntosh, P. and Charlton, V. (1985) *The Impact of Sport for All Policy 1966–1984: and a way forward*, Sports Council.

Maguire, J. (1988), 'Race and position assignment in English soccer: a preliminary analysis of ethnicity and sport in Britain, *Sociology of Sport Journal*, 5, 257–69.

Malcolmson, R. (1973) *Popular Recreations in English Society*, Cambridge University Press, Cambridge.

Mann, P.H. (1969) *The Provincial Audience for Drama, Ballet and Opera: Survey in Leeds*, University of Sheffield, Sheffield.

Marcuse, H. (1964) *One Dimensional Man: Studies in the Ideology of Advancing*

Industrial Societies, Routledge and Kegan Paul, London.

Marsden, D. (1982) *Workless*, Croom Helm, London.

Martin, B. (1981) *A Sociology of Contemporary Cultural Change*, Basil Blackwell, Oxford.

Mather, A.S. (1986) *Land Use*, Longman, London.

Mathieson, A. and Wall, G. (1982) *Tourism: Economic, Physical and Social Impacts*, Longman, London.

Mauldon, E. and Redfern, E. (1968) *Games Teaching: a new approach for the Primary School*, MacDonald and Evans, London.

Medlik, S. (1985) *Paying Guests: A Report on the Challenge and Opportunity of Travel and Tourism*, Confederation of British Industry, Centre Point, London.

Mennell, S. (1980) *Sociological Theory: Uses and Unities*, Nelson, London.

Ministry of Sport's Review Group (1992) *Building on Ability*, HMSO, London.

Morgan, W. (1983) 'Towards a Critical Theory of Sport' in *Sport and Social Issues*, **7**, 24–34.

Mulgan, G. and Worpole, K. (1986) *Saturday Night or Sunday Morning*, Comedia, London.

Murphy, P.E. (1985) *Tourism: A Community Approach*, Methuen, London.

Murphy, P.E. (ed.) (1983) *Tourism in Canada: Selected Issues and Options*, University of Victoria, Western Geographical series 21, Victoria BC.

Myerscough, J. (1974) 'The Recent History of the Use of Leisure Time' in Appleton, I. (ed.) *Leisure and Public Policy*, Scottish Academic Press.

National Parks Review Panel (1991) *Fit for the Future* (CCP 335), Countryside Commission, London.

Newton, K. (1976) *Second City Politics: Democratic Processes and Decision-Making in Birmingham*, Clarendon Press, Oxford.

Northumberland National Park Committee (1975) *Northumberland National Park Plan*, Northumberland National Park Committee, Hexham.

Oakley, A. (1972) *Sex, Gender and Society*, Temple Smith, London.

Oakley, A. (1984) *Taking it Like a Woman*, Jonathan Cape, London.

Orwell, G. (1970) *1984*, Penguin, Harmondsworth.

Pahl, R.E. (1984) *Divisions of Labour*, Basil Blackwell, Oxford.

Parker, S. (1971) *The Future of Work and Leisure*, MacGibbon and Kee, London.

Parker, S. (1976) *The Sociology of Leisure*, George Allen and Unwin, London.

Parker, S. (1982) *Work and Retirement*, George Allen and Unwin, London.

Parker, S. (1983) *Leisure and Work*, George Allen and Unwin, London.

Patmore, A. (1983) *Recreation and Resources: Leisure Patterns and Leisure Places*, Basil Blackwell, Oxford.

Pearce, P.L. (1982) *The Social Psychology of Tourist Behaviour*, Pergamon, Oxford.

Pearson, G. (1983) *Hooligan – A History of Respectable Fears*, Macmillan, London.

Pembrokeshire Coast National Park Committee (1985) *Pembrokeshire Coast National Park Plan: First Review and Policies 1982–87*, Pembrokeshire Coast National Park Committee, Haverfordwest.

Perkins-Gilman, C. (1979) *Herland*, Women's Press, London.

Phillips, A. (1983) *Hidden Hands*, Pluto Press, London.

Piaget, J. (1982) *The Moral Judgement of the Child*, Routledge and Kegan Paul, London.

Pryce, K. (1979) *Endless Pressure: a Study of West Indian Life-Styles in Bristol*, Penguin, Harmondsworth.
PSI (1991) *Britain in 2010*, Policy Studies Institute, London.

Rapoport, R. and Rapoport, R.N. (1975) *Leisure and the Family Life Cycle*, Routledge and Kegan Paul, London.
Reid, I. (1981) *Social Class Differences in Britain*, Open Books, London.
Rheinhart, L. (1971) *The Diceman*, Panther, London.
Richardson, J. (1985), 'Music, Dance and West Indian Youth Sub-Culture,' *Leisure and Youth*, Leisure Studies Association, Conference Paper No. 17.
Riesman, D. (1953) *The Lonely Crowd*, Doubleday, New York.
Roberts, J. (1979) *The Commercial Sector in Leisure*, Sports Council/Social Science Research Council.
Roberts, K. (1978) *Contemporary Society and the Growth of Leisure*, Longman, London.
Roberts, K. (1983) *Youth and Leisure*, George Allen and Unwin, London.
Roberts, K. (1984) *School leavers and their prospects: youth in the labour market in the 1980s*, Open University Press, Milton Keynes.
Roberts, J. and Sutton-Smith, B. (1971), 'Child Training and Game Involvement' in Loy, J. and Kenyon, G.S. (eds), *Sport Culture and Society*, Macmillan, London.
Rodgers, H.B. (1977) *Rationalising Sports Policies, Sport in its Social Context: International Comparisons*, Council of Europe Committee on Sport, Strasbourg.
Rojek, C. (1985) *Capitalism and Leisure Theory*, Tavistock, London.
Rojek, C. (1991), 'Leisure and recreation theory' in Jackson, E. and Burton, T. *Understanding Leisure and Recreation*, Ventura Publishing.
Rojek, C. (1993), 'After popular culture: Hyperreality and leisure', *Leisure Studies*, **12**, pp. 277–89.
Rojek, C. (1993) *Ways of Escape*, Macmillan, London.
Rothman, B. (1921) *The 1932 Kinder Trespass*, Willow Publishing, Altrincham, Cheshire.
Roweis, S.T. and Scott, A.J. (1981), 'The Urban Land Question,' in Dear, M. and Scott, A.J. *Urbanisation and Urban Planning in Capitalist Society*, Methuen, London.

Salaman, G. (1974) *Occupation and Community*, Cambridge University Press, Cambridge.
Sargent, P. (1987) 'Equal Access to Leisure,' in *Leisure Management*, August, 53–6.
Scraton, S. (1985), 'Boys muscle in where angels fear to tread' in Haywood, L. and Henry, I. *Leisure and Youth*, LSA.
Scraton, S. (1992), 'Leisure' in Haralambos, M. *Developments in Sociology*, Ormskirk.
Scraton, S. (1994), 'The changing world of women', *Leisure Studies*, **13**, July.
Selsdon Group (1978) *A Policy for the Arts: Just Cut Taxes*, Selsdon Group, London.
Shoard, M. (1987) *This Land is Our Land*, Paladin, London.
Sillitoe, K.K. (1969) *Planning for Leisure*, HMSO, London.
Smith, R.W. (1987), 'Leisure of Disabled Tourists: Barriers to Participation,' *Annals of Tourism Research*, 14, 3, 376–89.
Smith, S.L.J. (1983) *Recreation Geography*, Longman, London.
Spender, D. (1982) *Invisible Girls*, Writer and Readers Pub., London.

Spink, J. (1994) *Leisure and the Environment*, Butterworth-Heinemann, Oxford.
Sports Council (1988) *Sport in the Community – Into the 90s*, Sports Council, London.
Stanley, L. (1980) *The Problem of Women and Leisure*, University of Salford.
Stedman-Jones, G. (1983) *Languages of Class*, Oxford University Press, Oxford.
Stockdale, J. (1975) *What is Leisure? An empirical analysis of the concept of leisure and the role of leisure in people's lives*, Sports Council/Economic and Social Research Council.
Stokes, G. (1983), 'Work, unemployment and leisure,' *Leisure Studies*, 2, **3**, 1983.
Stonier, T. (1983) *Wealth of Information: Profile of the Post-Industrial Society*, Methuen, London.

Talbot, H. (ed.) (1992) *Our Priceless Countryside: Should it be priced?*, Countryside Recreation Network.
Talbot, M. (1979) *Women and Leisure: A State of the Art Review*, Sports Council/ Social Science Research Council Joint Panel on Sport and Leisure Research, London.
Talbot, M. *Relative Freedoms*, Open University Press, Milton Keynes.
Tec, N. (1964) *Gambling in Sweden*, Bedminster Press, Totowa, New Jersey.
Todd, M. (1987), Interview with P. Sargent, 'Equal Access to Leisure', *Leisure Management*, August, 53–6.
Tomlinson, A. (1979) *The Voluntary Sector*, Sports Council/Social Science Research Council, London.
Tomlinson, A. (1981) *Leisure and Social Control*, Brighton Polytechnic/Chelsea School of Human Movement, Brighton.
Tomlinson, A. (1989), 'What side are they on? Leisure Studies and Cultural Studies in Britain,' *Leisure Studies*, **8**, pp. 97–106.
Tomlinson, A. (1990) *Consumption Identity and Style*, Comedia, London.
Torkildsen, G. (1986) *Leisure and Recreation Management*, E. & F.N. Spon, London.
Tourism and Recreation Research Unit (1981) *The Economy of Rural Communities in the National Parks of England and Wales*, TRRU, University of Edinburgh, Edinburgh.
Tourraine, A. (1983) *Voice and The Eye*, Cambridge University Press, Cambridge.
Travis, A. (1979) *The State and Leisure Provision*, Sports Council/Social Sciences Research Council, London.
Travis, A. (1982), 'Managing the environmental and cultural impacts of tourism and leisure development,' *Tourism Management*, December, 256–62.
Tunstall, J. (1963) *The Fisherman*, George Allen and Unwin, London.

Urry, J. (1990) *The Tourist Gaze – Leisure and Travel in Contemporary Societies*, Sage, London.

Veal, A.J. (1987) *Leisure and the Future*, George Allen and Unwin, London.
Veblen, T. (1899) *Theory of the Leisure Classes*, George Allen and Unwin, (reprinted 1971) London.
Vonnegut, K. (1953) *Piano Player*, Macmillan, London.

Waites, B. *et al.* (1981) *Popular Culture*, Batsford, London.
Walton, H. (1983) *The English Seaside Resort: A Social History 1750–1914*, Leicester University Press, Leicester.
Walvin, J. (1978) *Leisure and Society 1830–1950*, Longman, London.

Walvin, J. (1984) *English Urban Life 1776–1851*, Hutchinson, London.
Weiss, P. (1969) *Sport: A Philosophic Enquiry*, Southern Illinois University Press, Cartondale.
Wells, H.G. (1905) *A Modern Utopia* (1967 edn.), University of Nebraska Press, Lincoln.
Whannel, G. (1983) *Blowing the Whistle: the Politics of Sport*, Pluto Press, London.
White, A. and Brackenridge, C. (1985), 'Who Rules Sport?', *International Review of Sports Sociology*, **20**, 1/2.
Williams, R. (1981) *Culture*, Fontana, London.
Willis, P. (1985) *The Social Condition of Young People in Wolverhampton in 1984*, Wolverhampton Borough Council, Wolverhampton.
Wolff, J. (1981) *The Social Production of Art*, Macmillan, London.

Yeo, E. and Yeo, S. (1981) *Popular Culture and Class Conflict*, Harvester, London.
Yorkshire Dales National Park Committee (1984) *National Park Plan First Review*, Yorkshire Dales National Park Committee, Leyburn.
Young, M. and Wilmott, P. (1973) *The Symmetrical Family*, Routledge and Kegan Paul, London.

Zurcher, L. and Meadow, A. (1971), 'On bullfights and baseball,' in Dunning, E. (ed.) *Sociology of Sport*, Frank Cass, London.

INDEX